SPIRITS IN A SPICE JAR

Sarina Kamini is an Anglo-Indian author now living in a pocket of paradise in small town Western Australia. A former food writer, food editor and food critic, she has spent twenty years working in Paris, California, Edinburgh, Barcelona and Melbourne. Sarina can be found among the trees with her husband, her two sons and her dog, DJ Chips.

Spirits In A
Spice Jar

Spirits In A Spice Jar

Sarina Kamini

SK Publishing

First edition 2018 by Westland Publications Private Limited
Second edition 2022 by SK Publishing
Website: www.sarinakamini.com

SK Publishing

Cover Design: Saurav Das
Interior and cover layout: Pickawoowoo Publishing Group - www.pickawoowoo.com

A catalogue record for this book is available from the National Library of Australia

ISBN 978-0-6455850-2-5 (paperback)
ISBN 978-0-6455850-3-2 (hardback)
ISBN 978-0-6455850-4-9 (ebook)

Also by Sarina Kamini
The Spice Companion

www.sarinakamini.com

For Mum and Dad,
When pain is passed.
Only love remains.

And for Scott,
Who always knew.

Contents

Prologue

I CAN TELL YOU EXACTLY when I stopped eating Indian food. It is the day I look Mum in the eye and can't see myself inside her. No, it's something else. That I *can* see myself there, and that's what disturbs me more. We are arguing upstairs in our big wooden house that stands sentinel on a windswept hill at the head of Australia's Great Ocean Road, the two of us facing each other in the living room that no one in our family ever uses. Mum's legs are folded beneath her on the Kashmiri carpet that had been a wedding gift to her and Dad twenty-three years ago. I stand three steps away, gripping the top of my Grandma's velvet-covered drawing room chair. The piece is part of Mum's inheritance; a pale robin's-egg blue. I am twenty to Mum's fifty-three. Old enough to come at her with a full quiver of frustration but too young and tangled to know whose battle I fight.

'But you aren't dying.' My words are as forceful as my distress. *But you aren't dying.* Fuck. That's not a statement, it's an accusation.

'You aren't *dying*,' I repeat. I'm mean, now. It's so much easier to feel anger than grief that I relish the flare of guilt-born fury. And yet not even its force can annihilate my awareness of her: I see the pain on Mum's face and know that my words have dragged the hurt up from her gut. It makes me wicked with distress.

'You *are* going to be fifty-five and sixty and seventy. Even if you do nothing in all of that time. You *will* get there. The doctor said it—you don't die *of* Parkinson's Disease, you die *with* it. So not making decisions because you're scared of what you'll be *like...*' I am furious with her. I'm terrified for myself. I have waited almost a decade for Mum to help me reinterpret my world in the wake of the diagnosis. To help me recalibrate my faith. We are Hindus. We are *believers*. But, Jesus, the fear that sets her mouth. It's as if, even after all these years—*she has been diagnosed for eight years*—she still has no idea what the challenge of this illness is.

'Sarina. I can't.' That's exactly how she says it. *Sarina.* A plea. 'You don't understand. No one understands. I can't think of the future. How can I? I don't know in five years if I'll be able to travel or to dance or to walk. I don't know how I'll be...'

'But why are you so scared?' My impatient need to have her see reason propels me to interrupt. 'Why won't you go and *talk* to someone? Just because puja, and having faith is enough for Dad doesn't mean it has to be enough for you. It's like you can't do anything without him making decisions for you. You can't do anything on your own.' My accusations spew forth. They cut her words dead and I feel cruel pleasure at stopping the flow. Her arguments are old. We've had this same exchange countless times as I have grown from an adolescent into a young woman, as I continue to fight to regain what had once been mine to claim: Mum as my guiding light. But we're both stuck. She, trapped in her belief that this disease is now her life. I, cemented in anger that she is incapable of helping me imagine a future where Parkinson's doesn't rule our world.

'It's easy for you!' she cries. 'You're not the one who's sick. No one else in the family is sick. *I* am sick. None of you can know how I feel.'

There is more but I've had enough. I've *heard* enough. Because she's right and she's wrong. I can't know how she feels and yet I can't escape it either. If she is wedged against disease and loss then so am I. I don't know how to differentiate my emotional landscape from hers. Not with her so close. So I leave soon after. I leave the house and leave this life. Leave it behind to move on: to marry and to travel and to have children of my own. I shed it all. Or at least I try. Family. Faith. Food. I leave anything that can tie me to the moment when I look into Mum's eyes to be flattened by the realisation that she can't lead me back to the place I have lost. Mum's faith in the future has gone.

But worse than that—so has mine.

CHAPTER 1

Turmeric

Turmeric is a root spice. Bitter, despite its
beautiful flower. Yet it is indispensable.
A base note harmoniser. Identifiable
only in its absence, turmeric is used
in almost every Kashmiri dish.

'WHAT ARE YOU COOKING?' THE shop girl's smile is open with interest. I stand at the till of Lygon Street's Gewürzhaus Spice. It's March. Wednesday, mid-week. A busy time when the new year finally chugs into high gear after the lethargy of February. The days are warm even as summer fades and orange leaves hold the promise of autumn. Change. I have driven here straight from dropping my two boys to their South Melbourne childcare centre, a twenty-five-minute drive across Melbourne's CBD, the City Centre, to Carlton. It's an incredible store. An aromatic wallop of exoticism in the middle of Melbourne's suburban Italian heartland. I put my collection of goods on top of the antique French medicine chest that serves as a counter—its hundred tiny drawers are now emptied of little white pills, filled instead with varieties of loose tea and spices. An alternative way to heal.

'I'm teaching myself my father's food.' I hear the hesitancy in my response. 'From Ammi's...I mean, my grandmother's recipes. They're Indian. Kashmiri. It's something I've avoided doing until now,' I pause, push through my reluctance to continue, 'but I think it's finally time I cooked.' The expression of polite interest on the face of the young saleswoman jars with the rawness of my confession. It makes me self-conscious. I let the tinkle created by small glass containers fill the awkward gap as she packs them side by side in a paper bag. Nigella seeds. Whole nutmeg. The rich sweetness of cinnamon. My hands fumble as I pass her the turmeric, nerves knocking it sideways. The lid has come loose. A pungent yellow spill. It was one of the first spice truths my Indian grandmother fed me in her New Delhi kitchen: turmeric is bitter and it stains. A mere girl back then, I swallowed the words as verbal titbits from my sari-clad Ammi and eagerly received the culinary secrets she dropped as grains of rice into my lap. *Sugar must always be put with turmeric. To balance it.* I stand at this shop counter and hear Ammi's words in my head, her soft tones barely masking the steel of her matriarchal strength. English was her second language after Hindi, her mother tongue. As my two brothers and I grew older we loved that she spoke like Yoda; Ammi had the same vocal quaver and irregular syntax. And yet the insights she gave me as I watched her cook were clear; designed to whet my appetite for knowledge of my culture, for connection to my heritage. I think of this as I return home to South Melbourne a few hours later, fingers a jaundiced flash as they turn the key in our front lock. This is the first time I have kept turmeric in my own house. Not a small plastic pack of McCormack's thrown to the cupboard's cavernous back, untouched and forgotten behind half-empty bottles of Worcestershire and Heinz tomato sauce, but a spice I am determined to use. One that is loud with presence and carried alongside the other spices whose names are as familiar to me as those of Cailean and Ashok, my own two pre-school-aged children. Ginger powder. Aniseed. *Garam masala.* Cumin seeds. Coriander seeds. Mace. Cloves. Cinnamon sticks. Red chilli.

Turmeric.

I know this spice from a lifetime of Christmas visits to New Delhi. There, it was a spice cupboard cornerstone with 1001 uses. The purifier when mixed with fresh buffalo milk to cleanse the Shivling deity in Ammi's puja room, her home shrine that was the point of contact between her prayers and our Hindu gods. An ointment when mixed with sandalwood paste and water to heal the back of my childhood knees irritated by eczema and dry Delhi air. As an emulsion to stain the unlined foreheads of my two brothers and me with the yellow markings of God. *Rani Beti, Raja Babus,* she would sing from the bedroom that smelt of ironing and incense, the last syllable of each sentence drawn out on a sharp upward inflection. My little queen. My little kings. We would run to bury ourselves in her shrine and in her lap. Wait for Ammi's cool thumbprint of orange-yellow tika to wet our foreheads. Her kiss on my crown was a blessing equal to that of any deity.

Ammi is dead, now. Her British Raj-era bungalow that once occupied a green corner of South Delhi is a renovated monstrosity in a street choked by cars. I am thirty-five, three decades older and a hemisphere away. Everything has changed. Everything but what this spice once meant to me. 'Bugger.' I step down into the kitchen from the narrow entrance hall and clock the time on the microwave. It's already past 1 p.m. That leaves barely three hours until childcare pick-up. I had hoped for more time. Though the centre doesn't close until after 6 p.m., my own mother's guilt drives me to have them home by 4 p.m. on each of their thrice-weekly visits. Especially now, as the night crowds in early on these cold autumn evenings. Cailean is five years old, Ashok, almost eighteen months. These are big days for little people. Long stretches of hours cleared to accommodate my freelance journalism career, to create space for myself. But sometimes—on days such as these—there doesn't seem space enough.

Sarina. I can't. You don't understand.

Mum's words scream at me as I begin to rearrange my pantry. I stop. Have to grip the edge of the faux-marble bench where Tupperware containers of flour and sugar jostle for space against jars of cumin seeds and cloves. It's the spices that have brought her back. Scents of sweet earth and smoke and fire that leak from these sealed ampoules despite their closed lids. The healing promise of turmeric borne on a wave of olfactory remembrance that has dredged up Mum's old plea—her words long ago stuffed into some forgotten part of my brain. It's a talent I have. To stash and seal away disturbed happenings. Ugly experiences. I was eleven years old when Mum, at forty- three, was diagnosed. Twenty when I gave up hope that her disease could somehow come to mean more to me than a life-defining tragedy. In the void of years between then and now I have whitewashed my own life's canvas whenever I saw fit. I have created new demons and strange heroes. Inverted roles. Reattributed blame. With his wry Australian wit my husband, Scott, refers to my tricksy internal landscape as Sarina World: the place where every Grimm life event is subjected to a forced Disney re-write.

I've only just begun to realise the depth of my gift.

I lied when I told that girl today that I had run from the food of my father. I refused to hear it this morning but I know it now. Knew it the instant Mum's voice leaped into my afternoon. It was an easy delusion for me to propagate: Dad is Kashmiri, after all. Mum, an Australian, the outsider who married into a world as far removed from antipodean suburbia as I am from my own identity. But those single sentence refrains tell nothing of who they are. And even less of the lives they lived. The truth is that Dad was the figure to frame my belief, but it was Mum who fed my heart.

We had two categories of meals growing up in our Australian home. 'Dinner' could be neatly defined. Sausages and mashed potato. Roast lamb and its sequel—a shepherd's pie prepared with the leftover roast routinely served the night after. Spaghetti bolognese. Meat loaf, a dish I still can't abide. The odd bakery-bought meat pie drowned in tomato sauce and surrounded by Bird's Eye frozen peas. But *khaana*. *Khaana* was nourishment with meaning. The word itself simply translates as food. It explains nothing of its importance. Khaana had an umbilical significance: it was the feeding cord that kept me attached via taste and ritual to the ancestry of Dad's Indian family. *Khaana* was never eaten on plates. My brothers and I were served on slick and round stainless steel *thaalis*. Daal was spooned into *katoris*; neat little vessels designed to keep the ginger-rich lentils separate from the one or two sabzi*s*—spiced vegetables dishes— that circled a mound of Basmati rice. *Salan* was lamb, not the sweeter mutton served by Ammi in India, but we devoured it all the same. And no matter what the dish served—no matter it was Mum who was the convert to both Hinduism and the Kashmiri kitchen—it was Mum who always cooked. *'Childrrren!'* Dad would call, while Mum finished up with a last stir of her pots, red hair slipping from its top-knot and gold bracelets jangling as she added a half-teaspoon of *garam masala* to whatever sabzi was on the stove in the minutes before it was served. *'Khaana's ready!'* My brothers and I would drag ourselves from the couch, roll two chatais across the living room floor, collect our *thaalis* from the kitchen and return to the floor to eat: cross-legged and seated three abreast in front of Sale of the Century on TV. If we were lucky, there were homemade *paranthas*. If not, then Old El Paso fajita breads became makeshift chapatti*s* when browned on a hot tawa smeared with ghee.

Dinner was food. *Khaana* was an emotional language with its own vocabulary that only we understood. It was the history of my family, made real with the pieces of herself that Mum built into each mouthful. Because, somehow, in her adoption of the Ganju family's philosophical and culinary customs, Mum was uniquely able to tell the tale of who we were as people in the dishes she cooked. As if she alone was the medium between me and our clan's fantastical past. The weight those exotic meals carried. For me to consume this food was to feed the legacy of all the things I was known to be. A Kashmiri Brahmin. A card-carrying member of the priest caste. Dad whispered in my ear from birth that I claimed a spiritual inheritance. One that connected our family intimately to the world of Hindu gods. *Thrice born,* he would repeat throughout my infancy, at the top of the caste tree and already three turns around life's cosmic wheel. These tales my Dad told; so rich it seemed the multi-armed deities were as close to me as the daal and rice he and Mum ladled onto my empty plate.

Dad's family—the Ganju family—has not lived on its Kashmiri mountaintop for centuries. Theirs was an exodus from an ancient homeland laid squarely at the feet of Emperor Aurangzeb. The Mughal prince was the third son of Emperor Shah Jahan and Mumtaz Mahal, the famed royal couple whose love built the beauty of the Taj Mahal. Yet Aurangzeb took on none of their golden qualities. Instead, it was he who imprisoned his father and murdered his two older brothers in order to clear his way for ascent to the Peacock Throne in 1658. From there Aurangzeb ruled until 1707, stripping away a legacy of religious tolerance that had defined Mughal rulers from Akbar the Great right through to the reign of his own father. So, with Hindu temples burned and Kashmir's Hindu Brahmins captured within the crucible of forced conversion to Islam or death by beheading, the Ganju family scrambled down from its historical birthplace. Houses were left. Possessions that could not be jammed into trunks forgotten. But recipes—recipes are easily stowed in an exiled person's heart. These dishes became the ancestral connection to Kashmir handed down the Ganju family line, from mother to daughter, within a community bound tightly by its place high up near the lap of God. *Salan wala chawal,* an earthy dish of mutton and rice cooked as one and infused with the black earth and shadow of whole black cardamom. Stiff white florets of cauliflower made smoky with ground coriander and whole cumin, reduced to mouthfuls of molten spices. Burnished triangles of paneer held in thrall by the sweet intensity of cinnamon, clove and mace. Like the generations of relatives who came before, these were *thaalis* given to me at each meal since childhood to serve as reminders of who I was. Plates to anchor me. Bites to concretise our status as chosen people, yes, but that also served as quotidian reminders of the ancestral land we had been forced to leave behind.

By the time I was born into a cross-cultural marriage in late '70s Melbourne, the pain of the Ganju exodus had long-since passed. The family had moved on. To the pristine hills of Dehradun, originally. Then the scattered crawl south. New Delhi. Hyderabad. Bangalore. Melbourne. But this idea of landlessness continued to feed in, to mould the people we thought we were. Without a geographical mooring to serve as anchor, our clan evolved to ground its identity in connection with God. It was in this way that Dad—tales told in his distinctly accented English and held together by his steadfast faith—made Hinduism come alive for me. It wasn't a religion or a philosophy. It became a *place*. And I grounded myself here. Grounded myself in the idea of a people who found their home curled up on the welcome mat of God. A space impervious to geographical conflict. It didn't matter, at God's feet, that I was a Hindu girl who lived between Australia and New Delhi. That I could not lay claim to one landscape. A single nationality. God's house was territory I had rights to occupy without threat of expulsion.

And so I ate up Dad's stories just as I did Mum's Indian *thaalis*. As a girl I sat on the banks of the Yamuna river and swayed in time as Krishna seduced the *gopis* of Vrindavan by playing on his exquisite flute. Stood with a lighted candle in the streets of Ayodhya and welcomed Lord Ram as he exited the forest triumphant after fourteen years of exile, loyal brother Lakshman and wife Sita by his side. Peered from behind a cupboard door as Shivji absorbed the Goddess Ganga into his matted locks, hiding his lover at the sound of wife Parvati's early return. My homeland this collection of fantastical topographies that seeped into my skin like the aroma of spice.

For the dreamy, book-obsessed child I was, that sense of exoticism was an intoxicant. And like all intoxicants it blinded me to an essential germ of truth. I cherished the notion that I existed between worlds. Being Hindu in a foreign landscape created a sense of untethered connection that held me for much of the year in a cultural limbo. I spent ten months in every twelve living in our towered hilltop house on farmland in the coastal hamlet of Torquay, another two roaming New Delhi streets between Ammi's Defence Colony bungalow and my cousins' neighbouring C Block home. At the time it seemed that God was my anchor. The power of Hindu mythology that connected me to an intersection where all the pieces of my life could meet. And God was. And those myths were. But only because I tasted it all from within the warm and safe shelter of *her*: Mum, who was my original font.

The spices have been put away and the close of the pantry door brings my attention back to the present with a click. I rummage around the kitchen looking for a place to tuck away my restless mood but can't seem to settle: I wipe down the kitchen bench; half-heartedly make myself a cup of tea; toy with the idea of sitting at my desk in the front room to work on a health feature for *Vogue* due next week. I don't even consider cooking. Today—despite my earlier professed intentions—I'm too agitated by Mum's reappearance in my story. By this twist in plot that I didn't write. Instead, I grab the car keys off the bench and head for the door. I'm driven to shake off my nervous static. Short of a mid-afternoon martini, I know just what it will take.

'Mummy!' Cailean spies me in the childcare playground, leaps off the climbing frame and straight into my arms. 'We haven't had fruit time yet, are you early?'

'Yes, Monkey,' I grin. Hold him close. My every cell aware of his tight little boy-grip. Focus zeroed on his reassuring weight. 'I am. Let's go find your brother.'

Cailean jumps out of my arms and I grab his hand. It is a beautiful afternoon. The sun past its zenith but still warm. We scour the playground. Check the wooden cubby in the corner that overlooks the car park. The sandpit that holds Ashy's favourite digger. Even his room, windows blacked out by curtains where a few smaller babies are just waking from afternoon naps. Eventually we find him waddling in the fenced-off area reserved for construction play, shirtfront a crust of dribble and lunch and sand. Flush-cheeked smile in place.

'Mama!'

'Ashy!' I let go of Cailean's hand to hoist Ashok's buttery body into my chest. Relish the press of his padded bottom against my arm. 'Okay, Monkeys,' I say, holding Ashy high on my body as I pull Cailean close with my free arm. 'Let's go home.' We exit the centre, waving goodbye to their favourite carers as we make our way through the lobby towards the car. I feel better for their company. But it turns out the thoughts I had hoped to shake off via their presence aren't so easy to forget. Thoughts of motherhood and loss and food and what this all might mean for me. I think of this as I coax them into their car seats, bodies wriggly and sticky from a day of high energy, sweat and play. I click my own seat belt into place, reverse carefully and make my way towards home.

I think of how I have come to realise the beauty of motherhood in the boys' presumption of my presence. Adult presumption in relationships threatens inattention. But a child? A child presumes your focus and returns it every minute with a fresh ferocity. It's what makes care of them so compelling. Cailean and Ashy demand I *see* what makes life joyous and painful. Tie me to precise moments with the newness of their world view: door shut to the future and bridge cut to the past. But sometimes, on days like today, sometimes even with the fresh hope of Cailean and Ashok's forms anchored against me, the knot still comes undone. Is that what happened between Mum and me? Was that all it was? As simple as a tether pulled to fray by the weight of Parkinson's? A tie come permanently loose? Maybe it takes less than we imagine to be torn from the children to whom we have given our hearts. An argument. A misunderstanding. An unexpected diagnosis. Their giggles drag my eyes from the road to the rear-view mirror. To see them laughing. The feeling that breaks through the skin of my chest. As their mother I owe them attachment to a past. A tribe. A heritage. But more than that, I owe them a relationship with the 'me' I once was—Mum's daughter of spice. Of course, to owe is not the same as to give. To give I must find it in myself, first. I must find *her*—that girl who once lived upon the step of heaven's door. One raised on the flavour of love and faith. It is a recipe I am desperate to remember.

CHAPTER 2

Daal

Daal is the starting point. When a child's
palate opens beyond basic succour, it's this
dish she will consume in a first hungry bite.
With the lentils soaked for up to twelve hours
before and then pressure-cooked to formless
liquidity, daal offers children a digestible
first understanding of their family's history.

As a baby, Cailean adored Dad's food: the taste of his
Indian grandfather, his Baba. Cailean has always been a
sweet and sensitive child, and the delight he took in eating was as strong as the pleasure Dad got from providing.
The enthusiasm with which Cailean scooped up mouthfuls of rice, daal and sabzi with freshly made chapatti
painted a divine tableau.

It was a sight I was afforded often: Cailean was born
eight weeks before I turned thirty. By then Dad had been

granted sole dominion over our family's Kashmiri stove. There was no contest. Despite being given Ammi's recipe collection upon moving in with Scott at age twenty, I had remained a self-determined non-starter. No pressure cooker in my kitchen and no shrine in my home—at least no shrine that I worshipped at with any frequency. That hadn't changed in the ten years since moving in with Scott and giving birth to Cailean. And Mum? By that time it had been eighteen years since her diagnosis and Mum was too debilitated to cook at all.

I call to the boys from my position at the kitchen sink, occupied with preparation of another night's meal that fails to include any of the spices I bought and stowed in my pantry the week before. I don't fumble for the rolling tub of coriander seeds waiting to be ground, nor shift the cache of red chilies as I reach for the Tupperware of turmeric. I leave aside the gur. The cumin. Forget the nubs of fresh ginger. Instead I re-heat bites of my faded past: *gajar mattar*; the carrots and peas Dad makes for his two grandsons balanced with the sweetness of gur to tamp the pervasive warmth of clove, mace and cinnamon, an overly fragrant trifecta of sweetness too pungent for young palates. A dish that was as much a part of my family time in Ammi's Defence Colony house as were the sunny winter mornings when I played barefoot on her rooftop.

This sabzi forms the foundation of the Kashmiri meal tower Dad has delivered in plastic take-away containers almost every week since Scott and I moved to Melbourne from France when Cailean was ten months old. For four years Dad has worked to maintain a link between my young family and his own Hindu gods through my eldest son: the dinner-table intimacy he has shared with Cailean a way to bridge my culinary and cultural omissions. Dad's gods that long ago held me through Mum's embrace, a lost homeland that no longer feels mine.

'Can we just finish watching *Bananas in Pyjamas* please, Mummy?' It's Cailean throwing me one of his soft smiles from a nest in the couch before turning back to the screen. The late afternoon light floods our back courtyard and falls across the floor and catches the fat round of his cheek. There is such innocence to his needs that I struggle to deny him. Ashy crawls at Cailean's feet, still a little young for his attention to be held by television; he is more enchanted with the bash of his big brother's old Matchbox cars on the rug-covered hardwood floor.

'Sure Buddy,' I concede. 'Ten more minutes.'

Returning to the task at hand, I pull the steamer from the heavy-bottom-pot drawer. I slit open the five-kilogram hessian bag of Basmati rice bought earlier in the week at nearby Limra Groceries and stowed beneath the kitchen sink. It's a child-like starting point. I dip a *katori* into the heavy sack's contents, tip the katori of rice into a stainless steel tiffin and then rinse the grains under cold running water in the kitchen sink. I rinse it, as Ammi once taught me. I swirl my hand through rice and water to remove dirt and starch. It's the secret to cooking rice that is fluffy and light. So I rinse and drain. Twice, three times, before I set it aside. And with each action, I duck and weave around the doubt that has dogged my step since the confession I made the week before to a disengaged shop girl. *Cooking Kashmiri food is something I've avoided doing until now.* Avoidance of spice is where I'm stuck. It seems I would sooner risk continuation of this lifetime of pain than trust my own ability to cope with the emotion that cooking this food will unleash. I try to ignore the similarity between my own behaviour and that which I so long ago accused Mum of enacting; to deny the parallel between Mum's inability to move forward and mine.

So to the noise of cartoons in the background I divide portions of Dad's *gajar mattar* into three, hold Scott's aside for his return later. I drain the rice placed minutes ago on the sideboard and swish it into a pot of water on a rolling boil. Fire up the gas beneath the steamer. I slot in the boys' two *katoris*. Regret that, tonight, this is as far as I can reach: to gather and heat and serve the flavour of someone else's passion. Later, I will lie to my Dad when he asks if I've eaten. But for now, I steal a carrot. Snaffle a pea. Run my finger through the empty plastic container's spice-rich slick before I cram both it and my disturbed thoughts into the sealed kitchen bin.

Parkinson's stole my mother. It is a spiteful disease, one that has used the last twenty-three years as an opportunity to strip her of normalcy, of all the parts and pieces and practicalities that once fit the puzzle of her. Her belief in God was one of the earliest casualties. Sleep another. Dyskinesia was the culprit for the last, a tasteless joke of a medical side effect that caused 'dancing' limbs in patients for whom just walking was a challenge; it didn't distinguish night from day and the ceaseless jerk and twist of her left leg made sleep a peculiar form of torture. Her ability to drive was taken away at the same time as I earned the right to get behind the wheel of my own car. And the cooking? I guess she held on for as long as she could. But it wasn't long enough for me.

'Okay, dinner's ready.' I call time on the day as I lay *thaalis* for the boys side by side on the table.

Cailean gets off the couch. Turns off the television. It is a little before 6 p.m. I help him up to the cushion on his seat. Settle Ashok in the high chair. As I do so Cailean sights his plate and frowns at the mix of rice and sabzi.

'Can't you cook your food tonight, Mummy?' As Cailean's questions, Ashy has already picked up his spoon to dig in: the same passionate nature that can make him an emotional handful also, thankfully, makes him an enthusiastic eater. Grains of rice fall liberally to the towel spread under his high chair, put there to protect the patterned Indian rug of amber, burnt umber and lapis lazuli blue that spreads across this patch of hardwood floor. But Cailean is still, his hands a hold on the chair's sides. 'I don't like Indian food, it's too spicy for me.'

'Just eat it up, Monkey.' I pass him a *roti* bought from one of the Asian food stores at the South Melbourne market. Heated on the tawa, it's warm and buttery with ghee. He loves them and the bread offsets some of the *sabzi's* spice when eaten together. 'Eat it all up, please. Baba made it for you.'

The hypocrisy of my instruction to Cailean is not lost on me. And I'm beginning to wonder if it's not lost on him, too.

Something happened when Mum stopped cooking. Dad took over. The changing of the guard was so seamless as to leave no empty space. There were no frozen meals or easy dinners of baked beans on toast. Food meant too much in our home for that. Alongside mantras it is the embryo of the Hindu Brahmin tradition. All incarnations in the Hindu pantheon have a character. Relationships. Foibles. A favourite food. To convey the personality of each god through bedtime story and kitchen table was Dad's way of providing me a moral compass and a deep sense of belonging. By making our gods people for us, Dad was helping to provide me with a series of powerful figures in whose image I might see myself reflected. As a girl, I realised Dad reinforced this daily through the interconnection of food and philosophy, what I understood to be the two pillars of my family's Hindu framework. He told me stories of Ganeshji and his passion for *gulab jamans*. Taught me that the dark pull of Saturn meant Saturday was a day to not eat animal products, get haircuts, nor wear black or new clothing. He explained why, when fasting, it was important to cook with *hing*, a pungent oleoresin said to contain none of the physically arousing and spiritually unsettling properties of garlic and onion, the two aromatics *hing* is used to replace.

But Mum was different in her approach. It's not that she didn't have Dad's knowledge of myth, but that she brought more of herself to the stories. The knowledge she had acquired much later in life had been so deeply internalised that it sounded not only natural, but softer. Mum had a way of interpreting the tenets of Hinduism without the heavy emphasis on religious strictures and spiritual regulation. Her comprehension refracted through love and luminosity. She didn't *tell* the stories, she just lived them. And when she left the stove, she took the lightness of that understanding with her.

Mum's gentle approach to myth and spice was something Dad couldn't replace. As I sit at the table with an empty place mat in front of me and encourage Cailean to eat more than *roti* and rice, I can't help but feel that his growing refusal to continue consumption of the food he once adored is merely an increasingly conscious reflection of my own reluctance. It's not a fanciful notion, but a universal truth: my children's behaviour within the family reflects all the pieces of myself that I prefer not to acknowledge; Cailean and Ashok show my beliefs in their actions long before I am ready to face what they see.

I sleep terribly that night. Dreams plagued by cuts of lost and stolen things. Scott comes to bed late and I leave it early, a physical indication of the distance that has crept between us. Scott has been the communicator in our relationship since the day we met. I have needed that. I have become, over the years, so tired of listening to the garbled sounds of my own voice and so confused by the absence of Mum's that I have let him be the one to finish my sentences and make my voice coherent by doing so. I have tuned into Scott because his tenor is different to the replacement that was Dad's: so strident and implacable, no space to hear or untangle a young girl's doubt. But Scott—Scott who has never lived in a sky filled with chariots and battles and cosmic intrigue. His world tied to the physicality of the Australian bush and the ocean and the soil beneath his feet. His voice that is earth and tree and tide. His home a place of solid earth where I could re-make mine.

But everything changes.

I slip from beneath the covers and pull on my clothes discarded by my side of our bed the night before, my breath the only disturbance. Slip a thick pair of socks on my feet so that I may remain unseen: this is my invisibility cloak. So shod I can creep past the boys' bedroom adjacent to ours on the second storey, pad down the stairs of our creaky Victorian-era cottage without a sound. I am alone in the quiet half-dark of a 6 a.m. silence. Restless. Impervious to the early morning chill. I open a few cupboards as a bored child seeking food. My attempt to find some *place* I might file these thoughts. Purchase of these spices that has been my pull of a loose string on a knitted sweater. I have tugged on the errant thread in the hope of fast putting my life to rights. But this itch to cook is wound into the fabric of who I have been and who I am. To unravel it is to be left me, a pile of formless wool. The fear is immense. If I bring myself undone, who can I trust to knit me back together?

Can't you cook your food tonight, Mummy?

And yet in the face of this fear I hear other things. Cailean's need of me that echoes the growth of my own desperate reach for the girl I left behind: each morning that I wake beside Scott I am pushed into a hollow of sorrow as I realise that not to cook the Kashmiri flavours of my girlhood is to lose the taste of who I am. And I don't want to be lost and I don't want to be broken. It hurts too much to be a victim of someone else's tragedy. To ignore the person I was. The woman I know that I still am: a vessel for generations of culinary remembrance. I am looking for a way to heal enough so that this journey can begin. I want a different future. One that might allow me to exist independent of my past. And I have no idea where to start.

I drift down the hall to flick on a light and stand before my tall bookshelf in the front room study. Only then, when I pull the crinkled plastic pocket of computer-typed pages hidden between Mum's old *Woman's Weekly* cookbooks, do I feel that first quiet shift. My soul sighs: *Here they are.*

Rajma. Keema. Sheer pulao. Palak paneer. Aloo parantha. Kheer.

Ammi's recipes.

As a young Hindu girl I was raised as a creature of myth. But Mum's diagnosis ended my belief that our family's love for God and myth kept us protected. Her illness caused a seismic shift to the dynamic of our family. Into the cracks created crept doubt. My doubt. With this distrust was born a determination within me to leave the tales I had been bred on, behind. I have taken myself as far away from my roots as I have been able. I thought I could survive forever, here, in a bubble of dislocation. Yet in this last week, as the leaves have begun their change, so have I. Now, lost in the empty hours before day, I can no longer ignore the obvious: I cannot survive a ghosted existence. I am too tired to run anymore. And yet I will need guts to recognise the look and the feel of my new path. Is it in Godlessness? In an altered faith? In food? Is it in separation from my parents' family? In the solidification of my own? Leafing through Ammi's recipes I know that, no matter where I end up, this is the place I need to begin; to dive into food and story, that is where I have to start.

'Cailean, turn off the cartoons, please, your Weet-Bix is on the table. Okay, Ashy, up you go.' I grunt a little as I lift his rotund frame up and into the high chair, then move his bowl from the kitchen bench to the tray in front of him.

'Naanees?'

'There are sultanas on your Weet-Bix, Buddy, you don't need more. Tea, darling? Cailean. Table please. Now.'

Is this the truth of infidelity? I feel nervous. Jittery. I can smell the sweat of my armpits though I showered only thirty minutes ago. The morning's discovery of that time-yellowed sheaf of recipes I have now stashed above the fridge, occupies the kitchen as a presence. I want my family gone so that I can cook. At thirty-five, I have already procrastinated for more than twenty years. I know the impetus to move forward is a delicate one and that it would not take much to discourage me, to knock me off course. I'm worried that fear will defeat me and leave me stranded—that the smallest distraction will provoke me to grasp at any one of the myriad reasons the scared little girl inside me has, *not* to cook. In this way, the two hours between seeing my family off at the gate and cooking from those papers feels an eternity.

'Do I need their kindy bags?' It's Scott, by the front door. He'll walk them to childcare on his way to work; the men's shoe store he owns and runs with a business partner and friend on Clarendon Street, South Melbourne's busiest thoroughfare.

'They're outside with the shoes,' I call back.

At the table I give Ashy's face a brusque wipe, unsnap his bib and carry him to the downstairs bathroom, Cailean on my heels. I barely have the patience to make sure both boys' teeth are brushed before I hand them over to Scott, waiting by the open front gate.

'Have a great day. I'll be picking you up later, Monkeys,' I speed talk. 'See you darling,' Scott and I share a perfunctory kiss, the kind parents of young kids perfect. 'I'll speak to you later.'

I had always believed a refusal to cook this food would bring me safety. Safety from pain and safety from sadness. Safety from *memory*. But as I shut the front door against the falling mess of silverbirch leaves and tread the hall to the kitchen, I understand something else. I understand that, at some point, refusal manifests its own presence. That instead of being known by the sum of all the things that I am, I have become framed by the sum of all the things that I am *not*. A life scratched in negative neon. I couldn't see it before. It took my son to show me; that moment at the dinner table last night when I saw him mirror signals I hadn't known I'd sent.

As a girl who felt emotionally deserted by her own mother, I fear that to not address my own emotional limitations would see my children pay a price that I know to be too high. But that doesn't take the fear away. My god I wish it did. But it doesn't. I'm not capable of being emotionally generous enough to place my sons' welfare above my own, at this point. Instead I worry what effect facing my past will have on *me*. It takes enormous focus to look beyond my internal conflict and move towards action. In the end a single thought overrides all of my fear.

I can no longer stand to be me.

With this thought to cauterize my pain I do what I have not been able to so far. I break free of safety, I turn my back on insecurity, I pull out my pots and I cook.

As I cut into a knuckle of fresh ginger, the knowledge floods back to me. The number of times I have participated in this very act. The peeling. The chopping. Knowledge I could not expunge in all these years, despite my active denial. The art of using spice that was absorbed in childhood from within the cradle of my family's embrace. I forget the day and the seasons. Feel only the effervescence of familiarity in my palms as I handle the ginger. As I run dusty yellow lentils through my fingers on the way to transforming them from hardened pellets to a rich potage of love. *Toor* daal. Flecked with cumin seeds. The first taste of India for my children and the one Scott misses most when absent from Dad's bounty of meals. The one Kashmiri dish I used to permit myself to eat, even during all those years throughout my twenties when I would eat no other, determined as I was to eat outside of my culinary heritage.

I remember all of this. I remember Ammi's fingers curled by arthritis and softened by glycerine and rose water as they handled lentils and vegetables and spice. I remember shelling peas with her in pallid winter sunshine on her concrete kitchen steps. And I remember something else. I remember why I couldn't cook this food before and when I felt as if I would never cook it again. I remember the helpless sadness of those tearful teenage exchanges between my Mum and I before my suffering turned to sober silence and a silent stove. When she was forced to watch me flounder. As if by drowning in her pain I could make her better. Hold back the tide of her physical deterioration.

The pain of memory is choking. But after so many years of depriving myself of this connection, the push to move forward is too strong. I have no time to soak the lentils. So a *katori* of daal routinely left to soften in water overnight is rinsed instead. Once. Twice. A third time and left aside. I swing the pressure cooker onto the stove and tip in the drained lentils, listening as they hit the bottom of the pot with a watery *schlump*. I swallow tears. Top with water and set aside. Spices are next, retrieved from the pantry and lined along the counter. Cumin seeds, turmeric and salt. Red chilli. A restrained nub of gur. *Garam masala*. Some of it instinct, some of it lessons from Ammi's notations given to me by my Dad in hope, years before, so that Ammi's spirit may one day guide my hand. She is here, today, I can feel her. Willing me on as I move forward. I grip her close in my memory. I need her now. Need that remembrance of my life when I believed I was still the favourite. The beloved of my faultless Ammi, not my faulty parents. Her Rani Beti. Her presence always consistent. And me held steady in her faith. Another regal daughter of God born to Earth.

I boil the kettle. Take three over-ripe roma tomatoes from the fruit bowl. Twist into their tops my favoured black-handled knife and, with a crank of my wrist, they are cored. A cross snicked in to their base then five minutes in a bowl of hot water to release the skins. Short cuts learnt at the feet of my parents. Next, spice. Into the pot I sprinkle turmeric, gur and salt before returning it to the stove. I replace the lid and turn it to medium heat, attentive for the stream of steam that will tell me it is time to seal the pot and wait for the pressure cooker's whistle. I set my clock for the seven minutes that will see the alchemy of cooking performed. Only then do I release the breath I am holding.

In the infinitesimal gap this exhale creates I see me: mine, the actions of a marionette, controlled equally by fear as by recipe and recollection.

There is a powerful motive why Indian daughters were taught to cook while still struggling to reach the height of their parents' knees. It is how I learned what to put in the pots and pans that cluttered our family's stovetop. Spices, of course. Measures and quantities. But the real magic was in understanding how much of the cook was liberally peppered through each meal. Truly transcendent food is that which tells the tale of the one who makes it. To do so is to be possessed of the ability to pass feeling through fingertips into the pot. An artist, only one with an edible palette. Ammi was the first person to teach me that. In Ammi's daal I didn't just taste the teaspoons of salt and turmeric. Two measures for the former, a three-quarter for the latter. Nor the ten grams of gur, the twenty grams of fresh ginger. I tasted *her*. Her joys and lessons and experiences and disappointments. I tasted the coalescence of her inner space, the axis where all the pieces of her identity met.

I tasted her ability to tell. I tasted the gift she had to listen.

The scream of the pressure cooker's whistle calls my attention. I note the time on the microwave clock. Switch off the gas. Place it in the kitchen sink to de-pressurise while I reach for another pot. This one smaller. A vessel for the *chownk*, the mix of spices stirred into hot ghee that is then folded into daal to serve. I consult Ammi's recipe. Thrill to the sizzle of cumin as it hits the ghee. I breathe in the warm burn of fresh-grated ginger before tossing it in alongside ground red chilli and coriander powder, quantities ordained on the page before me. I am rushed. Excited, yes, but also scared about the parts of myself I might re-find. I slice in diced tomato stripped of its skin before the spices stick and burn. Stirring over a medium heat is fragrant alchemy. The mix draws together as moisture and minutes evaporate, what was at first only liquid scent now a heady paste. Returning to the pressure cooker, I release the lid, pour in the *chownk* and stir. A half-teaspoon of *garam masala* the final addition.

I pull in a half spoonful of daal with my teeth. In that first swallow I understand exactly how much of Ammi's legacy has survived inside me. I am present in my food, all right. Just not in the way I had hoped. This dish tells the stark tale of who I am now. It's spicy. The back of my throat caught by a punch of fear in the forward spike of red chilli. I taste its knobbled texture as a choke of impatience; half-moons of lentils I didn't take the time to soak. As if any pause would set me off course. My journey consumed by a terrific drive to bring it all to a head with maximum speed and minimum feeling. It's unrealistic. I know that. But pain avoidance is a practice I have perfected. The habit is a hard one to break.

And yet despite all of this, it's not the daal's imbalance that releases the flow of tears. It's what's there. Hidden. Underneath. I discern it with a second taste, after the shock of that first bite has passed: the smoky warmth of cumin seeds; the echo of *garam masala's* complex sweetness. Soft depths now barely discernible that once penetrated the entirety of me.

It is an arresting moment. To know that today I have cooked *this* recipe: a bare beginning in the hope that, one day very soon, I may come to express a different taste of me.

TOOR DAAL
Yellow split pea *Daal*

Daal is integral to the cuisine of India. A sustaining bowl of protein and spice afforded as nourishment by both paupers and princes. Each region and each family will have its own recipe. This is ours.

INGREDIENTS:
2 *katoris toor* daal (around 350 grams)

1 large tomato

2 teaspoons salt

¾ teaspoon turmeric

10 grams gur

20 grams fresh ginger

1 tablespoon ghee

1 heaped teaspoon cumin seeds

1 teaspoon Kashmiri red chilli powder

1 teaspoon *garam masala*

METHOD:
Pre-soak the daal for at least a few hours or preferably, overnight. The lentils soak up a huge amount of liquid so make sure they are placed in a container with enough space to allow for a cover of water that is equal in height to the lentils themselves. When soaked, drain of all water.

Empty into the pressure cooker and add fresh water until the lentils are just covered. Add turmeric, salt and gur before closing the pressure cooker lid, leaving the pressure valve to the side.

Put on to high heat and place the valve in place once a steady stream of steam is whistling from the lid.

The daal will take from 5 to 7 minutes to cook, depending on how long it was soaked. I always release the pressure and check after 5 minutes. If not quite cooked, I put back on to high heat with the valve replaced for a further few minutes until cooked.

Thickness is a personal preference. I enjoy a thicker, more textural daal and will at times remove it from the heat before the lentils have completely broken down.

While the daal is cooking, prepare the *chownk*.

Combine the tomato and ginger in a food processor or finely chop.

Heat 1 tablespoon of ghee in a small pot. Add the cumin seeds. Once fragrant, add the Kashmiri red chili powder and the tomato and ginger mix. Cook on low heat for up to 20 minutes, or until it forms a thick paste.

Add to the cooked daal and stir through.

Add the *garam masala* and stir through. Simmer for a further few minutes on low heat.

Serve.

Comfortably serves eight as part of a larger Kashmiri meal.

CHAPTER 3

Salt

Salt is the accelerator. The intensifier.
It alone is the spice with the power to
explode the taste of what lies within.

WHEN I WAS TEN YEARS old, Dad told me a story of a book that existed as a record of every Kashmiri Hindu Pandit ever born, the names handwritten. It seems to me an impossibility, now, but back then I believed him. The book, he said, as we sat together on a wool rug, on completion of his morning puja, was preserved in secret on a Kashmiri mountaintop. Dad loved to embroider his tales, and I loved to enable him: I imagined a pulpit in a dark forest displaying a book somehow impervious to time and weather. It was easy for me to believe in magic over practicality when Dad spoke of our ancestral past, chiefly because Kashmir was a geography so remote from where I grew up: in the rugged newness of Torquay, a small

33

beach town on Australia's South East coast where summers are hot and dry and winter brings frigid Southern Ocean gales. Yet Dad's tale was so vivid that I could feel Kashmir's cold mountain air. I could imagine the gentle summer sun that lit wild forests. The river landscape. Inscribed within this book, Dad said, was the history of my family that dated back more than 5,000 years to our Ganju ascendants, the Seven Rishi Saints. Known to all now as the Seven Sisters, the open star cluster located in the constellation of Taurus, one of the nearest to Earth and brightly visible to the naked eye.

The night after I cooked that first daal I take out the bins. And it strikes me, as I look to the inky sky, that it's been years since I have remembered that tale of the stars. And even longer since I have seen myself reflected among them.

I don't return to Ammi's recipes in the day that follows my first daal. The shock of tasting where I am, is still too powerfully raw. It is the beginning of a pattern that will emerge as March moves into April: each new dish experimented with will demand of me a period of recovery. But for now all that is known is when Scott comes home from work the night following my first attempt at Kashmiri cooking it is dinner, not *khaana*, which awaits him.

'The boys have just gone to sleep.' It is dark outside. Just gone 8.30 p.m. I push out the sentence in a strained

stage whisper from the couch the second after I hear the scratch of keys in the front door, Scott's footsteps in the house. I crane my head forward in the hope that my voice will carry down the length of the hall. It must do, because I hear his movements quieten. The sound of his leather- soled shoes slipped off in the front study.

'Your dinner's in the steamer.' I turn to look at Scott over my shoulder as he walks in to prop his bag against a leg of the dining room table. He slings his jacket over the back of a chair before moving to see what's heating on the stove. I don't get up from the couch to help. The hour is late. Being a Thursday, the kids were home and it's been a long day. The television is on. Tonight means *Law and Order SVU.* It is more visual distraction than entertainment, the sound so low that I can discern no more than the timbre of vocal tone.

'Turn it up a bit.' It's Scott, carrying a plate to the table. I do as he asks before I get up to go and flick on the kettle. 'How was the day?' I drop a kiss to the top of his head as I pass. He doesn't respond to the affection, only to the question. I know why the coldness. Since Scott gave up executive life two years earlier to open his own retail business this has been a nightly conversation. It was Scott's dream to run his own business. After twenty years of working to make money for global companies, he wanted the chance to try and make a go of it on his own. And yet the switch from the comfort of an executive salary to the uncertainty of a consumer-led existence has represented a terrifying shift. Our family is now reliant upon Melbourne men and their seven-day-a-week willingness to spend hundreds of dollars on English leather shoes. Each evening that Scott walks in the front door, I shove my heart from my throat back into my chest and with forced casualness spit out the words that feel as sawdust in my mouth. *How was the day?* With these four words I pass him my anxiety. And he has become tired of holding it.

'Twenty-five hundred.' Scott grinds salt over the casserole without tasting. He says nothing more. It seems that, of late, the more reassurance I need the more determined he becomes to withhold it.

'That's not bad for a Thursday?' What begins as a statement ends on an upward inflection. *Is that amount what we need? Are we going to be okay? Is it working out? Will the mortgage payment be made?* The less he says, the more frightened I become. Fear that escalates in direct correlation to his growing intolerance of my unspoken petition for emotional support. A support I am in no condition to reciprocate.

And yet I know he needs me. He is fatigued. The stress of the transition has been immense, our life now a joker's hand of Western middle-class angst. For the first time in our married lives we are short of money and the pressure this deficit creates takes away both our time and our breathing space. Melbourne is one of Australia's most expensive cities, and raising two children while choosing to live in a pricey inner-city suburb without a secure, executive wage to bolster us, leaves us feeling financially unstable. I believe in him, but sometimes I wonder if my faith that he can hold us doesn't just add to his feelings of stress. In any case, while Scott works at keeping us from sinking, I work to contain my resentment: because after so many years of living a fairy tale of romantic love, travel and enviable experiences, this change in our financial status has been a shock. One that I am struggling to handle.

It is not about the money. It is about what the money represents. I walked into this marriage upon a boardwalk of certainty; Scott's love and steadiness that had lifted me out of the mire of sickness and family trauma. Our lack of money represents the introduction of uncertainty. I find the change as destabilising as Scott's new reticence around me. He who was once so tolerant of my needs is now too consumed with his own anxieties to entertain mine. Or perhaps it's Scott's desire to be my saviour that has disappeared. Either way the signs are there: in the fill-in noise of the television; the concentrated clink of his cutlery; in the sharp and heavy silences in between. Some nights the tension bubbles so close to the surface, I'm frightened it might push through. His frustration at my emotional indigence. Nights like tonight. Just like my mother, I have always shied away from confrontation, particularly when the tensions relate to the people I love most in my life. Those are the times I flee.

'Do you mind if I go up to bed?' I finish making my tea in one of the delicate porcelain cup and saucers

Scott and I bought in Paris a decade earlier. We had spent more than an hour comparing designs in the small boutique on Rue Mesnil, its space cluttered with dishware of stunning intricacy. The purchase was our response to the beauty of the city in which we then lived. Scott had carefully carried the box weighed down with plates and tea things and breakfast bowls the 200 metres home. One of the teacups is broken, now. I'm not sure it can be replaced. 'I want to get up early and run in the morning.'

'I've got work to do tonight.' He moves his plate of sausage and steamed vegetables to the kitchen breakfast bench and begins to pull the bookkeeping files from his briefcase. Spreads them across the table. I know Scott. I know that his non-response to my pronouncement is deliberate. He can't even begin to address my 'want' to run when there are so many of his wants and needs that I fail to directly address: his want for me to lean less on him; his need for me to understand, if only just a little, how my behaviour impacts him. 'Don't wait up for me,' he says, and I'm not sure whether or not I detect sarcasm. 'I'll be late.' We pass in the kitchen as he takes his dishes to the sink and I take my cup up to bed. He doesn't move to kiss me. I touch him hesitantly; feel all that is tightly held within him and wish that I was brave enough to allow him its release.

I spent the spare hours of my early adolescence reading Mills and Boon. Under the desk in year eight maths or English, once I had barrelled through the set work. On the school bus after my girlfriends had hopped off. Dad berated me; mine was an addiction to romance he deemed inappropriate for his only daughter. I recall a Bangalore day when I was fourteen, Mum lifted my mattress to find a library of second-hand romance novels bought in secret at a cluttered used bookstore on Bangalore's busy MG Road. Thick quadrants of hope whose sharp corners kept me lifted. Even as I kept them hidden. I remember the consternation. The confused reaction of Mum, as if she couldn't figure out if her daughter's secret fantasy life should be weeded out or left to flourish. But these books spoke to a central part of the woman that I was becoming. Romantic love has always been at the core of who I am. It was, and remains, intrinsic to me.

But as I labour up the stairs to our bedroom under the heavy weight of disappointment—in myself, in my marriage, in my life—I can see now why Mum worried about my teenage romantic obsessions. Mills and Boon storylines are no basis upon which to build a marriage. In real life, marriage begins where these fictional lives end: not with sex and with courtship, but with babies and sleeplessness and economic difficulties and the difficulty in remaining, not just cohabitees of the same house and life, but lovers and partners, too. I see this in the same way that I realise other things. That my need to seek a new way forward is complicated by the fact that I must learn how to bring Scott and the boys along with me, too. Failing to do so will lead to catastrophic loss. My changes must deepen my marital connection. At the moment I don't feel this is the case. I know Scott is worried all I am doing is creating a point of departure. For change can as easily drive a wedge as build a bridge, and to experience this certainty around my relationship with Scott is wordless terror. And yet the train is in motion. I brush my teeth. I slip beneath the covers. I reach out an arm to click off the lamplight and close my eyes against the future I'm reaching out towards, desperate to have it and yet scared by what its arrival might mean.

When a Ganju cooks, the way salt is used is an indicator of the nature of our faith. Mum's use of salt was soft. Ammi's piercing. Dad's, strident. And mine? I'm still figuring that out. These thoughts chase each other around my head as I stand at the benchtop and add the final touch of *garam masala* to yet another attempt at daal. It's been a week since I left Scott at the dining room table with his briefcase and accounts. A week of trying to work out whether or not I should continue to move forward with my plan to cook myself into another reality. Though I considered it, I couldn't ignore my kitchen forever. It took five days to catch up on work. After the Southern Hemisphere summer break everyone is fully back online.

It will remain busy now until August, when winter's dark pull draws us all into its slow and heavy vortex.

I filed a health piece with one of my *Vogue* editors, received the sign off on a first person piece from another, and won a few pitches with one of my longest-standing editors at *Epicure*, the newspaper food supplement that attracts attention as Melbourne's go-to culinary bible printed each Tuesday in *The Age*. In between there were trips with the kids to the park. Coffee dates with girlfriends. Then the domestic drudgery that has to be taken care of: food shopping; toilets cleaned; dinners prepared.

But these recipes have their own pull. To be back with the pressure cooker and spices means I remake my daal often over the next few days and the results vary. The single consistency is my inability to intuitively gauge the measure of salt. Though I have Ammi's recipes to follow, I want to make these dishes my own. This is where my experimentation comes in: playing with finding a balance between what Ammi cooked and what I taste like. She's my family, but as a woman, belongs to a different generation and a different geography. Her food was always more heavily salted, a preference Dad told me owed partly to the climate (salt being a necessity during the sweaty months of the monsoon), and partly just to the way Ammi cooked: her sabzis were heavily spiced, a reflection of her powerful personality. And yet I'm softer and lighter in my faith and in my strengths, than she. When I follow Ammi's recipe, the salt is too much.

Too sharp and too false, as a representation of me. Salt's strong burn is a distraction; it cancels out the nuance of warmth and comfort and sweetness that my daal should contain. And yet when I leave Ammi's written directions aside, the balance invariably falls short. I'm too frightened by that first taste of my own daal to let go, to see what my cooking might reveal. So I recede. Then the salt drops too far back, is folded up by the lentils' heavy neutrality. My daal becomes insipid. It lacks the strength of Ammi's belief, the thing that identified her presence in each meal's savoury profile.

For even as a child I understood that, in Ammi's hand, salt was powerful. With it she created clarity: the element that united roots and seeds and leaves, transforming food into prasad, an edible conversation my family carried out with God. At each of those meals I would watch as Ammi slid a small corner of rice and sabzi to the edge of her *thaali* with the dexterous fingers that spoke of her tailor's profession. Her long-time servant, Kishin, would wait until she had finished eating and then set this small portion of food aside. He offered it to the garden that was Ammi's open-air temple. I imagined that with this small taste Ammi fed the gods our devotion. I attempt to trick myself into a belief that it is Ammi's absence from my life that's behind my culinary confusion. But I know I carry Ammi in my heart. That where I go wrong is not the missed presence of Ammi, but my inability to create a culinary link between her and me that includes Mum.

I need to understand where Mum fits in the Ganju culinary story before I can understand where I do.

It was Ammi who taught Mum to cook. Then upon my parents' return to Australia in the months before my birth, Mum who taught Dad. Mum was a woman of depth and allure. The modern version of the traditional maternal archetype. Soft. A nurturer. She was sexy, too. As a girl I knew her from the newspaper clippings she had saved from her twenties as a stunningly slim fashion designer who had set early '70s Melbourne on fire with her risqué outfits. *Men fall off trains when I wear this outfit.* It was my favourite quote and, having as a teenager later tried (and failed) to pull her narrow diaphanous dresses over my own slim shoulders, I could well believe it.

Even as Mum converted to Hinduism after her marriage to Dad she kept her free, fashion-forward spirit alive: the two of them worked side by side in their family business, the manufacture and design of clothes and textiles for some of what were then Australia's biggest women's clothing labels. Portmans. Sportsgirl. Adele Palmer. The same affinity for colour and texture that inspired her youthful fashion identity and her design work, found expression in her food: plates that were rich and nuanced and bright. Mum never tried to recreate Ammi's taste. The strength of her identity and the natural aptitude she had to pour herself into the pot meant she mixed her own balance. A certain enchanting lightness that I loved. Hers was a talent Ammi and Dad deeply respected and it set the tone for the years that unfolded. The deference Dad paid to her judgement. *Jenny,* Dad would call, *how much* garam masala *should I put in this* daal? *Jenny,* he would follow, *shall I start timing the rice?* And yet if there was one element of Mum's cooking Dad would repeatedly call to question through all their years together, it was her light hand with salt.

Dad has always encouraged me to accept that there is no distinction to be made between in-laws and birth parents. It's the Indian way. So when a Hindu woman would marry she would cease to exist within her original family structure. She would become, instead, the spiritual property of the Other. Her husband's family. Complete absorption into the married family demanded that the new wife treat her husband's parents as her own. For this reason the wedding ceremony could equally be considered a baptism. Because alongside the diamonds and jewels her new family would place around her neck, would hang a new name. Chosen by her new mother. And as surely as her red and gold wedding sari would be unwound, this is the woman she would become.

The new wife's name was chosen from one of the thousands of monikers claimed by each of the Hindu goddesses, some of which were utterances of worship I was taught to recite daily in my prayers. With these words, I would highlight the essence of who these deities were in my eyes. Saraswati, Goddess of Knowledge. Padmakshi, Goddess Whose Eyes Are Like a Lotus. Or Kali, the One Who Is Beyond Time.

It follows that choice of this name carries the heavy weight of blessing and expectation: that this new wife will receive both the boon of her namesake's gifts, but also that she will realise this good fortune within the house of her new family. Ammi decided Mum would become Amba, one of the first names of the thousand claimed by the Ganju family's ancestral Goddess of Worship, Durga Devi. So, naturally, when Ammi taught Mum to cook, she instinctively made an ancient culinary tradition her own. Because even among all of those Indian women for whom exoticism was a birthright, Mum shone like the silver leaf that topped those diamond-shaped barfi sweets she so loved. Dressed in sheer and vibrant swathes. Lips red and jewellery bold and chunky and gem-studded. Mum had a wildness that sweated itself through her skin. Initially her spirit showed itself in the pans with just a lighter touch of ghee. But as the years slid by and Mum became increasingly familiar with these dishes, her presence grew: sabzis born of Ammi's essence twisted by my mother's hand with the same graceful elegance captured in her own dyed henna-red topknot. Less mace and nutmeg. The addition of garlic. Mum's food, like her presence, was a thing of ethereal beauty. And yet I think her soft relationship with salt confounded Dad. It had nothing like the force of Ammi's. But to me those white grains fell in a waterfall of gratitude from Mum's fingers. I saw her as blissfully contented. That she had found herself in a foreign space. As if she had always known it was her destiny to land in a physical reality far removed from the one she had grown up knowing. That it was this sense of wonder that kept her presence serene and her play with salt dappled.

I don't know how to find that space. Her Parkinson's diagnosis reared up right at the point in my early adolescence when my linkage to that matriarchal chain should have been secured, Mum the one to secure me. Instead she was distracted by her illness and her presence in my life was diluted. Her sickness required her attention, and Mum's guardianship of me in that important stage between adolescence and womanhood was not what it could have been. I felt alone at least some of the time, and it was within that void that my sense of security was lost. Lost along with all those other parts of myself I can no longer see. Contented wife. Devoted daughter. Child of the stars. As a girl I could look to the Seven Sisters in the night sky and see myself reflected in their light: back when I placed myself within the frame of a world that existed both on Earth *and* in heaven. When Mum remained a goddess untouched by age or time or disease. Now I just feel the cold light of her absence from the pantheon that once ruled my world. And me. Left to look upon my God, my kitchen and my life from the outside because of it.

The rest of the week passes in a blur. I wake up that Saturday morning sick with a feeling of dread. Scott will spend another weekend at work on the retail floor. I shall spend another morning alone with our two boys awaiting the arrival of my parents. A family endurance test made more difficult by Scott's absence. His solid presence has acted as my buffer. As always, I hope traffic on the hour- long drive from Torquay to South Melbourne might make it a later start; Mum and Dad never like to leave for the drive home any later than 2 p.m. But by 10 a.m. the doorbell rings. Surprise, surprise: it seems that even today God refuses to be on my side.

'*Namaskaaaarrr.*' It's Dad. I flatten myself against the hallway wall upon opening the front door to make way for my parents' passage down the narrow corridor. The March sun is weak this morning and a chill of cold air rushes inside. Now sixty-seven, Mum's physical incapacity is such that they must move as conjoined twins. Dad's arm twined under hers so that she does not fall. His focus on the burst of commands that have become—it seems to me—their primary form of communication.

'Jenny! Stop. You know how to walk. *Lift* your feet. Don't shuffle. Jennyyy,' the last, her name, said on a drawn out downward inflection that rings with a unique melange of warning, condescension and compassion. 'You need to turn yourself up.'

They limp the hall's length in a bustle of coats and shawls and plastic bags, their combined girth brushing the walls: cooking and eating have become their primary form of entertainment and communication and it shows in their shapes; their wide frames are confronting to me, so foreign from the slim and straight parents I grew up knowing. I follow with the heavy haul of food Dad had sent me to collect from the boot of his car in time to see Mum lurch sloppily down the single step into our kitchen and living room. Frozen feet that propel her forward in a staggered shuffle. For a second it looks as if she might fall. I feel my heart leap into my throat in the split second before fear ignites in a flame of anger.

'Be careful, Mum.' My mouth ejaculates the words. Voice sharp and loud. I can barely breathe for the band that has tightened across my chest. It's always like this. Always, always, always. I have come to dread their bi-monthly Saturday visits for the emotional toll it takes on me. All those years I knew her as the Mum who wore Chanel red lipstick to tend her beloved roses on our dry, five-acre bush block. I knew her as the Mum who advised me to always wear clean underwear because— she smiled with a wink—you never knew when an accident might happen that could require a fireman's rescue. The Mum once engaged to Scandinavian royalty. Who cleaned the house in a waft of Poison and a clatter of gold. The one who laughed herself silly watching *Fawlty Towers*. Who called me *possum* and *flea*. Who loved to take me shopping. Who never failed to kiss me goodnight. And now. Now I know her as *this*. The Mum whose girth equals my father's. The one who is apparently too tired to do her physio but can cross the house at a whip for a piece of cake. Who rustles in her embroidery-panelled handbag for the stimulator she turns up and down to control the pacemaker in her brain. Who joins Dad in a bizarre dynamic of grandparenthood that rotates them through the roles of crotchety bullies, detached bystanders or kiddy-crack pimps determined to seduce Cailean and Ashok with sugar.

'I said Namaskar, Cailean.' Dad deposits Mum in a chair at the dining room table. He berates Cailean, playing Lego on the living room floor, for not getting up to greet them and kiss them both hello. 'Don't you say namaskar to your Baba and Ammi anymore?'

'Namaskar, Baba. Namaskar, Ammi.' Cailean is nothing if not dutiful. At my signal he pulls himself up and away from his patch of sun to give them the kind of distanced hug and kiss that suggests fear of contagion. Ashy has no such qualms. He sits in the middle of the table, put up there by his Baba. He pulls at Mum's reading glasses. Loses a sock as he scrunches the newspaper that Dad immediately opens to read beneath his nappy-padded bottom. Ashok, their little Indian prince. I'm happy for his blind enthusiasm. It helps in some small part to relieve the stifling tension.

'Sarina, I'll need those plastic containers back,' Dad directs the comment to me, while Mum stays mostly silent. Over the years Parkinson's has combined with Dad's energetic expansion to stifle her speech. Our conversations, when they occur, are reduced to a few spare sentences. I can no longer bear to be assaulted by grief. To hear in the stilted form of our communications how far we are from each other is too much. And when I can't avoid it, the neutral tenor of her words contributes nothing to the rebuild of my shattered past. So I stand behind the kitchen bench. It's my buffer zone, a physical barrier that delineates my space from the sphere of their influence. Here I sort through Dad's sabzi*s* and various leftovers—some Chinese rice, gelatinous sweet and sour pork—he brought up in the cooler bag. I distribute its contents within my fridge. Pretend it's the chores and not the emotional baggage that keeps me at this physical distance.

'If you can turn out the food that's in my dishes and then wash them, I can take them home.' I try not to visibly grit my teeth at Dad's request. If Mum's voice inspires defensive sadness, Dad's draws me immediately to anger. I blame him for so much. For the failure of his faith to protect us from illness. I know it makes no sense. That I act as an irrational child in his presence.

I push out the offer of a cup of tea and proceed—at their acceptance—to make it in almost total silence.

Parkinson's opened up a whole new world to our family. Dopamine. Dyskinesia. Depression. The various medications whose copyrighted names that we came to recall with the familiarity of our own. Stimuli that fired up the recalcitrant chemicals in Mum's brain. In all of this my two brothers, Mum and I fought our own emotional battles. But Dad appeared to know no such conflict. His true north never wavered, narrowed to the point between spiritual patrimony, pressure cooker and prayer. This is where he found his compass and where he wanted us to find ours. Dad is a man of principles. The rightness of his presence on this earth. Hit. With. Blunt. Force. Into his every syllable and verse. It's how he has always been to me. So when the ground opened up beneath our feet it was with the power of puja that Dad attempted to bridge the chasm that cleaved our spirits.

He attempted it by sheer presence. The same force he exerts in my house today. In the insistent 'Namaskars', loud mobile phone calls and multitudes of dishes I am not permitted to turn away. For each night since Mum's diagnosis that Dad has taken to the stove, he has cooked from a place of spirit that comes as naturally to him as breathing. Flavours that have diverged from those taught to him by Mum so long ago. The power of what *he* is now pushes up from the bite. Pungently herbacious fenugreek. Strident cassia bark, the spice he prefers to use in place of a cinnamon stick for its stronger, more masculine flavour. A heavier hand with salt. Spice that is bigger and broader and believing.

Dad cooks to protect us from more pain. And yet in spite of his noble intentions, I have always been too terrified to digest the promise of emotional restitution his cooking contains. Dad can't *believe* Mum to wellness. Though I think he has spent many years trying to do just that. If I accept his food, then I accept his version of Mum's story; that our gods still protect her. Watching her ordained physical and mental deterioration over so many years, I cannot accept that truth. It's why I sit with an empty place mat, still. Why I continue to reject his food on my own plate, even as I feed it to my own children.

My continued refusal is irrational, really. But if I've learned anything in this life it's that deeply felt emotions rarely hold up to rational inspection: grief, love, jealousy, hate, desire—explaining the logic behind feeling while we're in its grip demands a perspective and clarity I certainly don't have possession of.

So as an adolescent I ate the food prepared by Dad but I chose not to keep its secrets. I wanted something else. Something I could control. It is what I have continued to search for my whole life. Control of external environments and the self-control required to shape my internal environments. I have wanted to exist in a different world than the one that Dad drew for me as a child once it was proved that his prayers couldn't stop tragedy. Little wonder that to have his food fill my fridge today feeds my resentment. In the wake of Mum's diagnosis, the salt of his belief may have been enough to preserve Dad's devotion. But for me, since the day Mum was snatched away, his faith has been a searing injury to my open wound.

CHAPTER 4

Raita

Raita is the first dish a young girl, new to her
mother's kitchen, will prepare. Made only of
fresh dahi— yoghurt—mixed with cucumber,
salt and vinegar, it's the raw power of black
pepper that kicks the dish into high gear. A
little-used ingredient in Kashmiri cooking,
the addition of black pepper shows how one
unfamiliar element can redefine expectation.

I *KNEW* MYSELF THROUGH MUM. Her awareness was mine.
So when I stepped in the car that day, her grief ravaged
the residual glow of my girlhood play. Eleven years old.
Cocooned on a random weekday afternoon in a single-
storey brick veneer house on Muirfield Avenue, the
Torquay home of a childhood friend. Mum had called.
Her car idled on the street outside. I was late. I didn't
want to leave; I was busy, completely entertained playing

the Barbie doll games my two brothers never allowed me to play. Mum's car horn beeped and the minutes passed. Reluctantly I ran, yelled goodbye. Pulled open the heavy steel of the passenger door.

'You're late.' I was surprised at the first words that came out of Mum's mouth. Normally so patient with me and my brothers, her voice was edgy and her body held tense. I became instantly still and quiet. I was sensitive to Mum, and this mood was not one I had witnessed before. It made me frightened. Instinct told me something was seriously wrong, and my intuition was proved right upon her very next cry.

'I have Parkinson's Disease,' she barked. And then the wailing.

Hunched over the steering wheel, she collected herself. Put the car into drive and pulled away. I shrank back in my seat. Bewildered. Confused. Fearful. I did not recognise this incarnation of hers. I couldn't comprehend what she said. Felt only shock at the foreign *thing* that she became—brittle with some monstrous pain. It consumed her. Telescoped the expanse of her into a fist-tight terror. Somehow she drove me home, parked the car in the garage and pushed out the driver's door. Not a word. Not a glance my way. I scrambled in her wake, watched from the front door as she stumbled to the top of the spiral stairs. She stabbed out a number on the phone to scream down the cord to Dad. Travelling in India. Continents away. The sound of her loneliness and fear stunned me. I curled at the bottom of the stairs and there I stayed, too scared to hide.

Looking back, I can see what it was that frightened me. It wasn't the word—at that point, for me, Parkinson's was a meaningless three-syllable sound. In Mum's moment of extreme distress, she had forgotten I had existed.

And until that moment I hadn't known that she could.

I cannot find dahi. I try. But the taste is never right. I drive across Melbourne to seek it, stockpiling each discarded half-litre tub of yoghurt in the back of my fridge: additions to an expanding dairy graveyard. My experience so far is nothing more than one mouthful of disappointment after the next. These swallows of the subcontinent are either too sour or too flat. Too sweet or too thin. Occasionally I will bring the boys on these treasure hunts, and these are the times I enjoy the best. Both of them buckled up in their safety seats. Ashok's head lolls as the softened April sun pours in through the windows. Any more than twenty minutes in the car and he will fall asleep. Mostly, we stick to the inner city suburbs. Carnegie. St Kilda. Brunswick East at a pinch. Our destination the Indian shops wedged between video stores and kebab joints. These exotic grocers with their dog-eared linoleum floors, wire shelving and flickering fluorescent lights. The young men at the counter—for they are always men—who sit with earpieces and mobile phones speaking in rapid- fire Hindi to family back home. Maybe I project onto them, but I always come away with the idea that these are displaced people, who travelled from their home to the land of opportunity only to find themselves tied to a crappy shop floor. Their stores reek of loneliness despite the overstocked shelves.

Unable to taste-test throughout my suburban trawl, I rely on visual cues. Pictures and words on the front of otherwise ubiquitous small white buckets. The dahi I buy for its image of a black-blue Krishna playing his sweet flute. Another for the bold red of the brand's capitalised Hindi script. Each time I peel off the lid and hope for a taste of memory. Each time I retrieve nothing but a bare and barbed hook. I am searching for a savour of long ago. In Ammi's house dahi was neither tart nor insipid. Not infantile sweet. It sat in the fridge in a curve-lipped stainless steel vessel: a thick white drift encircled by a thin moat of whey, it was sensual in texture. Calming in savour. Dahi that was the foundation for her taste of a true raita; a simple yoghurt dish found at every Indian table. 'Is it the right one, Mummy?' It's Cailean, chin lifted from beneath the bench. He stands next to Ashy who babbles in a high chair by my side. We have returned from another dahi seek and find mission in time for lunch and afternoon naps. If the taste is true, I will make raita alongside sausages and daal for our dinner. The kind of mixed-bag meal that is more and more common in our home as I gain confidence enough to begin introducing the flavours of my past into my family's present.

Cailean's question hangs in the space between us as I take the teaspoon from the top drawer, dip it into the newly bought tub and then take it to my mouth. The boys watch me closely.

'No, sweet pea.' I drop the spoon in the sink, disappointed by a swallow that is at once buttermilk-thin and slightly sour. No raita again, today. I can't see the point in making the dish when the dahi is wrong from the start.

For while the core ingredients for this simple accompaniment are pantry staples, the right dahi is essential. It is the base ingredient that will donate both depth and texture. Next is cucumber, grated. Sometimes finely diced onion and tomato. White or apple cider vinegar. Salt and white sugar. Raita's defining taste is punched out by a confident grind of black pepper. This is the special touch, for in the way of Kashmiri cooking the last is a peculiar addition: black pepper is conspicuous by its absence from a Kashmiri kitchen. As a girl I never saw it added to the sabzis created by Ammi or Mum, nor in later years by Dad. Theirs were dishes that spoke richly of a sweeter, smokier brand of spice. I have come to think it's because we use it so rarely that black pepper's foreign darkness holds so much power: in a good raita its inclusion skews the palate's expectation. The dirty heat of pepper is a kick to the taste buds; it's the catch of something raw.

I want raw. I crave it. Some stripped back taste of truth that could show me how to get it back. To get an understanding of *her* back. And maybe within that reclamation to rediscover a pristine piece of me. So I look at the preparation of these dishes—this raita—as a stab at redemption. My own SOS—Sabzis Of Salvation. It goes to demonstrate my desperate state of mind that, at this point, such a concept doesn't sound at all ridiculous to me.

'Okay, boys,' I rally, pressing the lid back on the container to round out yet another failed experiment, 'lunch'.

Still, as I slide the discarded tub of dahi to the back of the fridge and pull out the makings of the toasted ham and cheese sandwiches I will prepare for us to eat, I acknowledge that the growth of tension between Scott and I illustrates that my compulsion to use cooking as therapy could not have come at a worse time.

As a couple and as a family we are stretched. *More* than stretched. Stretched implies something else. Elongation. Like we might adapt to these difficult circumstances given time. What we are is *coinceé*. It is a French word I learned in a previous life. Before children. During the years Scott and I called Paris home. When, no matter our difficulties, there remained space enough for me to wake every morning and make the decision to fall in love with him again.

Je suis coinceé.

I am inundated.

C'est un peu coinceé.

The situation is difficult. Tight. Je me sens *coinceé.*

Can't. Breathe.

It is one word with a constellation of meanings and each one applies to me. To the life Scott and I lead. To the journey of self-discovery I have independently decided to take. There is no room in our day-to-day life for reflection or romance, a thought that strikes me with force as I wrestle the boys through lunch and then, amidst loud protests, into bed. Their afternoon sleep that will allow me the hour I need to meet yet another copy deadline before they wake and the whole thing begins again. Nappies. Snacks. Play. Bath. Dinner. Bed.

I know that Scott feels betrayed by my decision to step on the path I have only recently chosen to walk. He doesn't say so, but then he doesn't have to. I can feel it in the tight energy that flows off him. He intuits correctly that my quest could become that element in our lives which creates only more anxiety, more confusion. For right now we are barely holding on. Our attention and our energies once so aligned are strung tight. Pulled in different directions as we grapple with the change in me that has reshaped our lives and with the change in him that has come as a response: the fact that he is no longer so accepting of my idiosyncratic ways; my penchant for whimsy that, at its worst, looks more like denial and is ruthless in its ignorance of practicalities; my naturally introspective nature that stifles his attempts at communication and informs my particular brand of self-focus. He feels I have removed my attention from where it needs to be. He is right, I have. As I tend to our two children, I acknowledge it. Just as I acknowledge something else: that despite his concerns I can no longer be who I was.

And I have no idea how to take him along on the search for who I need to be.

When I was young I made raita for Mum. It was my one job on the nights we celebrated our Indian kitchen. It began as a tradition before her diagnosis and continued as a necessity in the years after. My help to support her emotional fragility that came to the fore after her diagnosis and was, in those early days, a far greater presence than any physical decline. She needed rest. She needed space. She needed to know that there was something or someone that could hold her up. So I tried. I tried as I stood beside her in the kitchen to make that raita. I made it in her Portmeirion bowls. She collected them, piece by piece. Dinner plates of dusk-pink cyclamen and violet clematis. Teacups of white campion and delicate harebell. These were *her* dishes. Florid contrast to the metallic gleam of stainless steel *thaalis* and *katoris* positioned for eating upon those unrolled bamboo mats set upon our living room floor.

I made raita under her instruction. Yoghurt, of course. Three or four heaped tablespoons. A four-inch spear of cucumber peeled, grated and squeezed of its excess liquid. The seasoning is where she kept a close eye. A conservative teaspoon of salt that was equal to the measure of sugar. A capfull of straw-yellow cider vinegar. A few generous grinds from the tall wooden pepper mill that had stood in her kitchen for as many years as I had. When I finished she would dip in her index finger to taste, then make the required adjustment: the burn of a little more salt, the addition of vinegar's acid break. If I concentrate very hard, I can place myself there again. To the tug of resistance in the second before I yanked open the heavy fridge door. The 250-gram tub of Peter's yoghurt with its green and white packaging, its sour taste.

It didn't seem to matter, then, that the balance of the raita was thin. Or that the pepper was sometimes too bold. What mattered was the ordinariness of the task. That the actions I performed to make the dish were the same before Mum's diagnosis as they were in the days and months and years after. That my actions kept me close to her even if she and Dad kept mute about the fact that her emotions were no longer capable of adequately feeding me.

Because the strange thing about the grief we felt at Mum's diagnosis was how quickly we all papered over it.

Once the initial shock and tears wore off, once Mum's roster of pill-controlled treatment began, Parkinson's settled into our home like a silent interloper: heavy with presence, yes, but soundless. It would take eight years before the change in her psychological disposition—that state of paralysed hopelessness—would become, like her physical symptoms, the only thing I could see. Before I would walk out of her home and emotionally bar her from my life. But in the years preceding that day I made a deal with my gods: if they could make the decision to annihilate my world, then I could make the decision to reconstruct a new one—only this space would be a universe that *I* could control. My private place, with boundaries that would remain impermeable to their influence until such time that I might figure out a new way to *be*. A way to categorise Mum's new reality and my place within it. The venture began as a temporary measure. I hadn't anticipated these fences would endure so long. That this construction would alter, not only my experience of the present, but the shape of my future, too. And yet even had I known, I'm not sure I could have reacted any other way. I never felt the choice I made was mine to own. More that it arose as a consequence of Mum and Dad's actions in the immediate aftermath of her diagnosis. A series of events that added up to communication of a message I am now sure they hadn't meant to send. But as a child? I hadn't the clarity. For instance, there was no suggestion of counselling. We simply did puja. Because who needed a psychologist's ear when we had God's? And as for Mum's parents, my Australian Grandma and Grandpa, it was decided that they should be kept in the dark: two years eventually passed before they were told. To my desperately reaching adolescent self it seemed to me that our family's overriding new script ran something along the lines of 'ignore it and it might all just go away'. So when I stood in the kitchen on those nights to make raita by her side, that is what I did. I pretended that this help was not help at all. I pretended that it was destiny.

'Sarina,' Dad would call, interrupting *Monkey Magic*, my favourite TV show, 'please get up and help your mother with the salad.'

Or: 'Sarina,' he would say, 'we need raita made and radish and onion cut for the table.'

I would grumble. 'Why me? Just because I'm the only girl...' The last I would speak with as much venom as I dared. The fact that he would never try to reason or refute my bitter mumbling reinforced the new internal framework I was building—that this near-nightly ritual wasn't about me helping my sick Mum, it was about training me as a Kashmiri daughter in the kitchen. About me fulfilling my destiny. But my destiny had been to become *her*. It was all I had ever wanted. Until the entrance of Parkinson's had shot that dream down. So as the years slipped past, my culinary rebellion became the internal armour needed to protect me against my own gut-deep grief; this became the world that I could control.

As my teens progressed and Dad's expectations became more demanding—'Sarina, I want to teach you to make daal,' or, 'come and see how I make paneer,'—I stood my ground. I reasoned to myself that, if I never learned to cook these dishes, then I could never be called upon to take Mum's place at the round timber table that was the centre of our family kitchen. Because as time went on her illness consumed more of her. She tired rapidly, a result of the physical wear and tear of dyskinesia. Mild depression took hold, both a symptom of the disease and a terrible side effect of the daily doses of pills she was forced to take in order to supply her brain with the dopamine it struggled to produce.

Dad increasingly took control of the stove and clearly hoped that I would do the same. My refusal caused friction but I was glad of it. He didn't force me. I think even then he knew that my recalcitrance found its origin in behaviours that went deeper than simple boundary pushing. That it was all a charade for something more: for me to occupy a more significant place in the family kitchen meant acknowledgement that Mum's presence had receded. In any case it was easier to adopt the persona of a difficult teen than an obedient and caring daughter. Because as a caring daughter I would be forced to accept Mum's sickness, to accept that my gods had stolen the model of the woman I had hoped to become. And so I cultivated that obstinate identity. I grew it into a character possessed of such strength and intractability that it became bigger than even I anticipated. So big that it not only blocked the shadow of Parkinson's, but simultaneously gouged distance between me, my family and my beliefs: the kitchen gave me a target, and each dish I refused to learn was for me akin to hitting a dart directly at the bullseye of my own defiance.

It worked for a while. Certainly to be angry felt less destructive than to be sad. But as I passed from my teens to my twenties and into my thirties, the incongruence grew. For a start, the emotional limitations of the universe I created at twelve became glaringly apparent as the transition from girl to woman took effect: I suffered with my body image, with ideas of self-love, and with creating spiritual resilience. I was an emotional adolescent in a woman's body. And yet it seemed that the higher I built the walls and the more I reinforced the battlements, the louder resounded the echo of all that I had left behind. The same call that echoes in my head, still. I haven't been able to just set my dial to 'forget' and leave it be. If anything, it's been the opposite. By desperately trying to ignore the physical presence of Mum's Parkinson's in my life I have created an even bigger monster. One relentless in its hunger for distraction. It's only interest to feed on more and more of me.

In my worst moments I imagine my gods laughing at the attempts I have made to escape their reach. But now, as my experiments in the kitchen begin to open my heart to the first cracks of light, I can *almost* see it differently:

not that they wouldn't leave me alone, more that they were unwilling to ever leave me completely be. The clarification is small. I'm not even sure I believe it. Yet the spectre of hope is a huge step towards recognition of the spiritual support that might await me in the world I have deserted. It's an insight that makes me feel courageous.

It is this courage that supports the burgeoning awareness that begins to reveal itself to me as I go through the motions of settling my two sons for their afternoon sleep; Cailean in my bed, Ashy in the boys' bedroom, laid down in the cot he has almost outgrown. I drop the curtains in each room. The afternoon cooled enough now that I cover them with blankets. That done I gently close both bedroom doors: though they sleep in the same room each night, their reluctance to rest in the day means I must separate them so that they will actually nap. Still, all of the abominable sleep training I endured with both of them as small babies—the suicidal hours I spent patting and shushing by their restless sides—has paid off. Now, within ten minutes of resting their heads on their pillows, they will sleep.

I descend the stairs of a now-quiet house. I know that work waits. But in the space provided by the silence, in my soft downward footfall on each shining timber step, a five-word mantra begins recitation in my heart.

I can't get it back.

The dahi in Ammi's kitchen. The raita Mum helped me to make.

I can't get it back.

The healthy Mum I used to have. The childhood security taken away.

I can't get it back.

The quality of the faith that once bloomed within. I can't get it back.

I can't get it back. No matter which recipe I cook. No matter what past tragedy I reshape. No matter the degree of belief I might re-find. Everything will be different. Because the problem—in the daal I cannot master, in the dahi I cannot find, in the raita I cannot make—isn't that nothing can taste or feel the same. The problem is that I *expect* it to. That's not moving forward. That is a futile attempt to recapture a life already lived. The understanding heralds both liberation and devastation: that I now see more clearly, yes, but payment for that sight might cost more than I am willing to give.

It also sounds the warning bell on another missed copy deadline: reasoning that an angry editor will cause me less upset than ignoring my own internal call, I move past the open laptop on my dining room table. With sixty minutes of freedom on the clock and a new awareness to light the way, the kitchen is my draw. I need to explore what moving forward might look and taste like. At this point to cook is my only way.

The first ingredient I check for in my pantry is black pepper. Raw awakening. I line up the stout glass grinder next to the half-dozen containers of dahi now retrieved from the fridge's bottom shelf. Next is cucumber: the long, slim Lebanese variety protected by shrink-wrap plastic. They are out of season. But as Cailean and Ashy are happy to eat thinly sliced spears as a snack I always keep a few in the fridge. Apple cider vinegar is another staple—a base for homemade salad dressings. White sugar in that Paris-bought porcelain sugar bowl by the kettle. Salt.

I take out a bowl from the cupboard beneath the microwave; dump into it a heaped tablespoon from each of the containers of dahi lining the bench. I swirl a spoon into the white drift. Slip the cold cradle of stainless steel into my mouth—it tastes like no memory I know and that seems the right place to start.

The familiarity of the task as I make this bowl of raita allows me to lose myself in a way that preparation of daal—still a mystery of alchemy to me—does not. I don't need Ammi's recipe, require no prompts to remind me which ingredient to add when and in what quantity. The recipe survives as a secret scripture, buried somewhere deep within me. And as I step through all of it I feel something I haven't for a very long time: I am alone and unattached. I am in my own space. Suspended in a delicious moment uncoloured by reference or reason or regret. I've rarely been able to cultivate that kind of physical or emotional independence. All my life I have allowed my internal shape to be defined via external comparison. Have weighed and measured myself against the intensity and brand of spiritual belief of those that I love. It's my habit. My security. The way I have stayed aligned with the people that I love. A compulsion that was only strengthened when Mum's compass was magnetised by illness. So to come out of that space and to be aware of myself feels entirely new.

Steps complete, I hold my breath and dip the spoon to taste. It's acidic. A slightly heavy hand with vinegar razors through the dahi's creamy density like a rotor blade. But there is an element of sweet neutrality, too; taste buds caught in a cool slipstream of cucumber before—bam— the unapologetic wallop of black pepper. It is a small taste of truth to satiate that still-ravenous monster in me. A savour that tells me I'm trying. Because this is not the raita I have known. Yet within it a sliver of me exists. The flavour of an identity wedged between the girl that I once was and the woman that I want the chance to be. The sensation is fleeting but I grip tight to it as a portent. Of course, as I drop the spoon back into the bowl, a part of me understands it is one thing to cultivate a sense of equanimity as I make a simple dish of raita. It is another entirely to attempt that level of clarity as I remake my life: to turn back and meet Scott's gaze over my shoulder, our children's hearts carried in my two hands. To attempt to reconnect with the presence of God in a way that feels honest and specific to me. To achieve any one of these things I know that I need to make myself whole, and am not at all sure that I can. What would it take? What tools would I need? Certainly more than a canny instinct with seasoning. I'm no spiritual wunderkind. What I am is a lapsed disciple. Yet perhaps my hope is that if one small recipe stuck, then other lessons might have, too.

So as Ashok's first waking cry finds its way down the stairs; as I hear Cailean's padding steps reverberate through the ceiling above; as I leave the mess on the kitchen bench to climb the stairs and devote my next few hours to meeting their innumerable needs; as I strip Ashy of his wet nappy on the change table; as all of this happens I attempt to keep the smallest piece of myself aside. And with this blessed fragment of self-awareness I think that, if my gods *could* hear me pray, then now would be the time to speak: *please show me who I need to be.*

RAITA
Cucumber yoghurt

To me, raita is always more than a simple accompaniment. It was the first Kashmiri dish I was ever taught to make. It was the culinary marker that, many years later, allowed me to see the outline of a new way.

INGREDIENTS:

4 to 5 heaped tablespoons of natural yoghurt
½ a Lebanese cucumber, grated
¾ teaspoon salt
1 ½ teaspoons apple cider vinegar
1 heaped teaspoon sugar
Black pepper to taste

METHOD:

Put the yoghurt in a bowl and whisk slightly until creamy.

Grate the cucumber, squeeze out any excess liquid. Stir through the yoghurt.

Add the seasonings. Adjust flavours to taste. Refrigerate until chilled. Serve.

Serves six as part of an Indian meal.

Kashmiri Red Chilli

Kashmiri red chilli is like no other spice in my
pantry. Its name suggests one thing—flame,
burn, alarm—but its complex profile evades
one-dimensional classification. The colour of
red Australian dust, its nose carries the scent
of a New Delhi spice market. And the taste.
The taste is clay and earth and humid heat.
It is not a substitute for classic red chilli when
cooking. Instead its use brings an alternate
character to an otherwise familiar dish.

I HAVE NEVER TOLD SCOTT, but the night we met my motives
had been fired by something more than honest attraction. At the age of seventeen, I had come out of my first
serious affair: a twelve-month sexual relationship with
my eldest brother's best friend that had ended with
my boyfriend's gradual disengagement and my broken

heart. I never really knew why he fell out of love with me, at the time he refused to say, but I had an inkling it had to do with Cricket—the spunky-looking photographer girlfriend of one of his mates. Nearly one year on and I was still mourning. So when my gaze hooked upon my ex-lover's Peugeot as it rocketed along Ocean Boulevard that long ago Friday in December, my breath stopped. The rest of my walk home along the cliffs from an afternoon shift at the local chip shop was spent imagining all the ways I could refuse him when he begged for another chance.

He never asked. His presence in my life that day was proved to be simply the domino that instigated my introduction to another man. A love put before me by God. A love that, one day, would guide me back to the trailhead of grace.

I am curled up on the cold grass of St Vincent's garden, the U-shaped park at the end of our street that sprawls across three suburban blocks. The grass is cold because it is night. And I'm lying here on the dew-damp soil because, after the fight Scott and I had, it seems only marginally less ridiculous than wandering the streets, sobbing. We never used to fight. Never. But it's been seventeen years since the December evening when the thought of that ex-boyfriend propelled me to turn and walk back into an emptying pub. To grab the hand of the man a mutual friend (between rounds of vodka and raspberry) had hours earlier pointed out as the catch keen to make my acquaintance. *Hello,* I'd said, tone a match for my strangely formal 1 a.m. handshake, *my name is Sarina.* He was visibly older than me. Tall, and with a wave of auburn hair that curled over the top of his tee shirt. I was unaware that, aged eighteen and only one week out of high school, I had just introduced myself to the rest of my life.

How have we strayed so far from where we began? 'I don't know why I can't seem to make you understand,' Scott had spoken through gritted teeth, earlier tonight. Words forced out like stone pips. I remained on the couch where I had been seated when I dared ask the question. The question, as he cleared up his dinner plate, that had escalated the tension in the house the week before. *How was the day?* My determinedly chipper tone and his end- of-tether fatigue collided. Pulled the trigger that shot him into fury. The spray of emotional lead shot that erupted surprised even me. I stilled. Arms wrapped around my knees. Wide-eyed, as he opened the door to our minuscule rear courtyard and stepped into the cold night. His body held tight in frustrated anger.

'I can't do it.' His back was to me, a hand to his eyes before he dropped it to his side and turned. Stepped back inside. 'I can't *carry* you anymore. Every night I come home you ask me, *how was the day?* What, like nothing is wrong? *Everything* is wrong,' he paused but I couldn't look at him, scared by what he might mean. 'We have no money. I'm exhausted. Working from 8 a.m. until midnight. Meanwhile you're running around Melbourne buying yoghurt and cooking. I don't need you to ask *how's my day*. I need you to acknowledge where I am. I'm broken. This,' he made some vague gesture that seemed to encompass the entirety of our life, 'is bad for me.'

'I'm *trying*.' They were the only words that had formed in my brain to say. His anger was so rare, its appearance had me paralysed. I have always preferred to write than to speak and never is my struggle to communicate more acute than when faced directly with another's anger or distress. The knowledge that my silence incited him only twisted my tongue further. I understood it; it was how I felt when Mum had greeted my frustrations with a blankness charged by her own emotional disconnect. Yet I struggled to find a way around myself. Conscious that anything I said would fall short of what he needed to hear. But I love him. So I forced myself to try harder.

'I know I'm cooking, but I'm writing and I'm getting more work in the next few weeks.' The words felt like marbles in my mouth. 'So that will be a bit more money…'
'Agggh, you just don't get it!' His words shot mine down. Frustration that tore the room apart. 'You just don't *get* it. It's not about your work or you or the money you make. It's about you and me; I *need* you to be in this relationship. Not off on some trip. It's the way that ringing me five

times when I've got a customer in the shop or hassling me when I'm late closing, shows me that you just don't understand. This. Is. Our. Life.' His fury lit a full stop at the end of each word. 'It *has* to work. And the only way it will work is if you are as committed as me.' 'But I don't know what you want me to say.' I was crying, then. Did he want me to give up cooking? To give up on me? I was too scared to ask. Too scared to tell him this focus on food is the only thing that keeps me from falling.

'That's the *problem*.' I shrank further in the face of his aggression. '*I* have led this family without your input for nearly twenty years based on what would be good for *you*. I left a promising career in California to get you to Paris. I've supported you as you've tried to travel and write. But now I am doing this business. I haven't surfed in ten years. The most time for myself I get is a Sunday pint at the pub. So if you don't like where you are then *you* change the situation. *You* find the solution. *You* make the money. *You* carry the stress of supporting an entire family. Because I can't do it for you anymore. I can't be the one to hold you up. I am almost done.'

My memory of Scott's last words press me to the cold park ground in a bitter sound wave. So heavy, I must eventually drag myself up to walk home for fear of sinking beneath the soil. Words that poke into my side as I toss through a troubled night's sleep on the couch. Whose outlines press into the bruise that, the next day, forms around my heart: Scott and I battered against a morning made sharp with unresolved emotion. 'It's not that I don't want you to cook or to work out this thing with your family.' He approaches me in the minutes before he leaves to begin his day. 'It's just that I need your help.' He is calmer now. Voice as soft as the kiss that lands on my mouth. It's been twelve hours since I walked out on our argument, though neither of us startles at his non sequitur. Instead, I use his momentary embrace to hide my tears from our two sons. He breaks off and I nod. I watch as he takes the kids and leaves for work before I turn back to rinse our breakfast dishes in the sink, my throat blocked by knowledge of what it all means. How much we have lost. That now *this* is our normal.

'I'm sorry but she's a bit caught up.' It is the girl at the counter of Gewürzhaus Spice. It's a month on from that fateful first visit. I've returned to speak with Maria, one of the two sisters who run the store. Research for that recent story I pitched to *Epicure* three weeks ago. It's the last thing I feel up to after the fight Scott and I had last night, but a deadline looms: 800 words for an article on spice. New trends. Odd blends. I nod my thanks for the information and then use my time to peer closer at the dozens of elegant self-serve dispensers: a sophisticated pick-'n'-mix of loose teas, exotic salts, infused sugars, all manner of herbs and unusual takes on blended spices;

laksa lemak whose elusive umami taste is donated by dehydrated prawns, or the 'kangaroo' mix of native Australian spice that, Maria later assures me, marries beautifully with steak. What I don't find is any flavour to represent the unbalanced dump of fire and spice that signifies the mess my marriage has become. I can only imagine it as discordant notes of chilli and black cardamom and fenugreek: dark and dirt and smoke without the softening layers of sweet to harmonise such savoury disturbance. I never imagined our relationship would be described in this way and it is a tremendous thing to face. I have always felt the love Scott and I share is sacred. Protected. Immune from the grudging, whining and bitching that appears to shape so many of my friends' relationships. I have *needed* to feel that. I lost hold of my mother. I lost track of my faith. Who would I be if I lost the security of my husband, too? 'Sarina?' Maria walks out of her back office. Her voice draws me back from the abyss.

'Maria! Thank you for giving me some time.' I take a breath. Compose myself with what I hope is professional speed. 'So, I'm looking for some spices that might be newer or lesser known to Australian home cooks for an article on what's new in the world of spice. Think you can show me a few things?' I click record on my handheld voice recorder as she nods her smiling assent and follow her around the store. The fact I have spent fifteen years working as a journalist allows me space to zone in and out of her conversation. Instinctively, I prompt when

I intuit a hole in her information. Make a mental note when my quote antenna is piqued: the moment a sentence leaves her mouth that I know will help shape the finished piece. But mostly I am occupied by thoughts of my husband. Heart filtering for a resolution my mind is too afraid to seek.

It was never like this before. The night Scott and I met had marked the beginning of a love bigger than either of us had known. In the wake of my handshake he had invited me home. Our path a side-by-side stroll along tall sandstone cliffs lit by moonlight. My two friends as chaperones. And we had talked. Tentatively at first. Then gradually with more surety. To this day I believe it was God's hand that turned me back to meet Scott. One of the last occasions that I listened to God speak. My behaviour certainly wasn't instinct; the idea of picking up guys in bars was so *foreign* to me. Though ostensibly Australian by accent and land of birth, my internal landscape belonged elsewhere: I was wild curls and tight black jeans on the outside, salwar kameez and braided plaits on the inside. At that point, aged eighteen, I could count the boys I'd kissed on three fingers. Those I'd been intimate with, on one. I had always felt that to so much as kiss a random stranger was to hack out a piece of my soul. But Scott. It was as if from the very first he knew who I was. As if he harmonised my whole.

'And this one over here,' it is Maria, her words shock me out of my reverie, 'is Kashmiri red chilli.' I am startled. 'I'm sorry, what did you just say?' Maria looks back at me as she repeats herself; she knows nothing of me personally and her selection of *this* spice catches me completely by surprise. 'Kashmiri red chilli. Typically it's ground from chillies grown and dried in Kashmir. It doesn't have as much heat as you might get from classic dried red chillies. Not a lot of home cooks here really know about it, but I think it can add a lot to a dish,' Maria pauses, lifts the lid on its clear container and encourages me to breath in its scent. It smells of damp, wet heat. And then I remember. Ammi called it Kashmiri *mirch*. Dad, though, rarely used it. He always preferred to cook with the brute heat of classic dried chilli. It was the spice he was handling the first night I brought Scott home.

So, what are you cooking, Anup? It was Scott's opening conversational gambit that long-ago evening. If my future husband had spent ten years plotting a path into my parents' collective heart, he couldn't have fabricated a more direct route. The question was asked just as Dad had reached up to pull down the glass jar of dried red chillies from his spice shelf. The one with the battered cork lid. As always, he threw a few into the coffee grinder that sat next to the kettle on the bench. With Scott's words, Dad whirred to life in time with the chilli he ground. By then a few weeks had passed since we first met. Scott knew that I was half-Indian. He knew I was an aspiring writer. Knew that I preferred tequila and orange juice to beer. That I had never considered myself athletic. That I loved books. My friends. That my Mum was sick. But Scott didn't yet know how deeply this food and our belief in it pierced to the core of my family. How much his enjoyment of it penetrated some forgotten piece of me: the paneer he hoovered up in great quantities that was the one Kashmiri dish I remember Dad making before Mum got sick; how his love for sucking out the sweetly spiced marrow from knuckled lamb bones instantly endeared him to my brothers—the three of us had grossed out our childhood friends when we did the same. Perhaps he felt all this. I don't know. But once Scott entered into our family home, it fast became apparent none of us would remain the same.

'Habanero peppers?' It's Maria. I retain the composure to make verbal sounds of agreeance at the suggestions she throws out—a recommended on-trend spice to pad out my growing mix; Melbourne currently in the grip of a Mexican culinary renaissance. 'Sure,' I smile, 'tell me more.'

At that point it had been coming up to seven years since Mum's diagnosis. Perhaps from the outside nothing about the five of us looked particularly changed. Families are inclined to close ranks around the internal workings that trouble them. But the fractures were there. Hairline cracks webbed through weakened foundations. Dad attempted to reinforce stability in the days after

Mum's shock revelation. He had returned from India to face my brothers and I in explanation of what Mum's diagnosis meant. My parents who stood in the upstairs office before the three of us. Their backs to the wild ocean view. Dad. Composed. Self-assured. Firm in his certainty. He could be a stirring speaker. And he tried. But it was hard to believe in him. His promises that were made hollow by the spectre of Mum's presence at his side: that our family could get through this, that Mum would receive treatment, that our gods and our guru would look after her and nothing would have to change. Mum, however, had displayed none of Dad's determined ease. She was brittle. A touch would shatter her. Even in my pre-adolescent innocence I knew it as the first visible division in the message of their marriage. Until then I had never considered that our quintet could be broken but from that moment forward I was braced for disaster. Nothing could ever be okay again. In all the years that followed, Dad and Mum were too embroiled in the fight to stay level. For Mum, Parkinson's was a slow-moving disease. She would be forced to endure its slow creep. We would be forced to watch its possession of her. What started with a stiff neck and a tremor in her left pinkie would over the years morph into a progressively severe, full-body stiffness. Stiffness that shortened her gait, causing her repeated and injurious falls. Stiffness that slowed and muted her speech. Stiffness that constricted her mental processes. Disturbed her thought. At diagnosis we had all of this dread to stare down. Knowing that no matter our front and our defiance, the avalanche of symptoms would suffocate us all in the end. Mum and Dad knew this from the start. Trying to stay calm and level in the face of a diabolically uncertain future meant they had no energy left to chase away my doubt.

But somehow, years after the fact, somehow Scott provided promise. It was as if the glow he manifested was the light to draw us back to centre. Scott fused our divisions: his appreciation of the food Dad made that I struggled to consume; the angle from which he viewed Mum that transformed her into something more than just a progressive disease; the way he saw me as a young woman who was whole and special and free. The beauty and generosity of the man that he was made all of us see anew the people we thought we had lost the chance to be. Yet of all the feats Scott unknowingly achieved, the most miraculous was in building a bridge to span the distance that had progressively grown between Mum and I. A side effect of the love he showered upon me. *Do you think…,* Scott had asked Mum one evening six months after the night we met—conversation as he built a fire in our combustion heater, a prelude to the Friday night Indian feast Dad had fast grown to delight in preparing for him each week—*Do you think that if I'm really good in this life, that Sarina and I might be together in my next life, too?*

Mum told me later she'd openly cried in response to his question. This twenty-five-year-old man, birthed and raised between Western Australia's wild beaches and the outback. A boy of quad bikes and bush camping and mangrove fishing trips. A surfer. And, at that point, a known lad. Yet there he sat. Devoid of embarrassment. Professing profound love for her only daughter within a cultural framework he immediately accepted as familiar. To this day it remains the most romantic expression of devotion ever bestowed upon me. With that comment Scott marked her soul and, in Mum's retelling to me, he marked mine, too. It was this story that became the common bond between Mum and I. For a brief time after that moment we became the mother and daughter I had always imagined we might be. We did things. Talked. Shopped. The spectre of Parkinson's overshadowed by the appearance of this *man* in all of our lives. At the end of our first year together, Scott bought his first home. A five-minute drive from the house I lived in with Mum and Dad. It was our opportunity to consolidate as a couple and I moved in the day he did. By then Mum had become my chief confidante. We cruised vintage stores for furniture and pots and pans. She gifted me a stunning—and stunningly expensive—leadlight lamp. At that time Dad had established a textile factory in Bangalore: no longer just an agent working as the middleman for Australian companies looking to make fabrics in India, Dad had decided to build his own small textile manufacturing base. This meant more travel right at the time I had left home. So when Dad travelled to India to check on textile production in the Bangalore factories, Scott and I would take Mum out for meals. A cosy threesome, curled around osso bucco, bottles of teeth-staining red wine, and sticky date pudding drowned in clotted King Island cream.

Those first intensely felt twelve months of Scott and my courtship peaked in a letter I found on Dad's desk that Mum had written. A love note. One I couldn't help but read. In it Mum described how watching Scott and I fall in love had flamed her own memories of what it had once been for them. I remember being startled at the time. Only from this vantage point of age and experience have I begun to understand: sometimes it takes one unfamiliar with our lives to bring into relief the texture and contrast and conflicted beauty in the relationships we take for granted. To give our sight new depth and outline what was always there for us to see.

'Can I give you something to take home with you?' It is Maria asking the question. I have survived the interview. I feel I don't deserve her offer; she has been so free with her time today. Me so distracted. And yet she gives more. It's something I've always loved about my work in the arena of food—the generosity of spirit common among those who find their fulfilment in feeding others.

'Really? You know that's not necessary.' But my protest is half-hearted, weakened by the remembered scent of that Kashmiri red chilli. 'No, I'd really like you to take a memory,' Maria assures me. 'Please.' At her insistence I leave with a bag in my hand, the particular shade of the desert-red dust that coloured my husband's childhood. More than any of my recent culinary acquisitions, this one rides alongside me in the car with all the hope of a new beginning. Another one. Because though I may be hopeful I am not deluded. Not yet, at least. Scott was once a new beginning and look where we stand now. The silver of newness mishandled is easily tarnished. Is that what happened to the shiny promise of Mum and I? As my left hand tackles the shifts of gear demanded by the build of early afternoon traffic so, too, does my mind gear back once more into the past.

When the house Scott bought was decorated. Once Scott and I had really settled in. Once he became familiar with all of the ragged undertones in my family that—in those early days—he had helped smooth over, Scott's hopeful influence faded. It wasn't that he failed. We did. Because it was one thing for Mum and I to find ourselves in him, it was another thing entirely to segue that emotion into a viable relationship with each other. To do so required discourse. It required acknowledgement of all those things unsaid. It required *change*. As the romance of Mum and my second chance became dulled by familiarity, we gradually reverted to how we had been. Less communicative. Less open. At the time I didn't know how to fix it. Whether it was Mum or I who was to blame and either way it matters little, now. Once again she and I found ourselves in a state of disconnection. Only this time it was worse. Having experienced so briefly what we *could* have been, to lose her a second time extracted an immeasurable emotional toll.

That was the terrible day of our argument upstairs in our family living room. *But you aren't dying.* The argument when I saw myself in her eyes. The loss of herself in her own life, pointing me to the loss of myself in mine. The day I walked out of her house in a fury, leaving my lost belief in her and life as I knew it behind. The day I made a decision to strike the pain of Parkinson's and its ramifications from my life. It was a decision I could take because I had Scott. We would be a new beginning. Just us. No flavour or faith from my past would cross this new threshold. And it didn't. Not for years. Not until now. Because *only* now can I see how my determination to keep everything else out has starved our marriage of the oxygen it needs to survive. Scott—whom I have forced to be my mother, my family and my belief for seventeen years—has finally buckled beneath the strain. I did that to him. I have done that to him. I do it to him, still.

And that's the secret of me I have been too ashamed to voice: since the day Mum's diagnosis reordered my reality I have run from any opportunity to change. To really change. Change the nature of who *I* am. On the inside. Truth be told, I am still scared to consider choice, of a new path. But I'm tired, too, I acknowledge, as I turn into our street and exit the car to carry my latest treasure inside. And in the aftermath of last night I think the possibility of losing Scott after all these months of tension, these years of pressure, has become too real to ignore. 'Okay,' I mutter to myself as I snap the lid on my newly turned out Tupperware of Kashmiri red chilli and slide it into the cupboard. 'I can do this.'

Piloted by some instinct I don't understand, I walk from the kitchen to the front room. Fire up my desktop computer and watch as the scroll of unread emails fills my screen. *Session with ERICA GODWIN of FLYING SOULS*, reads the subject of the only message in a multitude that catches my eye, sent to me by a particularly persistent PR, *healer/psychic and author.* I type out an affirmative response to accept the gift of a reading. If further change is what I need, then I decide that she will be my choice. Is the idea ridiculous? Quite possibly. But to find my way in life through faith is built into my DNA. That I can no longer trust my own Hindu gods—Shivji or Devi or Krishna—does not mean this is the end. It simply means I must find another way to communicate. So how to get a deity's attention when you have forgotten what words to speak? A hunch tells me they don't do Instagram. Short of crossing over, a clairvoyant seems the next logical step. Logical. Even as I type those seven letters I recognise the irony. Yet my need is stronger than reason. I hope that, with Erica's guidance, I may find a new entrance into my vacant house of worship. So I sign off on the email and press send. As I seal my next step, my own words spoken out loud in the kitchen come back at me. *I can do this.* For my young family's sake as much as my own I only hope that I can.

CHAPTER 6

Kaddu

Kaddu is the smiling assassin of Kashmiri
sabzi*s*. Made from pumpkin cooked to
baby food-softness, it looks like a benign
taste of infancy, a misconception that
lasts only until chilli and cinnamon
rise up to swarm the palate.

Namaskar Bhagwanji. These were the two Hindi words I
spoke as a girl each morning that I touched my forehead
to the floor before Dad or Ammi's puja. There is no literal English translation. If you asked, I would tell it to
you as this: *I offer myself to you, God.* For that's how I heard
the words in my own heart. The idol to whom I offered
this daily prayer was Shivji, deity of destruction. He is one
of the trinity of gods who create, maintain and renew
the Hindu cosmos. The third whose name we speak at
times when such things are spoken: Brahma, God of

Creation. Vishnu, God of Preservation. Shivji, the God of Destruction.

Given Shivji's edict it will come as no surprise for you to learn that he is a cave dweller. Four-armed and three-eyed. Cobras curled around his blue-skinned shoulders. A ragged triangle of animal skin his only modesty. Wearer of Earth's first man-bun and the Hindu pin-up for ascetics in India. Shivji was once my pin-up, too. Every Hindu family has its own favoured deity, one picked from the myriad personalities and incarnations that make up the pantheon. The Ganjus chose Shiv. There is a practical purpose to the singling out of one idol; chiefly, that it simplifies prayer. But the choice is also subject to esoteric reasoning. Each Hindu god represents specific qualities. Familial dynasties attach themselves to those gods or incarnations whose powers of import they would seek to manifest. Devotees of Vishnu are drawn by his omnipresent power to hold the present in his palm. Those that worship Kali, the black- skinned Mother Goddess, value her ability to protect the vulnerable and destroy evil. Or Krishna, whose many followers experience him as pure love's manifestation. But while I can tell you why others might worship their gods, I cannot tell you why we worshipped Shivji. As with so many of the rights and rituals of Hinduism that framed my life I was never subject to explanations. Why him, a figure of such conflict and power? Why that god? In all the myths of Shivji's temper, his lustless sensuality, his remorseless piety, why is it that he has been chosen by my Kashmiri ancestors? What is it that he should mean to me? I have no answers. And yet it has never mattered before this moment that I didn't know. Not as a child swept up by family and entrenched in the routine of worship, and certainly not as a woman removed from it. When I believed in him I had no questions. And when I didn't my heart was closed to the desire for answers. But it means something to me now. It would mean something should I hear his voice. In the way that Ammi's recipes mean something: I am aware that to comprehend who I am, it is essential I untangle the tight umbilical knot that stops movement of knowledge between body and spirit. Just as there is succour in spice, family culture has trained me to look for nourishment in the sound of Shivji's voice. Perhaps that no longer stands true. But how do I know?

It seems to me that I have little choice but to gather my courage and attempt to find out.

'So, I'm going to go and see a psychic this Wednesday.'

It's late autumn in Melbourne. Almost May and just a few weeks shy of Cailean's fifth birthday. Scott is enjoying a rare Sunday off and the weather is cooperating. We are together as a family. Scott pushes Ashy in the pram as I walk alongside. Cailean a little further ahead on White Lightning, his treasured and much-ridden bike. I attempt to introduce the clairvoyant concept between the stroll from house to playground. I hesitate to tell Scott everything. Certain he will flare up at my whimsical approach. Deem its efficacy as wanting. So I aim instead for straight generality. By that I mean to say, to broach the topic in a way that could be conceived as casual. But nothing is casual anymore. Every word. Every gesture. Every interaction. Outlined against a backdrop of wariness. Ours for our choices. Cailean's for our tempers. Scott's for my state of mind. Mine for his perceptions. The only one who appears unaffected is Ashy. Though perhaps his tight hold on me speaks of some peeling back I as yet refuse to see.

'I'm not paying,' I rush to add, hyper aware of his trigger points and keen to remove pressure from all of them. Conscious it is likely reservation and not interest that is behind his silence. 'I'm interviewing her for a story I'm writing for *Vogue*.' After years of working as a features writer I have become happy to muddy my boots in murky ethics—to trade column inches for personal gain in those instances when work topics are compatible with my life. 'I'll drop the kids to childcare and then go. She's going to do a reading for me beforehand.'

I'm not being a drag on you. I'm still working. I can do this and maintain my responsibility to our two sons. But it isn't those coded messages that concern him. It's the last. The one not even I am sure I can accurately interpret. *She's going to do a reading for me beforehand.* It could mean anything from *welcome to the beginning of an emotional wild goose chase* to *behind this door is the girl you love and fear is lost.* I hold tight to the idea of the latter. But Scott—his non-verbal cues suggest he's not so sure. 'Daddy.' It's Cailean, stopped at the curb. Patient as always in his wait for us. 'Can we kick the footy at the school playground?'

'Sure Buddy.' We all cross together. It's just gone 9 a.m. The morning is chilly and the roads are quiet. The school is less than 800 metres from our front door and we come upon it quickly. 'I'll take Ashy and go grab a coffee. Would you like one?' I lean in to Scott for a kiss as we slow before the unlocked school gate. I feel gratified by his reciprocal response. 'Ah, yep,' he says, with a lightness that was once as common as his new restrained silence. 'A strong latte with one.'

His is an outlook for which I am to blame: so developed by a man who loves me and yet must find a way to protect himself from the sharp edges of my increasingly turned around and fragile nature.

Over the years Scott has become a necessary expert at diagnosis of my state of mind. I use the term necessary because I am not a natural communicator. Words of vulnerability feel jagged in my throat. I will never volunteer information as to my own internal workings. In this way Scott's love has driven him to study me. He knows before I do that my stomach cramps come as a result of unspoken anger. That my snarky corrections of his word choices point to some anxiety that surrounds the relationship between my parents and myself. That a consuming drive to exercise indicates, not a run towards good physical health, but a sprint away from my disturbed emotional condition. But he has ceased this run of commentary now. Scott's shuttered gaze and silence indicates his deep fatigue with my battles, and his always-perceptive insights that once served as a diagnosis of my emotional health are now the secrets in our relationship that I have trained him to keep.

'And a babyccino for me, Mummy!' Cailean, so excited to have this time with his Dad. 'With marshmallows!' Even in my worst moments that child can make my heart sing. 'Okay, Monkey! We'll be back soon.'

Ashy and I keep on past the low green fence of Albert Park Primary School towards the village. The air is clean. The pavement littered with gum nuts fallen from the eucalypts that line the path. Our two-minute walk to the quaint street with its cluster of cafés and women's clothing boutiques and the one great bookstore, measured out in a babble of mother–son interchange. One ear on Ashok's emergent words and sounds. Another trained inward to my own internal dialogue. This won't be the first time I have seen a psychic. It will be the third, in fact. The first two visits occurred twelve months apart and offered up a mixed bag. My initial experience was with an obese man who faced me in a stuffy inner city Melbourne hotel room. Curtains drawn. The year was 2009 and he spoke of my conceiving a daughter that December. His predictive premise was correct, the gender was not: a few weeks before Christmas and after eighteen months of trying, Scott and I finally conceived Ash. He knew of the death of Scott's mother to breast cancer though didn't know that she was only forty-seven. And I like to think he described my maternal grandmother, Beryl Godkin: a stout and strong woman whose steel character belied her four-foot eleven-inch frame. My second dip into the ocean of clairvoyance was more of a disappointment: a wacky white witch who sat across a table in the crowded room of her semi-detached house, lost somewhere in Melbourne's innocuous middle suburbs. Her pronouncements were generic. Money. A new house. All the things we were furthest from at that point and remain distant to me still. 'Hey Darl, how's it going? Hey Little Man.' It's the part owner of my favourite local café. The one next to the small supermarket and the only place I can come to order coffee while waiting with the pram outside, always assured of quick attention. 'Coffees?' he asks. I smile. 'That'd be great.' I'm conscious that, these days, my only interplay with relaxed contentment is in the show I put on for outsiders. 'Two strong lattes, please, one with sugar and one without. Oh,' I add, my tone a smiling question, 'and two babyccinos for the boys to take away?' He gives me one of his nothing's-ever-a-problem winks. Ducks inside to place the order. Returns a few moments later with the treat of a cookie for Ashy, my voracious child, who grabs it greedily, of course, crumbs dropping like rain onto his buttoned up jacket. Though barely past breakfast it would seem petty for me to intercede. 'Five minutes,' he winks again and disappears.

I click on the pram's brake and set myself against the window ledge to wait. I have a complex relationship with the idea of Anglo Saxon clairvoyants. There was nothing in my upbringing that expressly forbade inter-action with Western psychics. But somehow the preju-dice seeped through all the same. I make the distinction between East and West because, of all the ways in which I was enamoured by Hinduism as a young girl, it was the storied proof of God's intercession in our lives that most captured my imagination: a cousin of Dad's who sur-vived a direct bomb-hit to the jeep he travelled in dur-ing a stint in the army, life spared, so the family legend goes, by his constant repetition of the *Om Trayambakam* mantra—the Hindu prayer recited to overcome fear of death and the unknown while giving health and lon-gevity; or the occasion when Ammaji, our family guru, reassured a distressed disciple all would be well in his life in seven days because—as she let her attendants know once he had left her New Delhi ashram with a new spring in his step, alleviated of his concerns—a week would bring his death. And so it did. Before I shut the door on grace, I had revelled in such tellings. These stories and others like them formed part of the daily conversation of my life, relayed by Dad repeatedly. They were exchanges intended to steady me. To paint divine context around daily uncertainty. *Our physical world is not what it seems*, the family fables said, *there are things we can never know in our existence and events we cannot control.* For this I gave Shivji jurisdiction over my destiny, as if Hinduism would protect me from harm. And look how well that turned out. Still a lifetime of conditioning is not so easily discarded: though I am having to re-find what spirituality means now to my life it is clear to me that I am not yet ready to call time on my heritage, to leave the idea of God and grace behind. 'Here you go, Love.' Gathering myself I flash a hit of direct eye-contact with my coy smile of thanks as I push myself to standing and grab the four-cup tray from my coffee crush: it's a scene that plays out daily in Melbourne—that of a flirtatious barista engaged in sexed-up conversation with a young and fed-up Mum. Moment passed, I balance the lot precariously on the Bugaboo hood as I turn the pram one-handed and steer the both of us back to the park. For while my faith has been cut out from under me, the need I have to believe in something bigger than myself persists. As if the notion of faith itself is a security blanket. It's an attachment that manifests in a million ways, both overt and subtle. In the given name of my second-born son. My spilling-over spice pantry. In the stories of Shivji and Krishna once told to me that I retell to my own children. The unattended puja, I keep in the front room as a talisman. Even the shawl I wear today, wrapped around my neck as material link between myself, my parents and the textured pantheon of Hindu gods.

'Stab pass! Stab pass! Aw, great kick, Buddy!'

I hear Cailean and Scott's laughter from the school crossing that dissects the length of Victoria Avenue. I note the sound for its rarity. Grasp at it, the same way I grasp at Erica and my imminent experience of her; all of my long fingers curled as flesh hooks around hope. In doing so I acknowledge that the clairvoyants in my past were mere puppets in the performance of my curiosity. Not this time. This time I desire to know nothing of the future. Seek simply a point of access into my past. A new language for a renewed dialogue with the gods I do not want to leave behind. Namaskar *Bhagwanji*. Words once rich with context that now project from my mouth as no more than exotic sounds. I require an interpreter to rediscover their meaning. A frequency converter. As Ashy and I enter back through the school, I decide that Erica Goodwin will become this. That she will be my guide. That I will make it so.

'More.'

That night I cook *kaddu*. Dad has been sending it up frequently. Pumpkin sabzi that has become a staple alongside daal and *gajar mattar* as late-autumn Butternut and Jap varieties currently fill vegetable shop shelves. I have no recipe for this. Competence in my Kashmiri kitchen proven by the ability I now possess to cook it free form. 'More.' The *kaddu* burns Ashy's mouth. He spoons it in anyway. Face red. Mouth that moves furiously in a movement that suggests extreme pleasure and the prick of pain. Discomfort marked by the tears that run down his face. It's not the heat. It's the burn. Cinnamon. Ginger, both fresh and ground. Kashmiri red chilli. Mace.

I make it as Scott and Cailean depart for a Sunday evening lemon squash and pint of beer at the nearby Montague pub. Feed it to a hungry and impatient Ashy before their return. In the immediacy of completion, I had felt pleased with the result but—watching Ashok's face now—I am suddenly unsure. Confused by his reaction, I withdraw his bowl. I am concerned for him. But he flails at me. Demands it returned.

More.

Scott named both our sons. Cailean was simple. We found out he was a boy during the twenty-week scan at an ultrasound clinic two steps off the Champs-Élysées. *C'est un petit garcon*, the doctor had announced. I'd squealed. Never in my life had I pictured myself with boys. Though Scott and I curled together around our longed-for future to play, tongue-in-cheek, with ancient monikers written down in the pages of Scott's impressive family tree (*Farquard Farquason? Cummin the Red?*) our first son's birth on 11 May created an obvious choice: Cailean, Scottish

Gaelic for Colin, the name of the Scottish paternal great-grandfather whose birthday he shared.

Ashok was different. I had expected a girl, for one thing. Kamini. It is my middle name, the first name of my Ammi. I had always wished it was mine, too. Me, the only one of three siblings whose autograph had roots that could not be assigned to our Kashmiri origins. So I plotted to strengthen my connection to that name. It was a tactical decision made in early girlhood: that I would pass on Ammi's moniker—the gift of inherited identity—to the future daughter I was so sure I would have. *You choose a boy's name, just in case,* I'd advised Scott in the weeks that led to Ashy's birth. I never believed we'd require its use. Needless to say it was a beautiful shock to pull our second son to my chest the night he was born in a private maternity hospital in Melbourne. Long limbs. Compressed face. Thick black hair. The image, in that moment, of his big brother born almost three-and-a-half years before. Scott named him Ashok Alexander. For two of history's greatest warrior kings.

I sit and watch, now, as Ashok cries his way through a bowl I had wished as soft nurture. My son. The one given to me by God, just as He had intended. The child I had spent my life imagining by another sex and another name. And though the realisation is there to be seen I close my eyes to it: that vastness that exists between desire and blessing—the benediction I think I want versus the boon that is mine to receive. In the stillness, a thought rises up from the darkness. That I have to walk into this experiment with Erica firm in the belief that it will give me what I want—a strengthened link to Shivji and the spiritual sanctuary of my childhood. My emotional state is still too fragile for me to acknowledge the reality: that to re-enter into a dialogue with God may not take me where I expect to go.

'Hi, my name is Sarina. I've got an appointment booked to see Erica?'

The speed with which Wednesday morning has arrived has been startling. A large part of this owes to the routine and pace of our life. The rotation of childcare pick-ups and drop-offs. The work both Scott and I squeeze into every spare bit of space. The relentless tedium of daily chores that is the scaffolding around which small children construct their new little lives. 'Sure,' smiles the blonde behind the reception desk at Flying Souls, 'she'll be out in a minute. Would you like tea or a glass of water while you wait? Water would be great, thanks.' I take a seat in the adjacent lounge, filled with chairs and crystals and books on finding a healing spiritual space.

But a degree of acceleration owes to the way in which I find time is magnetised to events weighted by fear: the dentist I am terrified to visit; the loom of a non-negotiable deadline I panic I won't make; the psychic and what I'm scared she might see. 'Thank you,' I murmur a moment later, grateful for the distraction as I accept the full glass. The fact is I am not at all thirsty. I drink anyway. The act of raising the glass to my lips—the sip and swallow— diverts my awareness from the sense of intense discomfort that threatens to overwhelm. I have become wed to the idea that spice and spirituality can save me. It is why the kitchen has become such a place of shelter: to be there on my own, to cook food from family recipes that I believe to be grounded in faith. Should this experience challenge the remaining bits and pieces of belief that currently hold together the broken pieces of my life, then where will that leave me? The heating is on high. I unwind my shawl from around my neck. Look blindly upon this room with its trays of crystals, with its shelves of self-help books and Doreen Virtue angel cards. It is unrecognisable. This is not my space. I am not at home. Just as panic would engulf me I hear my name spoken from behind. 'Sarina?'

Erica. I have never seen her before and yet she greets me like a long-lost friend. I lean awkwardly into her New Age embrace, then pull back to take the whole of her in: she looks discouragingly normal. Lank hair that falls in a brown slide to her shoulder blade. Tight jeans that cut into the rounded flesh of her waist. Wedged sandals high and cheap. I'm not sure what I expected. It wasn't this. But it's too late to go anywhere. And to whom else would I turn? So I wrestle myself down from the high pedestal of judgement and attempt to face the fear that would have me flee; follow Erica into a room where she encourages me to lie down on the blanket-covered massage bed. I refuse politely. Sit determinedly upright on a cushioned seat. Legs crossed. Carmine-red leather briefcase at my side.

'Oh, put that away for now,' Erica directs as I make a show of fishing in my bag for the discreet silver voice recorder I use to record all work interviews. It is my play to influence events. A subtle show of force. *You'll be done helping me in a whip*, my action says, *then we can get onto business.* Her instruction for me to put my tools of trade aside leaves me scared and defenceless. I feel as a collector's butterfly skewered by another's agenda. 'Maybe it's just best if you call me for the interview tomorrow morning,' Erica suggests, her tone washed in the pastel sympathy of kindness. Her hands begin to move in the air in front of me in what I presume is her motion of healing. 'Why don't you just tell me why you're here?'

Now that I sit stripped of my armour before her I don't know what to say. I stutter and stammer a bit. She waits in patient silence, like the psychoanalysts I have watched in movies. For the first time I feel the full weight of my own resistance to this process. So far, every step of the way, I have had to grate and slice and boil myself down into new shapes and strange forms that I do not want to fit. It is hard. But I have done it. Inch by painful inch I uncover the forgotten tastes of me. I have been on my own, in this, and desirously so. Driven to cook and agonise and cry away from the eyes of my loved ones. Shame is a large part of it. The perfectionist in me regards any failure as something to be concealed, and no fuck up is more shocking than to find myself completely outside of my own life. No vulnerability more fragile than the one that demands I ask another to help me back in. And right now that's where I sit. Beyond the ballast of my kitchen. Far from the reach of my recipes. Apart from my pots and pans. I sit on this chair in *her* house of God. One occupied not by Shivji or Devi or Vishnu, but by Christian idols and unfamiliar saints: Archangels Gabriel and Raphael and Michael. Ascended Master Quan Yin. Mother Mary. I sit in silent struggle, unsure what words to use to ask Erica and these foreign spirits to transcribe my desperation. She sits in wait to hear the shrill of my need.

I want to speak with my God again. I want to hear His call.

The room doesn't warp. There is no instant transportation. Neither Erica nor her celestial support act appears to hear my silent pronouncement. So she is not that kind of psychic. No Mind Reading, should read the sign on the front door. It seems I will have to speak. That my sounds must be formed. 'I need…' Oxygen whooshes from my lungs. I suck in more, fidget on my chair, shoulders a tight band around my ears and legs twisted pretzel-tight. I try again. Release all the breath that I have into one stuttered sentence of belief. I hope with all that is left in my heart that she can interpret what it means. I know that to voice these seven words will leave me spent. I know *that* even if I know nothing else.

'I need to find my way home.'

The words spoken are mine. A sentence that holds me roped to the room with the fear of one who feels certain oblivion awaits.

Erica's hands still. Her eyes close. And the silence in the room grows loud.

KADDU
Pumpkin sabzi

I first introduced *kaddu* to the children after Dad introduced it, in my adulthood, to me. It was never a sabzi we ate growing up. But something about the contradiction inherent in its composition makes it one I return to again and again. Sweet. Soft. Searing. Spice. Nurture and pain. The complexity of the human state expressed in its truest measure.

INGREDIENTS:

1 kilogram of pumpkin

3 tomatoes

2 tablespoons ghee

1 ½ teaspoon salt

1 generous teaspoon whole cumin seeds

2 teaspoons ground coriander seeds

½ teaspoon ground ginger

10 grams of fresh ginger, julienned

½ teaspoon turmeric

20 grams of gur

1 cinnamon quill, broken in 2

3 cloves

1 dried mace flower

1 whole star anise

¾ teaspoon Kashmiri red chilli (½ teaspoon if cooking for children)

METHOD:

Cut pumpkin into cubes of about 2 centimetres. Skin and dice tomatoes finely.

In a large frying pan, heat 2 tablespoons of ghee. Add all the spices together and warm on a medium heat until fragrant. Take the pan off the heat when adding the diced tomato so that the liquid doesn't burn the spice. Cook together over a low heat for around 15 or 20 minutes. When cooked down to a thick and fragrant slurry, add the pumpkin and stir through the spice. Add a little water—about 1 centimetre in the bottom of the pan—to help the pumpkin soften. Cook on a very low heat for at least 45 minutes, until the pumpkin is completely soft and fragrant with spice. Add more water as necessary to prevent the pumpkin from sticking and burning.

Serves eight as part of a larger Kashmiri meal.

CHAPTER 7

Cumin

Cumin is common in spice pantries
across Eastern cultures. But that makes
it no less significant to me. Scent that is
smoke and memory and dusky sorrow.
Present in every kitchen I have ever called
home, it is what—for the longest time—I
understood love's foundation to be.

CUMIN IS THE TASTE OF me. It is the spice with which I most identify. Should God permit me use of only one seasoning for the rest of my life then this is the one I would choose, for I could not live without it. When I first began my Kashmiri kitchen experimentation, cumin was the lone ingredient that I categorically understood. I experience no uncertainty in its measure, can imagine in four-dimensional savour its influence upon any sabzi that I cook.

I know cumin because it tastes of the love that raised me.

Scott descends from a very straightforward Australian family. Within the Lewis household love was dispensed alongside teasing, Southern Hemisphere sarcasm and a regular dose of *she'll be right, mate.* Though I, too, spent much of my childhood raised on the same large island as he, none of that was true of my experience. It wasn't how my family interacted. And while I don't know what's true of all Indian families, I do know what is true of ours—that Ganjus argue, Ganjus judge, Ganjus interfere. Ganjus love but they love hard and they love intrusively without commas or spaces in between. Ganjus love as they live, relentlessly in close quarter and always with the power of right on their side. To be raised within that space is a kind of magnificence yet it creates a certain internal intractability, too. That this is the only way to love. But it is more than that. This is the only way I understand how to *be* loved. Deeply. Directly. Defensively. The last is important. For by being in a continued aggressive state of emotional interaction, part of the game is in the pushing back. The counter-argument. It shows engagement and engagement shows a willingness to play, and a willingness to play shows your sameness, and your sameness shows love. What this chain doesn't allow for is shared vulnerability. And an absence of shared vulnerability—as I would only much, much later find out—will lead to the death of intimate connection. Maybe not straight away. But eventually.

All of this is what cumin tastes like to me. I could never conceive of a life where I am shaken free of such strange comfort. Find it impossible to imagine that I could ever let any of this go. For that is the only outcome I can conjure—if I am to move forward I feel certain it will require absolute forfeit of everything that has gone before. It must.

'Are we there yet?' Cailean's voice comes from the back seat. It is Saturday morning, a dreary May day that feels less like autumn and more like the coming winter. We are packed into our pint-sized VW Golf on the way to a weekend at Mum and Dad's. It's a little squeezy—though we will only stay a night with my parents, the hatch is filled with grocery bags of fresh food, a couple of backpacks with teddy bears and changes of clothes, and an array of Matchbox cars the boys couldn't bear to leave behind—but this is the only transport we have. We made the decision to sell Scott's Land Rover twelve months ago to reduce petrol and car registration costs. To lessen in some small way the tear of financial strain. Has it worked? The distracted weight that continues to sit at the bottom of my gut suggests not. 'Mummy? Are we nearly there?'

My mind is elsewhere. I have to look up and around to get my bearings before I can answer Cailean's question.

'Um, just about fifteen more minutes to go, Monkey,' I say it with confidence, having noted the landmark that is the Freshwater Creek cake shop, as we whiz past. 'Here,' I offer distraction as I sense his frustration with the journey, 'take some sultanas.' I twist around to face back. Hand out two opened packets to two sets of chubby grasping fingers. Know that at least a third of the contents of each will find their way squashed and sand-covered in the wedge between the boosters and our leather car seats. 'Is there a banana in that bag?' Scott joins in. The largest of the three males to whom I am indentured. We left just after 8 a.m. and in the rush neither he nor I had eaten breakfast. 'Yep.' My voice emits a familiar false cheer; being with Mum and Dad is a test of endurance and I have to fight hard to keep my mood from crashing. I reach into the rustle of plastic and pull out the last of our travel supplies. This familiar seventy-minute trip that always takes on epic proportions. It is a way of living with small children. The need for props and ballast and contingencies. I peel the fruit for Scott in a curve of yellow, return the softened skin to what is now a makeshift rubbish bag. Duties done, I hope for ten minutes of silence—the nourishment *I* need before I land as an emotional refugee at Mum and Dad's doorstep.

It has been three days since that morning with Erica. Three days in which I have been tied in knots trying to understand what occurred. Three days of my brain working to record and classify surreal events into known categories. I do not like the unknown. It is not a comfortable place for me to reside; have spent much of my life working to ensure that this is a territory I need never again enter.

Your breasts should be bigger.

It was in the seconds after the room had filled with silence that Erica had spoken. Her peculiar and unexpected entrée that reverberated through my solar plexus with the brutal impact of a bare-fisted punch. I was winded by shock. Capable of nothing more than an alarmed, non-verbal response. I hadn't known what to expect in that first meeting, but had been acutely aware of my reluctance to journey *here*: into some dark and muddy pseudo-psychic investigation of me. Had wanted nothing more than direct answers to the questions I held before me as a shield. *How can I change who I am and still hear God? How can I move on from my past and not leave my connection to Shivji behind?* Erica's opening gambit was instead an unauthorised revision of my script. I would have resisted her direction but for the next pronouncement that had torn my heart from my throat. *You stopped them from growing when you were thirteen—was there something that happened to you then, some tragedy?*

Arrested by her accuracy—her surety—my shield had fallen. I could do no more than nod. I was mute. Though she had pulled the rug out from under me I was too stunned for anger. Too willing to fall into the cradle of another's surety. For it was Erica's certainty that seduced me. Later I would see that this was the moment my faith cracked open: when the idea that clairvoyance might serve as an alternative to my Hindu gods manifested somewhere inside.

'Okay, so who wants to guess the time?' Scott's voice startles me back to reality. I am momentarily voiceless as I re-enter the car, as a diver with the bends shoots up too fast from the deep. 'I say 9.37.'

Cailean chips in next. 'Umm, I say 9.39.' By his voice and in the view of dry grassy paddocks and wind-battered gums blurred by speed outside my window I am returned. We are on the freeway and we have nearly arrived. This game is the signifier; a thing we do when we know our destination is near. A competition to guess the precise minute Scott cuts the engine at the head of Mum and Dad's orange gravel drive.

'I say 9.35.' Concentration shredded, my offer comes as a stab in the dark. Ashy's contribution—he is still too young to grasp the concept of time or number value— is even more so. 'Five!' At Ashok's exclamation I sense Cailean's intake of breath to be released as a correction. Before he speaks I shoot him a look of warning over my shoulder. *It is a game,* my frown says, *allow him his participation. He's a baby. It doesn't matter that he plays it wrong.* Cailean reads me correctly. Drops back into silence. I turn my body again to the front. My face once again intent on the rush past my window. Truth be told I don't really care if Cailean corrects his little brother. All I want in the car is silence. Silence that I may relive and explore and deeply inhale the power of the messages that Erica gave to me.

> *You have a sorrow so deep I feel like you could*
> *cry for years and still not reach its heart.*
> *Your parents are not long for this world.*
> *Let your inner child speak those words of hurt*
> *to your mother and to your father.*
> *Visualise that little girl. Pull her into your*
> *heart and forgive yourself for not caring for her.*
> *Forgive your mother and your father. They did*
> *the best they could.*
> *You will be there for your mother in the end.*

Ensconced in that small room with its massage bed and healing crystals and patchouli essence, I had felt the poison in each root of embedded thought that Erica pulled free. The release of it into my bloodstream provoked a spill of pain and anguish that stained the air with the stench of emotional vomit. I was triggered by her insights into anguished recitation of my weaknesses. I told it all. The books I no longer read because I am so fucking *furious* that I do not write; disconnected from what it is I need to say by a tragedy so oft-repeated that even I am tired of its retelling. The devil that has me convinced my parents must die before I can find peace. That I know in my heart I do not have the courage to nurse Mum to her death. That I cannot imagine a world where I am resolved enough in my own grief to be there for her, nor she emotionally whole enough to be there for me.

'9.36!' Scott calls out the time on the car clock as he turns off the engine. The hood of our car noses Mum's hedge of lavender. Its steel body parked against the fragrant semi-circle that demarcates her garden from the driveway. 'Right in the middle! A Mummy and Daddy draw. No winner again.'

No winner again.

Only today can I see that perhaps that pronouncement no longer holds true, at least not for me. I push open my passenger door and hear the crunch of my step on the drive. I *had* wanted resolution. Had walked into that meeting with Erica, desirous of a neatly spooled result—hopeful that the visit would loop me full circle to reconnection with my own gods. I never expected to find a substitute. But the more I consider it, the safer it feels. Shivji is demanding, after all: he who chopped off his own son's head as a result of what was at best a minor misunderstanding. No, Erica and her strange menagerie of angels is safer; her visions had pulled at each loose thread of my being and yet I had felt coddled there, transformed in that hour from an electrified ball of tension into a blessed release of unspooled humanity spilled upon her carpeted floor: a kind of vulnerable surrender to grief that I have never before been able to indulge. Certainly not here, not in this house: not with all of those memories of lying in bed—ages twelve, fourteen, seventeen—and hearing Mum's wrenching distress through the floorboards above; the dry sobs that drowned out Dad's verbal comfort as she cried herself to sleep.

'C'mon Ashy, out we get,' I grunt the last word as I heft his weight from the car and hitch him to my hip. Acknowledge his cry—'Bunny!'—in my reach and pull out his mangled toy bunny from the rear foot well. I push the toy into Ashy's small grip and use my foot to kick shut the door. 'Let's go and find Baba and Ammi.'

In the time it takes me to walk the garden path, I ensure that all my vulnerabilities that this week exposed are firmly tucked away. I hug Ashok's form against my body, a shackle to the present. So anchored, I force myself to leave aside thoughts of Erica. Instead I walk as a death row inmate toward the weekend of ambiguity and tension that I know from past experience lies in wait, beyond Mum and Dad's front door.

'Hello-o-oh.' Cailean squeezes past as I open the door with my hands full of Ashy. I follow closely behind, sing out the three-syllable greeting. The first thing I note upon entry is the scent of cumin seeds, its aroma seeped over the span of thirty years into the porous cedar walls; I note it for the longing it invokes, the aromatic threat it presents to my thin and newly acquired armour; the little bit of strength I have gained from the idea that clairvoyance might lead me towards a new spiritual peace. The second is the silence. At this hour it is not unusual. Mum and Dad's bedroom is upstairs and at the house's far end. Come the approach of 10 a.m. Dad can most often be found helping Mum out of their en suite shower. Mum finds it difficult to get out of bed before 9 a.m. First she will wake, sore and stiff. Then she will cry at the realisation of another day in the body that betrays her. It is Dad's responsibility to scrape her heart off the floor. To fortify her will with a cup of tea taken with her favourite morning television show and her bedside pills. But Dad must have heard our car pull up. In the time it takes to kick off my shoes in the blue slate-paved entrance hall, I can hear his heavy footfall reverberate through the carpet-covered floorboards above.

'Sarinaaa? Chaitanya? Ashok? *Namaskaaaarrrr.*' Dad comes to the top of the second-storey landing. Scott joins the boys and me at the bottom of the stairs. I see from his body language as he puts down our bags in order to take Ashy from my arms that Scott, too, is braced for the weekend to come: I know he feels like the glue between my parents and I, that he is worn out attempting to hold us together. But to view his efforts is all I can do. I feel no capacity to own up to my part in all of this. To relieve Scott of the burden he carries for me.

'Hi Scott,' Dad calls down. 'Chaitanya come upstairs with Ashok and see Ammi.'

'Hi Anup!' Scott sounds determinedly upbeat as he straps Ashy into the motorised seat that corkscrews on a solid steel rail up the spiral staircase. 'Sending one of them up!' It is Mum's purpose-built lift. The lift is clunky and obstructive, attached to the smooth curve of the cedar handrail that is an elegant twist upward. To me it presents an apt visual metaphor to the ways in which Parkinson's has colonised our lives.

As a family we hesitated for years before adapting any part of the house to Mum's changing needs. We would all counsel caution as she lifted her leaden and increasingly recalcitrant feet up and down the dangerous procession of stairs. But it wasn't until after she had fallen multiple times—the last of which resulted in a severely broken ankle requiring surgery and a steel plate—that the idea of the lift was manifested. It seems that, for as long as Parkinson's has been a part of all our lives, we have each been reacting *to* it. As if the disease was the master and we—Dad, Mum, my brothers and I—were powerless. Either unable or incapable of finding a way to counter its bullying threat. Communication was our only weapon— our magic key—but that was long ago forsaken: even today we all continue to do anything but talk of how the disease continues to ravage Mum. The refusal to speak of it chews at the insides of us all. But no matter the degree of frustration the sight of this mechanical seat incites in me, Ashok loves it. His excitement as his Baba rides him up to the top of the stairs with the push of a remote button is voluble.

'I'll send Cailean up to say hello to Ammi in a minute,' I call up to Dad as Cailean follows Scott down into our bedroom where they will proceed to unpack our bags. I think Dad hears what I say, though given the volume of Ashy's excited babble I can't be sure. In any case by sending Mum her little Indian prince I have bought myself the few moments required to gather my thoughts.

Restless and anxious and momentarily alone, I do what I always do to find an internal corner of calm and security when I am here. I get busy. Material precautions taken to ensure that my footprint throughout this weekend is as light as possible. This must be done in myriad ways. The first is to say less; Dad and I rub each other the wrong way, and so not speaking has become my defence. The second is to be seen less; this I manage by thrusting forward the children so that I may step back into the shadows. The third and perhaps the most important is to make my actions invisible in the kitchen. Given the food prep I am required to do for the kids this is, unfortunately, the most difficult of the three.

'Right,' I mutter to myself, hauling the grocery bags Scott put down from the entrance hall into the kitchen, 'let's get started.'

Over the years, Dad's replacement of Mum in the kitchen has moved from necessity to a hard and deliberate kind of ownership. I know that Mum feels the pain of the loss: she is forever lurching up from her seat in order to peer into pots on the stove. If movement is too hard, then she will call out instructions from her chair at the dining table—reminders and questions that speak of her desperation to hold on to the role of family nurturer, the position from which disease has forced her abdication. But as much as Mum wants to remain the most integral point of connection for our family, she is completely physically incapable. As such, the room's configuration no longer resembles hers—the cans of condensed milk from which Mum had eaten secret spoonfuls are long gone as are packets of savoury and sweet biscuits that competed for space with boxes of pasta and sliced loaves of bread in the pantry.

Instead the kitchen environment is now categorically Dad's domain. Tubs of hokey pokey ice cream in the freezer and slabs of milk chocolate are stacked above the two porcelain Portmeirion canisters in the pine hutch. Sweets oriented towards his tooth. The fridge is filled with ingredients suited for use in his Kashmiri dishes: difficult vegetables like eggplant, overripe tomatoes, okra and lotus root. Perhaps a bit of iceberg lettuce for when Mum craves a sandwich or a salad. In the pantry, bags of spicy namkeen supplant biscuits; deep-fried morsels of daal and peas and crunchy batons of chickpea batter that taste of nigella, chilli and cumin.

None of that would impact me at all, but for the changed attitude that has come as part and parcel of the altered contents. As I said, this is Dad's domain. But unlike the fuss-free approach that reigned throughout Mum's kitchen rule, Dad regulates with vigilance any movement that occurs within the kitchen borders. He achieves this with regular pronouncement of implacable rules and pointed remonstration directed towards those that dare flaunt them.

'Don't chop up that cucumber there, Sarina, I need this space free for my bread-making.' Or: 'The ham doesn't go in that drawer, it goes wrapped in paper with the medicines and the cheese.' And then: 'Don't use that frozen bread for toast, that's not as old as the other one. Use this sliced loaf first.'

It doesn't sound like much. But over years and months and weeks and weekends and hours and minutes of constant micro control the heart of this home—the kitchen—has become a conflict zone. It grates upon me that—for all of the things that we do not talk about—these are the conversations Dad chooses to have. This domestic territory Dad defends against me. A culinary Gaza Strip. The *Garam Masala* Strip. Can I make that a thing? For the kitchen is no longer a space engendered towards reunion and communion. I don't know why Dad has moved in this direction. Is it to make his carriage of the domestic mantle seem as if it was his choice? A behaviour to distract from the cruel truth that it was Mum's disease that forced the new familial configuration? Does he find within the relentless regard of his new order a place to evade the hurt—a bubble where he can plan and organise and time his actions; exist outside the uncontrollable realities of Parkinson's? Perhaps if I had perspective I might recognise this behaviour as *his* defence mechanism against the hurt I inflicted by repeatedly making the choice not to learn to cook. The way I chose to shy away and not confront what Parkinson's has done to our family.

But I cannot see that yet.

All I do know is that his choices have meant I must exist within my childhood home in a heightened state of spatial awareness. So it is with trepidation that I proceed to unpack the groceries I purchased this morning at the South Melbourne market. I am cognisant of the admonishments that will come as I slide cucumber and broccoli and avocadoes into the vegetable drawer (*I can't find anything, the veggie drawer is too full*). I am braced for Dad's judgement when he stumbles upon my loaf of sliced commercial bread in his pantry (*What are all these loaves of bread for?*). I hear in advance his imminent critique as I slice a rockmelon for snacks and store it in a Tupperware container on a middle shelf (*You Western people waste so much food by cutting the rind off with the skin*). I know all this will come to pass, just as I know that Mum will stay silent in the face of the weekend's barrage. That she will neither join in nor defend. That the only thing that angers me more than his tactics of domestic demarcation and hers of frightened hesitation, is that

I am required by their actions and by the familiarity of my own response to regard this dynamic as functional. I have minded this development. I have minded very much. The transition of kitchen from place of nurture to familial battleground. Without the words to articulate our distress. Mine. Mum's. Dad's. Each verbal exchange carried out within this room is symbolic of the fossilized emotional positions we occupy in relation to each other. Dad desperate to prove there is no piece of his family's trajectory he cannot control. Mum too frozen by present pain and future fear to do anything other than make herself so small and so silent that God's glance may skip over her entirely. Me prone to confabulate any negative comment into a dramatic crisis, made irrational by their prolonged denial of my grief and my distress. 'Mummy?' Cailean walks out from his bedroom as a well-timed distraction. 'I'm hungry, can I have some 'tanees?' He skips across the television room and up two steps to the raised kitchen where I stand. 'Just a small *katori*, Buddy,' I concede. I turn from clearing the last of my goods from Dad's island chopping table to scrabble for a handful of sultanas from a glass jar in the pantry. 'Baba told me last night that Ammi had made you and Ashy some special lunch. I don't want you to lose your appetite.'

'Thank you, Mummy,' he says, serious and grateful in his acceptance of the small silver bowl. 'Can I watch a few cartoons?'

'Have you been upstairs to say hello to Baba and Ammi yet?'

'Nooooo…' His reluctance draws out of him on a long breath.

'Okay, well I'll keep your 'tanees safe here. You go and do that first and tell them I'll be there in a minute. Yes,' I insist as his face falls and his displeasure thrusts forward as a sulky pout.'Off you go. Go on. I'll be up in a minute.' As Cailean disappears I put the last of our fruit atop the big red apples that fill the bowl in the centre of Mum and Dad's round glass dining room table. Neatly stow any stray plastic bags inside the calico sack designated for this particular use that hangs on the inside of the pantry door. In doing so I catch the edge of the rounded glass jar of Dad's cumin seed stash. It would have tumbled but for my reflexes and the primal instinct to guard this piece of kitchen history. I place it back on its shelf; neaten a few of the other spice jars that rest alongside. At last, when I can put it off no longer, I follow Cailean's tracks up the stairs to greet Mum and Dad in their bedroom. My heavy footfall echoing my five-year-old son's.

Belligerent and resentful and resigned and burdened.

CHAPTER 8

Aloo Parantha

Saturdays when we were growing up were a day
for being vegetarian: atonement to mitigate
the influence of black Saturn. It was always
worth it when Dad made aloo paranthas.
Edible compensation for penance served.

I CANNOT HELP BUT SEE Mum as a ghost. I know that is how
I write about her. How she comes to half-life on the page.
She is not a spectre of threat or menace. But a wrung-
out phantom. A wraith in my life who holds a shallow
physical presence. The pain I feel that is wrought by her
emotional absence. She who barely talks. Whose motiva-
tions and dreams I no longer know. Whose non- being
as she sits in an armchair at the dining room table or
slouches into the couch cushions is contradicted by my
remembrance of the spirit she once was: that goddess of
my girlhood. I remember the promise of our burgeoning

friendship. The shared shopping trips. The cappuccino outings when I would scoop froth and chocolate from her white coffee's top. I remember her lit by a sense of magnificence contextualised by the way in which Dad spoke of her. The tales he told of how Mum won his Kashmiri mother's heart.

There is a framed photo that still hangs in Mum and Dad's bedroom taken in the weeks after they first met. Mum, with her pale, sharply beautiful face and long thin limbs. Braless. Head wrapped in a paisley print scarf. And Dad. Seated beside. Elbow balanced upon one raised knee in the way that he still sits today. His laughing face focussed on her. Grin framed by a black spring of Afro. Body cut by the shape of a lean seventies suit.

West-meets-East.

At the time of their New Delhi meeting, Mum and Dad both worked as successful designers in an era when fashion wasn't fast. When a girl from Melbourne's whitely affluent South Eastern suburbs found herself on a three-month subcontinental work adventure. When a handsome young sailing Indian with the heart of a poet channelled his creative spirit into a successful second career. That they met at all was kismet. What followed next was faith. Kashmiri *Brahmins* do not marry non-Kashmiri *Brahmins*. India's caste system was outlawed in the 1950s. Yet in the early '70s it remained ultimately defining. Caste was conceived as a system of social definition and the Brahmins were at the top of the pyramid. An imaginary sense of 'purity' of the bloodline has always been heavily guarded lest a *Brahmin* family lose its resonant prayerful voice. But Ammi saw past this. Sensed, perhaps, that the addition of this white woman to an old and respected Kashmiri *Brahmin* family could create an alternate way for us to be heard by our gods. Those idols into whose ears we whisper.

This Australian girl, Jennifer, my Ammi called out to Dad one night from her Defence Colony bedroom in the weeks after his Saint Valentine's Day conquest. Dad was sleeping in his parents' home, his bedroom across the inner courtyard from Ammi's. Her husband, my Papa, was still alive and lay asleep beside her. The strength of Ammi's position in the family, the power she had to veto Dad's hoped-for marriage, it was all carried in the question that echoed to Dad, then 30 years old, in the early spring New Delhi air. *You love her?*

Yes, was my Dad's straight and quick reply.

After so many years of protected Ganju legacy, I do not know why this single positive response was enough to convince Ammi to let her cultural drawbridge down. Why Ammi gave permission for Mum to enter into her clan and put an end to generations of marital tradition. I do know that the telling of it was a story more romantic to me than any Mills and Boon. Back then I liked to imagine that Ammi, a tailor and herself a beauty, felt a piece of her spirit embedded in *this Australian girl*. Mum, a woman outside of Ammi's cultural experience in every way, and yet recognisable by her strengths: her acute ability to not only perceive life's wonder but spread it outward with intelligence and warmth. These qualities that Ammi deemed of equal value to any spiritual lineage. At least that's how it went in my head.

But years have passed now and I no longer know how to marry luminescent family folklore with my uncertain view of the woman Mum has grown to be. The composition of her painted in my mind that confusion has washed out and set deep. The way I struggle to bring her to life. The way I fail to recall her words. Is it that I can no longer place her, or that I refuse to? Perhaps it is my mechanism for self-protection: better she exists as a whole person in my past than a debilitated woman in my present. Without perspective I cannot see the parallel between the bubble I create and the same shell of self- protection that serves Dad in his kitchen. Yet on some level I comprehend: if I cannot find a way to look upon her, I will never have access to a clear-gazed view of me.

'Sarina, can you help set the table, please?' Dad. It's Saturday lunchtime. His call demands I break from playing with the boys on the living room floor beside the combustion Scott has lit for warmth. That I heed routine. 'Mother has made some minestrone soup for the boys.' Dad's pronouncement of Mum's effort in the kitchen is weighted. She is too constrained by her physical degradations to cook routinely, anymore. The effort it takes is enormous. The danger of her falling is inherent in bending over to open drawers and pull out heavy pans; she hasn't the strength or balance to move a pot of hot soup from stovetop to benchtop. That Dad has helped her to make this effort tells of Mum's deep desire to nurture her family through the straightjacket of disease.

'Okay.' I attempt not to convert a two-syllable acquiescence into a forced sound of irritation as I move to do as he asks. This requires extreme force of will. For if Dad becomes the archetypical father over these weekends, then in the role-playing stakes he is bested only by the cameo of adolescent me. I sound sulky even to my own ears as I extend the barest of courtesies to Mum. 'Do you want soup too?'

'Yes, please,' she says and I set the table for the three of them: Mum and my two boys. Place mats and spoons and those same Portmeirion bowls.

It is not an affectation for metaphor that has me speak of role-playing. The brief early morning respite offered by the joy Mum and Dad experience in receiving the boys is fast replaced by re-establishment of the social order. Theirs as parents and mine as child. In this way in this house in the company of these two people I am an adult who seeks shelter in the shell of teen angst. As if time stopped the day Mum was diagnosed, as if we have prevented its progression by carrying forward all these years of silence. As such I am cranky. Short-tempered. Volatile. Sometimes I think this energy must transmit itself, that it then influences Dad's behaviour. Or is it the other way around? In any case, I morph into a caricature of adolescent dysfunction. And he, the disciplinarian. I hate it. It's vile. An out-of-character mode of behaviour that invades my psyche and leaves me brooding for weeks. 'Chait-an-yaaa. A-sshhhok. Come up to the table please. Ammi made you boys some minestrone soup for lunch.' Dad doesn't need to explain to the kids what this means—even Cailean knows the significance of the offer of Mum's effort.'You're not eating, Sarina?' Mum's voice comes out of her soup bowl as I walk up to help settle the boys. 'No.' My answer is short. It is a cruel refusal of a small piece of her and I loathe myself even as the words leave my mouth: to refuse food in any culture can be hurtful, but in our household, where meals prepared equal love offered, my actions are especially hostile. 'I'm not really hungry.'

This has become the extent of our conversation. Falsities. Hidden messages that sound to others as benign conversation. They are anything but: for the result of not being able to talk of our emotions directly means that, as a family, we have come to speak in code. *You're not eating?* means: *you're not going to accept this part of me?* My response, *I'm not really hungry*, translates as: *this all just feels as too little, too late*. In any case the silent exchange is quickly dropped. Mum is nervous around me. She worries that to broach any sensitive subject directly will be to push me away further. That I will misconstrue the most compassionate of her comments. I hear it in her voice. And the truth is she is right. After all these years spent waiting for either of them to own up to how fractured we have all become, I have fallen beyond easy reparation. Instead I am a predator ready to pounce. I scour sentences for the chance to attack. If not that, then silence. For the only way I know not to spend every minute in their company crying is not to say anything at all.

I am aware that this is a bitter trade.

'Mmm, the soup's nice,' Mum murmurs into her bowl. 'Can you butter me a piece of bread, Sarina?' I get up to do as Mum asks. She and I who are trapped by loss into a pattern of interaction we both feel as deep lack: it is less that we have given up, more that the paralysis of long-term despair has set in. Mum. Dad. Me. We all feel deprived of that single thing we feel will fix us and that no one is able to give. I want apology. Dad wants wholeness. Mum just wants to know why. Why *her*? It is a desperately sad trifecta of hopeless resentment that tears up the guts of us all.

'Sarina, did you use my special knife?' Right on time, Dad walks towards me. Mum has her bread and I am once again seated by Ash at the table. I say *right on time*, because, over the years, as the chasm of silence between Mum and I has become too wide, Dad has become louder and more insistent to fill the painful gap. Sometimes they are words in jest. Often they are judgements spoken in irritation. Always they are loud enough to shout down the threat contained in the void of undiagnosed grief. *Did you use my special knife?* In this instance Dad brandishes exhibit A in his right hand: the special knife. His tone makes it clear this is an accusation in a question's cloak. It is an altercation. A hierarchical tussle guaranteed to repeat multiple times over the next twenty-four hours. Only with the perspective of distance will I later come to view our mutual aggressions in clear light. Dad and I. So talented at rubbing each other the wrong way. Our fiery conversations that fast convert quotidian interaction into an exercise of verbal flame throwing. It's the same old story: preferable to being witness to each other's pain is the default distraction of annoyance and anger.

'Yes *Dad*.' There is an ugly emphasis. My tone laced with anticipatory aggression. 'I had to cut some bread for Mum.'

'This is not my bread knife.' He is straight-faced and serious, voice stern. There is a little wave of the knife in the air. 'This is the knife I use for cutting meat. This one,' Dad walks five steps back to the two magnetised knife strips that line the walls on either side of his gas stovetop, pulling a long serrated blade from the rack to demonstrate correct procedure. 'This one is the knife I use to cut bread.' I use the little energy I have, that is not directed towards stopping my head from exploding, to nod in his direction. Though no amount of threat on earth could force me to look towards where he stands. It has been decades since anyone in my family could sustain eye contact. Easier to look away.

'Wow, soup looks good, Jenny! Did you make it?' Scott chooses this moment to swing to the rescue, emergent from 'our' end of the house. He is six feet of well-timed pressure release. Though that grand passion, once ignited upon his first arrival into our lives, has faded, my husband yet retains power. To diffuse. At times to uplift. His presence has me at once relieved and chastened: spared another argument with Dad and yet bruised by shame that my capacity for resilience remains as shallow as this. Unfortunately the reprieve lasts only as long as the pause between Scott's sentences. 'Darling, did you tell your Dad you made aloo paranthas at Cailean's kindy this week?' Scott introduces the news blithely as he ladles himself a huge bowl of soup from the stovetop and makes his way to the table to sit between Cailean and Mum. I want to sink beneath the floorboards. I can only presume that he must not see the look upon my face because he keeps on. 'Monkey, did you tell Baba? Mummy said all your mates loved them.'

I know Scott is simply doing his best to facilitate connection. But his pronouncement is thrown into the room as a live hand grenade. Because that's the other thing: I have yet to tell either Mum or Dad that I have started to cook. It's too close to me. Even all these weeks in. Too new. I am not yet equipped to cope with their reactions.

Usually, when emotions are heightened Mum and Dad and I react towards each other in one of two ways: either with casual disregard or a conversational reroute. Both methods aim to diffuse connection. To create spoken distance when closeness feels too dangerous. But this time is different.

'You're cooking?' It's Dad. His tone strikes some note I can't decipher. Shock? Hope? Disbelief? In any case he needn't qualify what *kind* of cooking. There is only one cuisine of significance within my family. 'Yeah, a little bit. I guess,' I stumble; it's strange but I feel like I should make an apology. Whether for not having told him before now or for not discussing with him prior, I'm not sure. 'I found Ammi's recipes a while ago and I've been doing a little bit at home...' I feel fidgety. Electrified by current. Not sure where to go with it. Made uneasy by Mum and Dad's familiar response to awkward moments—that uncomfortable, stuck kind of silence. 'Just easy stuff, you know? daal and raita. No meat,' I feel myself begin to babble. 'Just a few sabzi*s*. Ashy, don't do that, Sweet Pea.' Ashy takes this precise moment to signify his fatigue with the high chair in a clatter of soup-covered spoon to floor. I am indescribably grateful for the distraction. Relieved to hide behind the clean up. The truth is that I feel proud. Proud that I am learning on my own to become the kind of woman I was bred to believe I ought to be: one who cooks and feeds and nurtures her family into the possibility of a deeper connection with God.

And yet that fragile pride makes me vulnerable. Self-satisfaction is a language that Dad doesn't speak. I need a minute to gather my thoughts. To find the words. So in place of attempting further explanation I wash and rinse a dishcloth in the sink. Wipe down the floor and the gorgeously grubby culprit. I appreciate the chance to turn my face. I'm afraid it radiates with the glow of something that feels a lot like vulnerability. And exposure in front of my parents has never been a safe space for me since Parkinson's came to call.

'The aloo paranthas were just something Cailean wanted me to do,' I blurt, not keen to continue but uncertain how to end the discussion. 'The kids helped. Just cooked them on a little electric fry pan.'

And right then. Into the opening I created and with his very next comment, Dad does exactly what I had hoped he wouldn't. He makes it about him. Some small piece of me understands it is the way he knows to release emotional discomfort. That perhaps it is even the only avenue he has to connect a piece of himself to a piece of me. But the child that I become in his presence feels only resentment: that in one neat segue, Dad's conversational diversion manages to undermine the magnitude of what we all know these small steps mean to me. 'Remember when I used to make aloo paranthas, Jenny? Actually I haven't made them for a long time. That's a good idea!' he says, comment directed to the air above all of our heads. He talks like that a lot. 'I should make them tomorrow for the boys for lunch. Would you like to eat Baba's aloo paranthas tomorrow, children!'

The exclamation mark at the end of a sentence that for anyone else would finish in a query is pure Dad. So, too, the uncanny facility he has to redirect conversation to the central point of himself.

It is so easy for me to be upset that I fail to see how difficult this has been for him: to lose a planned future with his beautiful young wife. I fail to see how his deep love and devotion compels him to act as Mum's full-time carer, how much bravery this takes on his behalf. Just as I fail to see how his own grief at watching Mum deteriorate has made it difficult for him to help me. I don't see that in all these years of not talking, it is not just me who teeters upon eggshells around them, but they who have been habituated to similarly fear conversation with me. No, I don't see. Instead I cry in bed later that night as Scott reassures me that Dad doesn't mean any of it. That his own insecurities leave him incapable of validating the things that give my life meaning. That *need* he has to contrast the achievements of his children against his own in a way that mitigates our efforts. *I'll make* aloo paranthas *for the children!* I could scream. Why I still require his validation at all is beyond me. But I am enjoying the upset too much to dive down that particular rabbit hole. *They always do it,* I sob to Scott. *That's why I didn't tell them. Dad always makes it about him. And Mum's no better. She doesn't ask anything. Doesn't say anything. I don't even know her anymore.*

It's like they can never just say, Wow, that's great for you! *It's just about him and what he thinks I should do and the amazing lessons he's learned and all the stupid stories we've all heard a million times before...*

It goes on. I spew out poor me-isms as the broken twelve-year-old who tonight occupies my heart. Scott is empathetic. He doesn't risk further upset by saying what is obvious: that my stupid anguish over Dad's comments only serves to further underline this role-playing dynamic in which we all participate—Dad's ownership of family recipes that props up his feeling of security and my distance that similarly strengthens my own. Eventually I cry enough to fall asleep. But in that sliver of space before I dive into unconsciousness my working mind drags up one loose thought—at what point did a grief so dark begin to feel this good?

Aloo paranthas seem like a relatively simple snack to make. Atta flour. Ghee. Water. Potato cooked to a soft mash. Whole cumin. Chilli. Salt. But it takes practice. Something Dad has had a lot of. So the next day I watch under the cover of a newspaper from the dining room table, as he works instinctively in his kitchen. I don't want to come under his direct tutelage. Consider such an interaction too flammable. But I am curious to learn. So I watch as he reaches up high to pull down the heavy glass vessel of atta. He mixes it with water and salt and ghee in a stainless steel bowl to exactly the right consistency. The boys are by his side. Dad has called them there. Though not much for child's play, Dad does like to have them watch him cook. Cailean and Ashy don't mind this. At least for a little while. They stick with him until they tire of throwing flour to the kitchen bench. This step is a precursor to the actual making: the flour-covered surface is where Dad will begin to roll out his dough into small flat rounds. The boys depart just as the serious work starts. A true parantha differs from a chapatti in one key respect. While a chapatti is rolled out once and then flipped onto a hot tawa, a parantha must be layered. A heavier form of unleavened bread made rich with generous use of ghee. There is, of course, a technique. First, to roll the dough into a saucer-sized round. Next, to dot its centre with ghee. Fold the sides around the sunshine yellow dollop until the circle of dough becomes a rough triangle. Roll the triangle out again and again use ghee to dot its centre. Fold once more. Repeat. The more times this is done, and with the more finesse, the flakier the end result. A talented home cook might manage seven folds. Dad can, and so he does. Of course, aloo parantha by virtue of its name requires the addition of one other element: a soft mash of peeled potato fried in a rich slurry of ghee, chilli, whole cumin seeds and salt. Lots of salt. Rolled into lychee-sized balls, one is placed in each parantha's centre. Wrapped snuggly. One more gentle roll and it's time for the tawa.

I watch Dad do all of this and think of how I made my own. With far less elegance, though no less focus. Crouched over a low, child-sized kindergarten table. Fending off little hands and making room in my interaction for the answer of their beautifully strange curiosities. But Dad doesn't know any of this because he doesn't ask. And in return I, too, look away from his efforts. We do a lot of that. The looking away. Strange practice for a family whose chosen idol is possessed of that dynamic Third Eye. Shivji is eternally represented thus: midnight blue face framed by his strong black eyebrows, between which is positioned this extra organ of vision framed on each side by three stripes of turmeric tika. This eye is positioned vertically. Its appearance is mystic. Cosmic. Alien. For Shivji to blink that Third Eye, Dad used to tell me, means the end of life as we all live it. Open, it represents wisdom and insight. Closed, it means death.

These thoughts fill my head throughout our Sunday lunch. Blind ignorance that kills connection. Is this the legacy I am transferring to my own small children? I regard their faces as they dip bites of parantha into *katoris* of cool yoghurt. My careful regard combines with threatening thought to distract me as I nibble a parantha between bites of Patak's mango pickle.

'I hate it how I lose you whenever we stay down there,' Scott speaks as we hit the highway. It's 4 p.m. The ordeal is over and we are headed back to South Melbourne in our re-packed car. The sky is grey and low. A reflection of my mood. 'It's like you totally disappear into your shell from the moment we get in the car to drive down there until the moment we leave.'

I can't deny it so I don't even try. 'I just don't know how to handle it,' I admit. I turn back to glance at the boys in the back seat before I continue. They are asleep. I'm not sure if it's the tension or the fresh air that has wiped them out. Either way we are free to talk. 'I just get so *mad*. No, mad is wrong. I get so upset. It's like, after all these years, are we *still* doing this? Really? No matter how much I try to go down with a different attitude, or how much I try to prep myself or talk myself through it, it never changes.'

Scott lets go of the wheel with one hand to grab mine. I feel his touch as a soft comfort in the few seconds before he speaks: 'When Mum died it was this huge grief. But then, once she was gone, after a while I forgot about all the sick years and just remembered the good times. I know that it's almost harder for you because you're grieving while she's still *alive*. But I think, in some way, you just need to let go of her—of him. The idea of them being parents you can talk to. Think of them just as doddery old people.' He glances my way with a little half-smile at this. 'And then the whole thing will be a lot easier.' Scott gives my hand one last squeeze before letting go to re-grip the steering wheel.

I turn my head to look out the window. I understand what he means. I just don't understand how. *How* does one do that? How does one kill off an attachment to a parent? How do I let go of all the things they have taught me to be? Where is the precedent? That is why my grief feels so good. It's comfortable. I know it. We all do. It is an emotional language that my family understands. As complex as the bite of cumin. As digestible as Dad's aloo parantha—even at my worst I can swallow it. And at my best, it reminds me of all the things that we used to be. But release—I feel the slow of the car into South Melbourne as we exit the freeway and hit our first traffic light, turn my head to watch as the momentary halt of our car brings Cailean and Ash back from sleep—what would that actually look like? Of what would I need to shake free?

ALOO PARANTHA
Potato-filled flatbreads

My version of Kashmiri comfort food, the familiar spice of aloo parantha feels for me as an edible fortification during moments when ballast is required against my own internal warring.

INGREDIENTS:
2 cups atta or stoneground wholemeal flour
½ teaspoon salt
1 teaspoon ghee
1 cup hot water
3 potatoes (Royal Blue are soft and fluffy)
1 tablespoon ghee
1 heaped teaspoon cumin seeds
1 teaspoon salt
1 teaspoon Kashmiri red chilli
Extra ghee to cook

METHOD:
Mix the flour with the salt and the teaspoon of ghee. Add enough hot water—a little at a time—and knead with your hands until the parantha dough is well combined but slightly sticky to the touch.

Wrap in glad wrap and place in the fridge to rest for 20 to 30 minutes.

In the meantime, boil or steam the potatoes in their skin until soft.

Peel and mash them. Heat one tablespoon of ghee in a pan set on medium heat. When hot add the cumin seeds and cook a minute or so, or until fragrant.

Add the salt and red chilli. Cook off until fragrant. Add the mashed potato and coat in the spices and ghee.

Remove from the heat and allow to cool slightly.

Take the dough from the fridge and divide into 4 balls. Roll out slightly. They should be thick and round, perhaps a little smaller than the size of a tea saucer. Place a dollop of potato mix in the middle and close up the dough around it.

Scatter flour on your surface and gently roll the dough with the aloo inside. This must be done very gently to ensure the potato doesn't ooze.

Heat the tawa until very hot and place a dollop of ghee in the centre. Cook the parantha until browned, before flipping with some more ghee and browning the other side.

Serve hot with pickle.

Makes four aloo paranthas with some leftover mixture.

CHAPTER 9

Green Cardamom

*Prasad from Dad's puja didn't always mean
sugar rock, almonds or* kishmish. *Festivities of
profound consequence called for something
more: the black seeds from pods of green
cardamom. Just one more experience to have
us know a taste of God is not always sweet.*

WHEN AMMI DIED, THERE WAS little left of her world to dismantle. It was 2005. She was eighty-one and by that time widowed for more than twenty-five years. Towards the very end she lived in a room in my Bapu's—Dad's elder brother and my uncle—house. At this point there was nothing she owned that her wooden almirah couldn't hold, for within the span of the past three decades she had given away most material items of significance. It is a traditional diktat: that a widow wrap herself in *saris* of white or cream and refrain from adornment. Anything more than the base essentials were passed into the care of others. Ammi's beautifully coloured silk *saris*, her jewels and her dowry were distributed amongst her daughters, daughters-in-law and granddaughters, as gifts to mark various significant family celebrations. In my jewellery box rests a pair of exquisitely enamelled paisley earrings rimmed in gold and dangled with tiny perfect pearls. Those Ammi gave to me on the occasion of my Chachu, my youngest uncle's wedding. Chachu is Ammi's youngest child, her fourth and the last one to wed. It had been in my very early teens.

As it is with most devout Hindus, Ammi's body was cremated within twenty-four hours of her death, her remnants submerged to the sacred Ganga river. I knew the Ganga from my childhood as the majestic spout of water that sprung from the centre of Shivji's topknot. Her ashes were released at Haridwar, a sacred spot that is considered by Hindus as the gateway to Shivji's abode. With Ammi's ashes returned, there was little material evidence that remained to mark her existence in the world. It followed then, that those things left after her death radiated with a highlighted significance: her circular ring of black onyx with its central diamond, a talisman to ward off the evil eye; the large and brilliant diamond she wore in her nose; her gold bracelets, looped circles as thin as the *kajal* I once applied in my eyes.

But nothing held more of Ammi than the small black *Shivling* she bathed each morning in turmeric and milk during her puja. The phallus-shaped object that is said to mark Shivji's formless omnipotence. It may have looked like a stone. It was more than that. It was a piece of hardened earth that mapped her internal world. Within Ammi's care of that symbol—the muttered mantra*s*, the small silver spoon she used to drizzle it with the yellowed milk—was contained the seed of devotion for the entire Ganju family. Her focus and her intimacy held us all in the lap of Shivji. For she knew *that* god as well as she knew herself. This is the way of a true disciple, a practice that demands daily communion and conversation with the godhead within.

It fed something in me when, as a young girl crowded in among the rolls of fabrics in her busy tailor's studio, my mouth full of sticky sweets, I would listen to Ammi explain why godhead was found within. It was Brahma's big joke. One played upon humans who had once occupied the heavens but whose terrible behaviour had caused them to fall from grace. These humans who had to be punished. Their penance was vicious, determined by a council of deities led by Brahma, the Creator and Lord of Heaven: that human divinity be forever concealed. Each god agreed, the only question was where they might keep it suppressed. *Let's hide it deep inside the earth*, said the council. *No*, said Brahma, *humans will dig to find it*. The council offered: *Let us plunge it into the ocean's depth*. But Brahma was not convinced. *No*, he said, *they will only use all their means to dive down to the seabed and below.*

The council remained undefeated: *We shall carry it to the top of the highest mountain, far beyond their reach.* But Brahma slowly shook his head: *No,* he refuted, *it may take time, but one day they will find a way to scale the heights.* No matter how many times I heard this tale I always held my breath at this point. *Of course Brahma,* Ammi would remind me, *was wise. We will place it deep inside the humans themselves,* Brahma announced, *for humans will spend their lifetimes digging and climbing and diving and exploring but they will never stop searching for long enough to find what already exists within.*

I always felt secure when Ammi retold that myth because I knew that her eye was turned within and that if her eye saw God, then we were all safe. Ammi, who felt the power of Shivji deep inside her own depths. Who not only knew *where* to look, but how: with great stillness and still greater faith.

Chai enters my lexicon in the aftermath of the tumultuous weekend with Mum and Dad. I return home as always, washed in resentment. It has taken weeks for that feeling to ebb. I am left in a fugue state, filmed with fatigue. I try everything I know to sluice it free. Coffee. Wine. Rest. On the days that I am alone in the house I can mostly be found under my quilt. Autumn days are darkening, and so am I. I write. Check emails. Sleep. I spend a lot of time asleep. Not polite naps. But aggressive absolute losses of consciousness. I might lie down at 1 p.m. and resurface with a start just before 4 o'clock. I wake groggy and wrong-headed. As I might if I were drugged. Or depressed. But I have not the luxury in this life of falling into either state. To pull myself up I take refuge in a drink made with one part longing and two parts nostalgia.

The pack of green cardamom is as yet unopened in my pantry. I bought the bag of pods on instinct on one of my first outings to Limra Groceries, months ago. I have never stepped into an Indian kitchen that is without them. Today, as I drag up the recipe for chai from deep memory, I open the plastic packet and shove my nose inside. It is a wallop of scent. The pungent aroma is menthol and aniseed; a nasal burn that sits on just the right side of unpleasant. It demands use as a contrast spice. One that threads between the sweet and smoke and heat of my sextet of compulsorily used classics: turmeric, chilli, salt, coriander, cumin and gur. In the months to come I will grow to think of green cardamom as a sharp B note at the tail of a harmony: a savour that introduces a distinct change in timbre. I will come to use it to inject my dishes with a shock of the new and, even in the bombardment of those green husks, remain centred enough to perceive which savoury tonalities might combine on any given day to express the truest taste of me. But today is not that time. Today green cardamom is nothing more than a handle rail. The spice I need as I drag myself upright.

A drink that frames this Southern Hemisphere winter with remembrance of another set worlds apart.

In that sweet time between infancy and adolescence, I would walk with Dad and my brothers from Ammi's New Delhi house, through January-cold streets, to the nearby taxi stand whenever we needed transport. I treasured these outings for what they were: opportunities to bite into the welcome of a beautiful community. Today in my mind this reel of memory plays in black and white. Tall straight trees at even spacing. A small convoy of mint-condition black Ambassadors lined by the roadside; voluptuous, rounded grand dames designed in the '50s that ruled India's roads until well into the late '80s. And the men. Sikhs. White pyjamas. White turbans. White beards beneath a twirl of elegantly curled moustache. Rangy and leanly muscled, they would sit and watch the pass of hours upon coir charpais set outside in the welcome winter sun. On constant boil was a battered stainless steel pot of chai: an umber cup of liquid, opaque with spice and sweet. Reward for the walk there would be twofold: a thimble of the saccharine cardamom brew chased by fifteen minutes of catch-the-squirrel fun while Dad and the taxi *wallas* spoke.

There are no squirrels in my kitchen. But I do have these aromatic husks. And so as I make the boys breakfast I pull out my favourite mid-size Mauviel pot and conduct a daily experiment in sensory memory recollection. With my chai I play with ratios of milk to water. With differing quantities of gur to green cardamom. Whether or not to add ground ginger and mace and cinnamon. Maybe turmeric? Eventually I land upon a recipe that seems to work. Slightly more milk than water to fill almost half my pot. A generous scoop of strong and loose black tea leaves or two PG Tips teabags. Two, sometimes three green cardamom pods pounded a little by the mortar and pestle I keep next to the kettle on the bench, husks cracked to release their fragrance. More gur than I know to be acceptable. If I want it simple that's how I play it. If seeking a little more depth I'll throw in a broken quill of cinnamon and a quarter teaspoon of ginger powder just before the cardamom: the penultimate to add warmth more than spice.

So close do these sips bring me to nameless contentment that I take to carrying quantities of the spiced liquid whenever I leave the house. June is almost upon us and it is the season for hot brews, after all. The weight of the silver bullet-shaped thermos makes my bag heavy. But its reassuring heft is *my* talisman: an anchor to keep me from drifting farther from shore. In this way I place the thermos on my desk on the days I work from Scott's upstairs office. Secretly fill my cup beneath café tables when meeting friends out for coffee. This chai satiates me. But more than that, it works as a stopgap. A magic potion to keep me raised above uncertainty when I must occupy space outside of the kitchen and away from the growing security of my own stovetop. Because this is who I have become, now: a disciple of the leapfrog school of spirituality, hopping from one stepping-stone of promise to the next. Forgetting Ammi and her internal gaze. Certain this is the only way to safely cross my river of doubt.

This random Tuesday afternoon I am at home giving a final stir to my current chai mix when the doorbell sounds. 'Hi Lady.' It's Taline. I had texted to let her know that the kids were occupied with *Sesame Street* and that my 3 p.m. pot of chai was on and she had come riding. For that's the other thing. As time and practice elevate my culinary skills, I have been taken with the urge to draw friends into this circle. Invites to Sarah and Jennifer and Taline for quick lunches of sabzi and homemade chapatti on the days the kids are in care. Occasional five-dish dinner parties at which my paneer is always the centrepiece. Acts that are not so much about sharing as they are about drawing people into my orbit. As if the more bodies I can gather close, the more magnetic drag I will generate to keep within reach this outward sense of *something* that I cannot quite touch. 'Oh my God, how do you do this?' Taline loves melodrama. She groans in pleasure at the first sip. 'This is special. I want to know how you can do this.'

Taline is not speaking of the recipe, but the x-factor of me that the chai contains. For she has been given the quantities, has attempted reproduction of the drink in her own home and yet, she confesses, it is never imbued with the same balance of bittersweet that mine contains. I try to answer but to be honest I don't know. How *do*

I do this? What makes it special? Like everything else it feels as if the essence of what this growing thing is, slips through my fingers in each moment that I think it's caught. As the June afternoon empties alongside my pot of chai I begin to think that to encapsulate the essence of *how* might answer in me a huge need. And I become newly determined to find for myself an incisive response.

When I wake the next morning it is with the first weak rays of the winter sun. Scott and I always go to bed with the window open and the curtains raised. It is his preference. As a husband and a father he has lost his boyhood connections to boats and bush camp trips and mud crabs in the mangroves, caught in an urban life of adult rationalism and responsibility. His interaction with the environment is largely reduced to this, now: to wake and know the mood of the day. He guards it fiercely.

And me? I like that, from the angle of my head on the pillow, I can see out. Across our corrugated iron rooftop and into the heavens. I like to watch the hot-air balloons that float past every day when the weather is calm. I like them because, sometimes, to witness the mute and weightless nature of their flight gives me hope for what the future might be. I had made the decision, once Taline left yesterday afternoon, that I must return to Erica once more. I had been compelled to push my experience with her into the background the Saturday morning I walked into Mum and Dad's. As if I couldn't hold those two platforms together in my being: the dual pressures of psychic and parental disturbance that combined as an overload of emotional confrontation. But time and distance and my centring sips taken from many mugs of chai have combined to do their work. There is space to think once more of God and nurture and connection. Of my need to draw a line between those three points and link them, as one might rig a kite with a piece of string. Airborne freedom. The thought turns my eyes from the ceiling to my bedroom backdrop sky. I note that the hot-air balloons are there, today, and I just may be light enough to take flight.

'Tea?' Scott rolls over for a cuddle and asks the question into my neck. I can't see the clock, but presume it is before 7 a.m. The boys are not yet stirring and the sky is only slowly coming awake. 'I'll make it.' I drop a quick kiss on his temple and slide out from his embrace.

Quickly bend down to grab and pull on my over-sized jumper and soft pants thrown off the night before. 'I want to make chai for me anyway. You stay in bed and have a cuddle with the boys.' It isn't until later in the morning, with Scott gone for work and Cailean and Ashy dropped to childcare, that I realise how much I seem to be fizzing. For that is what it feels like. A carbonated bubble that makes my head light and causes my limbs to ever so slightly tremor. It comes from anticipation. Whereas my first visit to Erica prompted anxiety, this second experience feels as the scent of cinnamon: zingy and festive and with a promise of warmth and sweet. What that promise is I cannot yet name.

Only later, months from now, will I be ready to admit that my infatuation with this process owes everything to the illusion of surety. It is the one thing Hindu gods refuse to promise; they demand discipline and devotion in their worshippers, unrelenting in their message that there are things we can never know in this existence, and not a single moment we can control. As a girl it was made clear to me—in the weight we placed on puja, in the protection we sought in observance of traditional rites— that within such uncertainty is born the promise and the magic of God. While my life was golden I accepted the understanding that, in order to keep my path, it had to be greater belief and not reason that lit my way. But when Mum was diagnosed the curtain came down and that theory meant less than nothing to me, a pre-adolescent girl—my gods, the deities in whose shelter I had grown, had taken an axe to my world and then looked on as I struggled to accept the carnage.

Yet I allow myself to birth none of these thoughts, this morning. Not as I slide a shaking hand across the counter to grab my take-away coffee. Not as I step out of my car at Flying Souls in Brighton and realise I retain not a second's memory of the twenty-five-minute trip. 'Hello,' I say to the smiling girl at the reception, in a repeat of before, the front door closing behind me, 'I'm Sarina. I have another appointment with Erica this morning.' The response is a cheery, 'She won't be long!' This time there is no repeat offer of water or tea. I decide it is a good sign, that I mustn't look needful or nervous: indeed, seated in Erica's waiting room once more, I am calm. As I sit and wait, my mind wanders back to my previous visit, to the intense experience of letting go of so much toxic grief: emptied of that pain my hope swings forward to address the prospect of revelation—that perhaps now is the moment to uncover the mystery of what food and cooking and faith definitively means to me. To answer Taline's *how* and, in so doing, begin to draw the circle of this experience inward.

'So how did it go after the last visit? How was the article?' Erica has come out to greet me. She makes small talk as we walk side by side to a healing room towards the building's rear. 'The article was good,' I reassure her. 'I submitted it a few weeks ago but it won't run until

November or so. There's always a fairly long lead-time on the glossies. I'll send you a copy when it comes out.' We reach the end of the hall. Erica pauses before a closed door. There is a strange shift in atmosphere. Time gathers to a still centre. My pulse slows a little. It is at that moment that she turns the knob and waves me through.

'So,' Erica breathes out the word. I sit on one chair, shoes unlaced and removed. She seals off the room and sits opposite. Face soft. Hands folded in her lap. 'What can I do for you?' I tell her. 'I wanted to come back and see you again because, after the last visit, I felt like we didn't have time to get close enough to what I wanted to say.' My words flow with relative ease this time, stem from the confidence that I have had time to quantify the worth of this experience. I have become comfortable with the idea of Erica as a replacement—this kind of clairvoyant experience that promises a form of spirituality though with none of the uncertainty that is implicit in the Hindu faith. It feels safer. Softer. I rationalise that it is not such a monumental shift—that the wealth of all that cultural and philosophical wisdom still lives within me. I am not leaving it aside so much as seeking a gentler entry to a changed cosmic landscape, less weighted by history and heritage.

'Okay.' Erica acknowledges my full stop when it appears I will speak no further. 'Did you want to lay down on the bed?' I do. She pushes a pillow beneath my knees and covers me in a blanket. I feel coddled. It is nice. It is wonderful, actually. I relish the texture of the smooth and cool round crystals she places in the centre of each of my palms. In the fresh and spicy scent of that she dabs at my throat and holds for a small space beneath my nose. 'Frankincense oil,' Erica informs softly, 'will help to soften your fifth chakra block and allow you to speak your truth.' A brief and condescending flash threatens to push out a hard bubble of speech; I am uncomfortable with her choice of language. But the scant touch of her hand a centimetre above my belly button sucks it back down. It takes with it any objection or speech.

'Are there clairvoyants in your family?' Erica's opening words make an imprint on the silence. As I feel their press thoughts take shape. But the lines are blurred. The sounds elusive. I feel the importance of what I'm struggling to say. 'Ammi, my Indian grandmother, she is a Kashmiri *Brahmin.*' My language is slow and measured. I sense my response is important. My way forward laid down with the enunciation of each thought-out word. 'She is part of the priest class. She's always been devout.' No, not a clairvoyant. But this is the link that I make.'In some ways I see her as a kind of Hindu priestess, I guess.' A pause. The thinnest of gaps. But with volume enough to create space for perspective.

I think: *this is the moment I have craved.*

'Ghamkar.' The voice is mine. All the air in the room stills. My edges loosen. I can no longer feel the bed beneath my back nor locate Erica's presence in the room.

My eyes remain closed but the blackness is replaced by line drawings of a Kashmiri mountaintop. 'That was my Ammi's maiden name. Ghamkar. It means *taker of sorrows*.' I pause. 'What do you see?' It is Erica. Her question drops me into a verbal free fall—I am in the grip of words that ring inside me and yet I make no claim of ownership: the answer to the question of their origin, in this moment, both unknown and unimportant. 'I see Ammi. And a line of women. They are Ghamkar women.

They stretch back. I can't see to the end. Just back and back until the beginning of Time. They are waiting for me. Ammi is at the front. She is holding a big heavy stone. She wants me to take the stone.'

'And what do you want?' Erica's voice is quiet. I begin to cry.

'I want to give the stone back to her. It's not mine to take.'

'What's not yours to take?'

'The sorrow.' I sob. Lids glued shut. Body no longer in the room but elsewhere. Standing in some suspended place before a matriarchal line-up devastated by my insistence that theirs is not a spiritual legacy I can carry forward. 'They want me to take the sorrow,' I say the words again, 'but it is not mine to take.' My heart empties with my mind. Nothing exists but this. I do not know if it is true. It is the only truth I know. I need this story to be told. I need Erica to understand why: 'Back then, in India, women had no power. The power they had was…' I hesitate. Laying on my back in this bed in this room in this suburban world one million miles from where this tale began, it is very important that I find the right word.'The power they had was in the *taking*. In taking care. In taking prayer. That was their strength. That was their healing power. That was their purpose. Their insight. That was the gift they gave and the divinity upon which they drew.'

My closed gaze shifts. I forget Erica once more. It is to Ammi that I direct these words now. I direct them to her but I say them out loud. It feels strange. Affected. But what must be said is too big to be contained.'This sorrow is not mine to take.' Those same words. A third time. I see the run of tears down Ammi's face as I hold out this weight of a stone and ask her to take it back. To take it away from me. This edict that no longer serves. We have too much of it. This family that is full, full, full of sorrows and needs no more. My Ammi who needs reassurance that this legacy will continue. I assure her that it will. In a different way. 'Things have changed,' I tell her. 'You had to be so strong. So strong. To take all of that weight. But the world has changed and it is the time to give. To give love and to give light. Let the taking be done. I need that the taking be done.'

The room falls into silence. I'm not certain how much time passes. Only gradually do I come to note air that was as syrup becomes simply air again. The feeling of Ammi's presence in the room slides away. The etched world behind my closed lids elides and fuses into the present and the light becomes a lightweight black once more. The silence in the room becomes translucent. As the minutes pass it releases the possibility of speech.

'How do you feel?' It's Erica. I struggle to open my eyes: 'Good.' The word is facile and inadequate. I attempt to compensate by sitting myself up. I try again. 'I mean, good.' I see my idiocy from a distance. It does not belong to me. I feel displaced. Not quite here but no longer there. Erica nods. Only later will I think; *she must see this behaviour all the time.* But right now I stare blankly at her half-smile: 'I'll leave you a glass of water on the table and then you can find your way to the front.' She pulls the door shut behind her and I heave a breath out. Shit. That was. That was wordless. Adjectiveless. That is what it feels like to be in the lap of something larger than myself. To be big. Boundless. And safe. In a really peculiar way it felt safe. As if I had been pulled into a vacuum filled, not by white noise anxiety, but by some kind of universal truth. But that place, I think as I hang my legs over the edge of the bed and slip off to land lightly on my feet, that place had no dark corners. There was only what was and nothing more.

Another heave of breath. I walk to the small coffee table at the room's far end. Throw back the glass of water Erica left. Reach down to slip on and tie up the laces of my polished brown brogues. I walk to the door and open it slowly. I hesitate there, half in and half out. Feel compelled to case my glance over the room. *I am missing something*, I think. The weight in my body feels wrong. I tap my jean pockets. Bulge of wallet. Cold slim length of phone. Car keys in hand. It takes me what feels like a minute though is likely much less. To realise I no longer feel in my gut the weight of sorrow in that stone. It's gone.

MASALA CHAI
Spiced tea

I never tire of making and drinking chai. It is a prayer in a cup.

INGREDIENTS:
½ cup of water
¾ cup of milk
3 green cardamom pods, cracked open
2 shards of cinnamon
3 cloves
1 teabag or a tablespoon scoop of loose black tea leaves
Gur to taste. I use a healthy knuckle

METHOD:
Put all ingredients in a small pot and heat on a very slow simmer until the liquid is caramel-brown and viscous. Strain and serve. Makes one cup.

Kheer

Indian sweets are calorific concoctions.
Kheer is no different. This Indian-
style rice pudding is grounded in the
bitterness of green cardamom.

I WOULD MASTURBATE AS A teenager. Sometimes in my bed at night. Quietly. Any sound muffled beneath the quilted weight of my rose pink and lemon yellow floral doona. Sometimes in the bathroom during the day, having wedged closed the unlockable bathroom door. I don't know if I was unique among my high school girlfriends. I do know that it was behaviour in strange contrast to the innocence of how I otherwise chose to view the world. Even at fifteen and sixteen, I loved to play imaginary games with my best friend; was made uneasy by thoughts of all-night parties fuelled by bottles of cheap vodka and hidden-by- dark feel-ups with random boys. I never touched myself directly, only ever through my clothes. It was not carnal. What I loved about masturbation wasn't so much the pleasure. It was the fantasy. In my romantic visions I was always being rescued. I was always the innocent. Always seeking of a gentleness that was given freely and without me having to verbalise my need. I wanted others to read me. To tell me. To protect me. I wanted someone other than myself to create my ending. To supersede any notions of self-determination. To ensure there was always someone else I could blame when pleasure inevitably gave way to pain.

The immediacy of change that follows my visit to Erica is a revelation. I walk out the door of Flying Souls and into my car as a woman of altered shape. I am expanded. I am hollowed. I am livened. I do not feel the cold. Fail to note the frigid wind that chews up bare branched tree-tops. With Erica as my guide, I have communed with some process of thought and experience I recognise as belonging to the cosmography of my youth. That world where the portal to all possibility is wide open and freely passable: where God is Man and Demon and Nature and neither Good nor Evil are distinguishable by Act or Presence. It was not that I *had* it or *saw* it, but that for those brief moments I *was* it. I was in contact with that nameless power. Was receptive to its message and its might.

As such I am alive. Capital letter no punctuation necessary shout it from the rooftops ALIVE. I rev my car into gear and speed up the Nepean Highway towards South Melbourne. Impatient to transport my changed body home. To walk in the front door and bend the energy of our lives to fit my new will. The drive to convert my internal shift into a show of the outward and the physical is enormous. To display. I want to display. My vibration thrums as the frequency of a hummingbird's flight. I am certain, as I swing the car into our street to park, nothing can leaden my ascent.

'Right,' it is my self-directed call to arms, 'garbage bags!' The words echo in the empty house. I march inside and down the hall. I grab the black roll from beneath the kitchen sink and race with it up the stairs. I fling open my wardrobe doors and recklessly begin making a single great pile of my clothes on our bedroom floor. The synthetic drapey black dress with scattered butterflies, picked up cheaply in Barcelona that falls to mid-thigh: out. The cumulus-grey Burberry duffle coat Scott selected for me soon after we met at a department store in Melbourne, unflattering in its wide and short cut: out. The two pairs of knee-length walk shorts—one pair beige, the other powder blue—bought in Paris at a mixed-brand boutique on the Avenue Victor Hugo: out.

What looks like organisation is not. This is not practical.

This is not about fit or style or fashion. It is metaphorical. A shedding of memory and skin. Of some specific emotion or other I have embedded into each garment tossed aside. I am in the process of an anthropomorphic assignment: the now enormous pile of clothes on my floor that says, *these are the outward expressions of the things inside me from which I now feel freed.*

So that is not a Burberry coat but a cover for the loneliness and inadequacy that cloaked me as a hungry- for-meaning twenty-five-year-old wife joining her executive husband on a business trip to Europe.

These are not ill-fitting walk shorts, but the conservative costume I reached for to smooth over the wild uncertainty I felt as a first-time mother in Paris.

That black dress that was not purchased for its body-skimming drape but for its soft volume that made my form seamless at a time when I had moved from Paris back to Melbourne. Cailean still a babe. And me, with no idea what my new outline might be.

Pull and toss. Pull and toss. The tangle of empty hangers grows to rival the tumble of clothes. And my shoes! The pointed toe and pointed heel boots with their patchwork leather that bound my feet just as living near my parents bound my life. The strange oxblood Campers whose clunky shape had me feel completely out of place on Paris streets. Tossed aside, now, along with all my old wounds of inadequacy.

It feels incredible. To lighten my emotional burden in such a quantifiable and material way. I don't stop for a second to question whether such profligate shedding is wise in this heightened state. Whether I should exercise some degree of thoughtful hesitancy. Of caution. I am only concerned with release. As a hot-air balloon pilot jettisoning ballast in the hope that such weightlessness might carry me to the stars.

'Wow, this is amazing, thank you.' It is the woman behind the counter at the local charity shop. My view of her partially obscured by the glasses and vases stacked in front of the till. She watches, wide-eyed, as I cart in garbage bag after garbage bag. Each one stuffed to splitting with boots and shoes and jackets and dresses. 'Can I give you a hand bringing any of it in?' she asks. I smile. 'Nope, that's fine.' I heave another bag atop the pile. 'That was the last of it.'

Job done, I preen and strut back to the car. I would go home but feel too effervescent to rest there alone. It is barely midday. There remain hours before I need to pick up the kids. No deadlines press. So instead I take a detour to Port Melbourne's Bay Street. The beach end. Its block smattered with boutiques of just-for-the-hell- of-it shoes and clothes. The day is gloomy, I feel anything but. My vision is laser-like. Have I ever been possessed of such acuity? I zero in on the stomping sex appeal of big and black and buckled ankle boots that have me teetering as if I walk on stalks. My legs taken on the appearance of Bambi's. Sold. Across the road for two pairs of cheapish round-toed heels: one is aquamarine suede, the other violet leather. Tights next. Tights in their multitudes. Mustard yellow. Sunset red. A pair with its psychedelic black and white pattern that recalls Twiggy and her sixties cohorts. No black. Nothing so pedestrian. But a pair of forest green. And blues: midnight and peacock, both.

'Looks like a fun morning.' It is the woman who sells me the tights. She eyes my shopping bags. 'Special occasion?' I grin. 'Sort of.' Take back my card. Saunter out. Saunter. How long has it been since I've sauntered?

Have I ever sauntered? But after my revelation with Erica my body is possessed of a fluid ease. *This sorrow is not mine to take.* Was it ever that easy? Was that all that I had to do and say? I listen to the crumple of sound my bags make as I open a rear passenger door to hoist my shopping in the car's back. I know I couldn't have done it on my own. I have always needed someone to be there for me. To hold my hand. If I thought about it—which, as I start up the car and head for home, I choose not to— then I might experience a sense of alarm at the pattern that comes into view. My systematic reach for equilibrium through the anchor of myself to another. Seen through a lens of honesty, it proves more a parasitic relationship than a symbiotic one. From Mum to Scott to Erica. My hosts have failed: Mum, whose gaze has been so arrested by Parkinson's that she can no longer find room to hold me in her sight; Scott, so worn out by my demands that he be everything to me—safety, compass, parent, provider, guide. To me it feels they have drawn away. And so there I find heady relief at location of a new supply. Not so much my appetite for fresh blood as fresh hope.

But, no, I do not want to think of the repercussions. Of what the end of Erica might mean.

Of where I will go, then.

For it is a pattern after all. And a pattern unchanged is a pattern continued. If I entertained the truth of my actions for a scant second I would see the forthcoming emptiness. But I direct my focus to other things. I direct it to high heels and flamboyant tights. I direct it to psychic truths and the divesting of symbolism. I direct it towards creation of a physical expression of all the ways in which I feel internally freed. I direct it thus and choose to ignore Brahma's wisdom. Instead I refract my light outward. I refract it outward to illuminate high mountaintops and deep caves and bottomless seas.

My *kheer* forms the centrepiece of the picnic table. A windswept bench settled into a grassy verge overlooking the beach. Jimmy has called a gathering. He is an old high school mate of Scott's. The friend with whom I fell in love for his whimsical approach to life. His fellow love of the written word. A newspaper editor in a past life, it was also Jimmy who gave me my first career break: a two-week work experience stint that allowed me to begin my folio of clippings. I was nineteen and focussed.

Jimmy lives in Red Hill. A country town on the Mornington Peninsula, a ninety-minute-drive from Melbourne distinguished by its incredible bushland, hilly landscape, cultivated food and wine scene, and proximity to the coast's wildly beautiful beaches. We stand upon one of them, now. It is late on Saturday afternoon. The ocean is a violently playful display of turgid blue and frosty white, the wind sharp as the cheap sparkling wine. No matter. It is liquid warmth for those in less-than-effective jackets. All in attendance are in high spirits despite the buffet of winter weather. Us especially. Ashy loves the playground. Cailean is enraptured by having so many adults willing to kick him his footy. And Scott and I? Against his better judgement, he permits himself to remain wrapped in my continued euphoria. Arms wrapped around me on and off throughout the afternoon, he keeps me close. Eyes soft when they look my way. Swept into my hope in the wake of that second psychic visit. *It was amazing*, I said. It was Wednesday night after Erica and the boys were tucked up in bed. My eyes shone. My body was angled half towards Scott, hitched upon the kitchen bench, and half towards the *kheer* I was stirring on the stove. *Really?* His body leaned into the conversation. *What did she say?*

It wasn't what she said, I told him, *it was what* I *knew. It was incredible. So different to the first time. Like, I saw Ammi and I had a conversation with her and I just knew all these things. It was like whenever I said the right words I could feel this sensation of fullness in my jaw. It was bizarre!* His gaze was trained on me: *Really?* And so I told him. I told him all. About Ghamkar and the stone and the sorrow. About Erica's desire to label me as claircognizant. *This means,* I said to Scott, *that I* know *things. That I can kind of download information.* I said this and I watched his eyes go wide. I noted his excitement but I chose not to shoulder the loaded gift of his confidence in me; a confidence I knew to be threaded with non-negotiable expectation: *fix yourself and get us out of this mess.* Apparently, my new powers of insight were blinkered to this particular message. Instead I told him from where the claircognizance descends—an open channel about six inches above my right temple. Not directly overhead, *more a little forward and to the right.* I told him all of this as I stirred and stirred my big stainless steel pot. Watched the rice and *kishmish* turn fat and fragrant with rose water and lactic sugar. The milk reduced and yellowed and thickened until a caramelised parchment hue replaced the starting colour of thin and opaque white.

'You must try this.' A voice snaps me back to the beach. In this parallel present an older woman spoons up mouthfuls of my *kheer* from a large rectangular Tupperware container. Comment directed toward Jimmy's father. Her name escapes me though I know she was once a winemaker. 'It's a type of barfi.'

'No, it's *kheer*, actually.' Though I know she is not aware of me I cannot help but correct her. It matters, this identification. To work so hard for clarity means another's misplaced presumption cannot be disregarded as an insignificant slight. At the sound of my interjection, her head twists on her neck to take me in. I smile from where I stand, a little off to the side. Continue: 'Like an Indian rice pudding.' I spell it out for her. K. H. E. E. R. *Kheer.* Pronounced as *seer.* She tries again: '*Kheer.*' The word a stopgap in the journey of spoon to mouth.

'Is there cardamom?' It's Jimmy's father. 'Yes,' I flash. Taken aback that he noticed. 'There's also rose water and almonds and sultanas. A bit of sugar. It's beautiful but rich,' I warn, even as I help myself to another small serve. As we speak others begin to gather around. To put down their navy blue napkins stained with cakey black chunks. Crackers and dips are left to the sand flies and seagulls. All of these friends of Jimmy who pick up clean bowls to fill them, try out the foreign word on their tongues. *Kheer.* Spoons that dip back into the rapidly emptying container for seconds. 'It must take a long time to make?' The old lady winemaker's statement ends in a question.

Thirty-five years, is what I want to say.

'About an hour-and-a-half,' are the words that fall from my mouth. Jimmy's friends form a casual semi-circle around the *kheer* container. Though their hands and mouths are occupied with tasting, their eyes are concerned with knowledge: the way they are trained, eyebrows slightly raised, upon me, serves as a silent encouragement. So I give them more. I tell them that it is my Ammi's recipe. That we ate it at our New Delhi wedding. Rich and condensed, it was served in red clay bowls and scattered with the slivers of almonds that Ammi and I cut; the last adventure in the kitchen we were to share. I tell them that Mum preferred to make it with angel hair spaghetti to a more watery consistency. That growing up I ate it twice a year at the break of Devi puja, a nine-day religious fast. I tell them that I like the rice version. The milk reduced heavily to a lush density. I don't tell them that I have never made it before this week. Neither do I reveal why it is that I make it now.

Why is it that I make it now? I make it for its sweetness, I think. For its heady rush of lactose sugars intensified by time and evaporation and heat. A dish to shadow a feeling. Of lightness. Of spiritual release with the sunset. Buckle the kids into their car seats for the long drive home. Sandy and cold and sleepy. Unpack them in the dark of our South Melbourne street and tuck them up without showers or a brushing of teeth. As Scott heats a dinner of leftover *gajar mattar,* daal and rice in the steamer, I dive back into what remains of my *kheer.* The day's *katori* number three. Then. Ten minutes later. Number four. In so doing I am compelled to acknowledge what Jimmy's father already has. That the compulsion to taste and to keep tasting that was felt by myself and others today is not propelled by the *kheer's* overt saccharinity. It is in the unexpected bite of the black seeds of green cardamom spilled from the half-dozen whole pods. In the compulsion to place one's finger upon a darker cause.

To quantify the source and the depth of that taste of bitterness that hides beneath.

I wake the next day with a heavy feeling of morning after. My stomach is a *kheer*-filled protrusion beneath the doona. Soft. Rounded. Scott nuzzles up to me but I refuse his entreaty. I feel his slight sag of disappointment and so avoid his gaze. It shames me. And yet I continue to ignore his needs just as I have for all the mornings of all these months that have come before. For if to masturbate was to recede into fantasy, to have Sunday morning sex with my husband in my bed with my children asleep in the room next door, is to thrust me completely and wholly into the shared space of family and connection and communion. 'I'm getting up to go for a run.' I whisper the words and kiss his head as I slip away. As if this might put another face upon my rejection. And even as I dress in my seen- better-days running clothes—quiet, so as not to wake the boys—I recognise the repetition. How often I do this. How often I force him into the role of spectator as I run off to chase down something to fill the hollow inside.

Slip away.

In our early years of marriage—when I desired to wash Scott in love—I would cook. Not Kashmiri. Not then. But cook in a way that best expressed my want for sex without having to engage in the physical act. This path was safe. Via this method, the vulnerability of transition from wife to wanton could be avoided. It was an act that circumvented nakedness and invasion: primarily Scott's of my body, but also the insertion of my own awareness into that slot I had long ago attempted to seal shut; the space where I felt the internal workings of my own body and the sadness that had turned my blood to rust. The idea of it is complex and strange but it was my way. My way to simulate intimate connection; the exchange of sexual for culinary orgasm. I liked to imagine it worked for me. But the conflict and defeat Scott felt at my evasion of him—the troubled hollow that gouged his cheeks during these tense conversations—made clear that he did not consider mine a sustainable strategy. *If you cooking a beautiful big dinner means that you are too tired at night to even hold my hand,* Scott said, eyes filled with pleading even as his voice revealed frustrated exasperation at my behaviour, *then I'll just have toast.* I lace my sneakers on the sound-gobbling carpet in our front room and silently, as silently as I can, slip out the front door.

Slip away.

Years later and right now, as the plosive sound of my toe pads launching me off concrete becomes the stand-in for my usual mental noise, the answer to the question of my resistance rises as reluctantly as this morning's winter sun: for me to lower the shield of cooking may have opened a universe of connection with Scott, but the problem was that toast would never have taken me far enough away.

'On your left!' I move to my right on the concrete bayside trail and let the Sunday morning bike rider fly past. And so where do I find myself now? How does my current approach to cooking affect my marriage? How does it frame me? I am too close to see what is in front of me. No X marks my spot. As I run, the *kheer* amasses as a stone in my gut. Is it the same shape and heft of the Ghamkar stone I had in Erica's room, already thought to leave behind? Or is it another, something that is new? A fresh grief that has arisen to fill the vacuum of space the evacuation of generational sorrow has left behind? If that is the case, then perhaps to rid myself of this malignant weight will bring me nearer to my goal. But what is my goal? In these months of headlong rush I have not stopped to quantify, to capture it in my sight.

'Oops! Sorry!' Lost in spiralling thought I don't see the woman walking with her pram until I am almost upon her. Stepping sharp left to avoid collision, I instead thrust my elbow into the side ribs of a tall and lean middle-aged man who had been running up on me from behind. He barely misses a step. Leaves me in his wake with a dismissive cast of his backward glance.

Is it my final thought that stops me? Or the interruption to my stride? Whichever, my rhythm is tripped. I cease movement. Feet now held to the earth by a magnetic pull of gross stasis. For it is one thing to categorise and recognise past behaviour. It is another thing entirely to have the courage to unpack it and leave it behind. 'Excuse me.' I look up with surprise to see the blockage I create on the path. The woman with the pram I had just passed only moments before who now bumps *me* aside. I am surprised that she can. That I am more solid than the deconstructed abstraction of my thoughts. I am still here? I am still here. I am still *here.* No matter that I slip away. That I cook and pray. That I travel to some secret place in me. Some place where Erica helps me be.

I am still here.

Perhaps it is that I must go deeper. I turn on my heel to thud home on now-heavy legs. Lips numb as I head into the cold wind. I hadn't wanted to keep seeking, to keep searching. The day I returned to shop and sort and discard I felt my realm was defined. That I was done. Complete. For how could one who was not done, experience such freedom? Except that it didn't last. As I flashed all of my progress outward—in high heels and new red lipstick and *kheer* at a windblown beachside birthday table—my new strength and certainty dissipated into the air around me.

Threads and loose ends. There are now so many. So many that I do not hear the heavy thwack of my feet that taps out the rhythm of cumbersome thought. I do not see the beach nor the grand Sunday morning promenade of early-morning movement. All I see is how I falter. Mum.

Food. God. Stories that I have begun. And yet in all these months of diligence and introspection, I have failed to tie a single one. It shouldn't take a genius to decipher. And yet as I slow my tread to a dragging walk upon the final turn into my street and home, I refuse to grasp what is there for others to see: that loss and shame has become the place where I feel at home. I do not think of any of this as I swing open our cream picket gate. I will not. Instead I kick off my sneakers. Leave them askew on the deck. Strip off and carry in my sweaty socks. 'Hi guys, I'm back.' The screen door's whine announces my entrance. 'Hi Mummy!' It's Scott, a smile in his voice. I am surprised that he sounds chirpy. A little jealous of his capability to apparently shake off his morning's disappointment so swiftly. 'How was your run?' 'It was okay. Good!' I correct myself. Step my way into the kitchen, prints left on the wood in the shape of my sweat-filmed feet. Sunday morning cartoons are set on a low murmur. Scott stirs a cup of tea by the sink. The time on the microwave reads 8 a.m. 'The air was nice and fresh. Hello, Monkey. Hello, Mashy.' The greetings are barely out of my mouth before I swoop down to drop a sticky kiss on each of their heads: both just visible above the brown leather curl of the couch. They are still warm from bed. 'Hi Mummy.' Cailean. 'Mama!' Ashy. 'Tea, Darling?' Scott. Three voices that speak of the love that encircles me. I hear the welcome they strive to create with their greetings. A way of encouraging me to stay close and safe. And yet I walk away.

'Um, I might just go up and take a shower first.' I ignore the need I see in the boys' eyes, the sudden silence from the kitchen. 'I'll be down in a few minutes.' In the bathroom upstairs, I strip off my running gear. The nylon tank peels from my hot skin. A mirror covers the better part of the wall behind the sink all the way to the ceiling. In it I see my face. Red. My hair. A maniacal ponytail frizz. As I step into the shower, the noise of my thoughts crashes back in. I will not say it aloud. But I know, as I soap and wash and rinse away both dirt and delusion, that the high I experienced following my visit to Erica is transient. That my inner light brought forth by the revelations I experience in her presence dim with each day I am away from the source. And while the source may yet be in me, my mode of access is only via her.

Yet if I am truthful this arrangement suits me. I turn off the taps and step one wet foot outside the glass-walled expanse to grab my towel. I like it. The compartmentalisation: that such depth of awareness is relegated to a set space. This is to say that *I* decide when an hour of psychic experience will be made available to me. It is my decision to enter into that zone. And once entered into, it becomes Erica's responsibility to keep me safe. Within

Erica's cradle of knowledge I become the child Mum's illness disallowed.

And as much as I see it. And I taste it. And I know it.

I cannot face my own weakness.

That was the exhaustion of this morning. As the high of the week ebbed, that was the residual emotion that rose to drown me as I emerged from sleep. The bitter truth pushed up from beneath the sickening volume of *kheer* consumed the night before. The realisation my passivity in the process has brought me to stand firm and tall in the way of my own progress. I drop my towel before the open doors of my cupboard. I have no idea what to do with such a revelation. No idea other than to dress it up. To conceal it. In defiance of both myself and the weather. I do it well in fire-engine-red tights, an embroidered skirt and sky-high heels. A literal and meta-phorical adornment that is my last attempt to fight the bare reality of what is happening to me: solidification of that terrible awareness that I have nothing left to face but the truth.

I struggle against it because to transition once more would mean alteration of the new foundation I have laboured and anguished over these recent months. A foundation that portrays me as victim. A victim of fate and family and abandoned faith. I cannot let that go. To think in any other way would mean acknowledging that I have let myself become lost. It would mean seeing that it was not Mum, or God or circumstance that has let me down; that my own salvation rests apart from fantasies of spice and Shivji and psychic intervention.

It would mean I am responsible for the vertical climb out from my cavern of sorrow. There will be no fantasy rescuer. The ending is mine to write. And I must word it on my own.

KHEER
Indian rice pudding

Even Indian sweets are not without their spice. I have always tasted *kheer* as both light and dark; those bitter black seeds of green cardamom that speak of all the pieces of ourselves we hide beneath.

INGREDIENTS:
1 ½ litres full-cream milk
¼ cup of rice
300 grams sugar
¼ teaspoon cardamom seeds
A handful of sultanas
1 teaspoon rose water
10 grams diced almonds

METHOD:
Soak the rice for 30 minutes before cooking.

Add one cup of water to the milk and put to high heat in a pot.

Drain the rice of water.

Once the milk starts to boil, add the rice. Turn down the heat to medium-low and stir frequently while simmering.

Simmer for around 30 minutes before adding the sugar, stirring frequently.

After another 30 minutes of frequent stirring, add the sultanas. Keep stirring the milk until it becomes a thick mixture.

Once you have attained the desired consistency remove from the heat.

Now add the rose water and cardamom and stir.

Serve immediately.

**Kheer* can also be made by substituting rice for vermicelli noodles.

Comfortably serves eight people.

Black Cardamom

One cannot play culinary hide-and-seek with
black cardamom. It is a balls-out spice of
masculine intensity that affords no compassion
and no quarter. Use it distractedly and a
dish is ruined. Handle it with awareness
and it will be the making of a dish.

MY WORLD HAS FALLEN UNDONE. It is no small thing. Not
as I spent so many years in attempts to clamp the damn
thing together. I have made no grand or foolish gestures.
Instigated no flash-point conflict. It has instead been a
slow collapse. A glacial collapse.

I do not quite know how to convey it. Still struggle
to understand exactly what it is that I have done, or even
know where it is that I find myself. Is it a giving up? A
giving in? A relinquishment? I have been going back and
forth this way for months—moving through all of winter

cloaked in a dense and impenetrable mental haze. Is anyone else aware of my change? I do not know for I cannot see beyond myself. Others have faded from view. Others and their concerns. Scott. Cailean. Ashok. Mum. Dad. How do I explain it, the way I have supplanted them in my thoughts? Erased the things that might matter? Replaced the importance of their concerns with the incomprehensible nature of my own? I am unmoored. And to be unmoored is to be alone and lost at sea, buffeted by the vagaries of wind and tide. If I were able to take stock— if I had the distance, the acuity—then I would see that this is where I stand: there is a great distance between my parents and myself, only *this* chasm has been wholly created by me. The concentration of my frustration and resentment and silence these past years has cut them off, figuratively more than literally. For we still speak. And yet each time we do, I can hear their soundless confusion at the pieces of me that I do not offer to them. I find no pleasure in this, though it does permit me an altered perspective: that I may begin to assess the scale of past damage done. I still see Erica. Though since that early June morning when I returned from my run, her psychic healing bed has vacillated between being a place of sanctuary and a slab of nails—at times a space to recuperate, at others an arena of unspoken ghosts who painfully needle me to an awareness of all the hidden aspects of my self buried deep. And Scott? Scott. Now *he* has set himself apart from *me*. Not in anger. But in the belief that I can find a way to take care of myself. Can restore the secret and inner piece torn out at the onset of Mum's illness.

So it is that the walls I have sheltered behind for many years have been dismantled. And me along with them. I do not know if it is obvious to others; by grace of the season I am afforded at least some ability to hide, to mask my deep lethargy and paint it as something other than that which exists inside me. For the winter has been long, now. Long and wet and cold. Melbourne is capable of exceptional bitterness. Winds that scream into South Melbourne's old Victorian houses with their built-for-summer insulation. Its bleak assault this year seems to me a blessing, for as June moves into July and July sinks into the four long weeks of August, winter becomes my disguise—I look only as hollowed as those around me.

What saves me from completely crumbling? I cook. I cook with intensity. I cook so that my kitchen becomes its own landscape. I do this because all other geographies have retreated: on the weekdays we are all home, the boys and I rarely spend much time out of the house. It is too desolate. Dark clouds weighted low. Cailean and Ashok don't mind. They have their cars. Their cubbies and their cartoons. And me? I have this new topography. A virtual land. The cupboard beneath the sink, my cave that holds five kilo bags of premium Basmati rice and wheat flour. The square space of bench to the left of the kitchen sink a plateau upon which I knead and roll the salty dough for fresh made chapattis. My lower pantry shelf, the valley that hides a brightly coloured bounty of whole seeds and ground spice. The map that interlinks these landmarks is printed upon the palms of my hands. I no longer require Ammi's recipes as my guide. I keep them close, of course, as any new explorer would. But I am immersed, now, in tracking my own path.

If I had some distance I would recognise the beginnings of hope in my new way. I would see, for instance, that the formation of my own internal landscape is a powerful metaphor for change. A deeply personalised world that, had I not been tossed out of my childhood cosmography by disease and disbelief, I may never have been forced to colonise. I am all these years later at the very beginning of creating my own sovereign territory. One whose colours and textures solidify with each and every turn of the spoon in my spice-filled pots. A place of curves and holes and rambles and skyline fitted to the shape and nature of my thoughts. My philosophies. My own particular viewpoint on God and grace and grief and the vast desert of loss that exists in between.

But I cannot see it that way. Not yet. I am living life in close quarters and all of this fantastical *construction* feels forced by necessity more than desire: the past presses so heavily upon me that, in my current state of terrible fragility, its weight is more tearing than I can bear. It feels to me that I am forced to grow away from my old life. To grow away from everything that came before. Right now, as I stand in the kitchen and begin preparations for the chapatti and sabzi I intend to make the three of us for lunch, my mood is flattened by a profound sense of isolation. I cannot see the possibility inherent in finding a new way to be. I am instead held under by the prospect of inevitable loss. Loss of all that I have been in the past— those aspects of me that will not survive the walk across into this new land. The people I love that I will not be able to carry with me.

'Mummy?' Cailean appears under my feet where I stand—my sentinel post—by the sink in the kitchen. It has rained all morning and, though the clouds have lightened a little, outside is a grey-brown mess of dirty puddles and wet concrete. We are all feeling a little hemmed in and Cailean is tired of my entreaties that he and his brother play on their own. Ashy—almost two-years-old and entirely more sure-footed than he was in the autumn— tags along close behind. 'Mummy, can we help you?'

'I guess.' I am too fatigued to even attempt to hide my reluctance. Brain leapfrogging over any moments of possible pleasure to the mass of cleaning my two messy *helpers* will leave behind. It is a telling indictment of my current state of mind. 'Pull across a chair, Cailean, for you and for Ashy. There isn't enough room for either of you to sit on the bench.' Cailean senses my antipathy and provokes no argument. With abnormal speed he does as I ask. As he drags closer two wooden dining chairs, the tear of them across the floor grates. Grates with the same teeth-aching frequency of the thoughts that drag across my mind. 'We're ready, Mummy!' Cailean clambers atop the chair closest to me. I break free of my thoughts long enough to help Ashy to do the same. 'What can we do?' 'Alright, well if I give you a cucumber, can you cut it and let Ashy put it in the bowl? Ashy, can you put the cucumber in the bowl? Woah!' I reach across Cailean to grab hold of Ashok's chair as he leans back and threatens to tip it over. 'You can't do that, Buddy. You'll fall. Okay? Okay. So, cucumber…' I retrieve it from the fridge and put it on the board in front of Cailean and then reach around his body to pull a butter knife from the cutlery drawer. 'Knife. Ashy here is your bowl.' I give him Cailean's favourite melamine plastic one with the cartoon pirate depicted on its curved interior. 'You guys get busy and I'll put the sabzi on and finish up the chapatti dough.'

I turn my back on the boys to face the stove. I can hear the thump of Cailean's blunt knife hit the board as he hacks his way through the cucumber, his small and serious voice that instructs Ashy when to reach for the pieces sheared free and when to pull those chubby fingers clear. The thwack of my own blade hitting my chopping block sounds as their echo. I will make aloo, I decide. An easy lunch of spiced and ghee-fried potato. I do not even stop to think that a dish I now consider *easy* would have been, a scant six months ago, as much an impossibility as the task of building an emotionally autonomous life now appears. Because whether I choose to acknowledge it or not that is what I am doing.

And yet I am afraid of the spiritual self-determination that I can feel creeping up on me from behind. *Thwack!* The potato splits in two. I work quickly to lay one half on the flat and dice it into centimetre cubes. But my growing autonomy is there on the board anyway, reflected in all the small ways I now make my own decisions when I don my Kashmiri mantle and cook: the way I keep the potato in its skin and cut it small, so much smaller and more delicate than those my Ammi once so long ago cut for me; the way I heat an obscene amount of ghee and yet omit to add Ammi's onions or Mum's garlic or Dad's brutal dried red chilli. I colour the buttery fat instead with a softer blanket: whole cumin, turmeric, a smidge of Kashmiri red chilli, a generous hand of finely ground pink Himalayan salt, a restrained teaspoon-and-a-half of ground coriander and a disproportionate knuckle of gur. At the very last I spy my black cardamom and throw in one of the dark and wizened pods. I do not take the time to notice that I am feeding myself with a soft complexity I have never undertaken before.

The question of why I don't pause and reflect is tied up in the answer to a life's worth of behavioural patterning. My fear means I am tricking myself into moving forward by neither looking forward not back in case my progress overwhelms me. This blinkered form of forward movement is familiar. I am a Cancerian after all. A crab.

More comfortable with a sidling sideways approach to life. It is my defining character trait. Only this time the trickery does not have me trained to retreat but is sending me forward. It doesn't seem possible—I cannot even move to form the thought—but perhaps the same devastating tic of personality that tangled me up in this mess may also be the thing that drags me out from beneath.

'We're finished, Mummy!' 'Fin'nish Mama!'

'Okay, okay,' I mutter, upending the board of potato squares into the hot pan in a spit and sizzle, 'just let me stir this and we'll do the chapattis.' I rush a little, in the dredge and coat of hard white squares in a rainbow of spice, before I turn the gas to low and let the flavours draw together over the idle of a slow burn. Pull my chapatti mixing bowl from the heavy-bottom pot drawer and join the boys on the bench opposite. 'Can I put in the flour?' It is not the hope but the doubt in Cailean's voice that has me acquiesce. As if he is already prepared for me to say no. 'Alright, Monkey,' I concede, conscious that they do not deserve my shortened temper, 'just try and be a bit careful.'

Repudiation of change. Even what one might feel compelled to label as *positive* change. As I heave the bag of wheat flour onto the bench so that Cailean might spoon it out into the waiting bowl, I can't help but think it: isn't this deeply ingrained aversion the axis upon which my whole sorry mess turned? On one of our recent good nights—when our words did not come at right angles and the wounds of the day had not cut too deep—Scott and I had shared the type of late-night conversation that had once been so common. *I think,* I had said to Scott, *that what upset me the most wasn't that Mum got sick, but that there was this underlying thread of propaganda that she hadn't changed. Dad was always so adamant that by being positive about what had happened to Mum, we could get around the emotional distress. I think his idea was maybe that it was a physical disease, but it didn't have to change her or us. But how could she not have been changed? How could you receive that kind of news and ever hope to remain the same?*

'Oops! Sorry, Mummy.' I try not to sigh too volubly. 'That's okay, Monkey, don't worry about it.' I reach for the dish cloth to clean up the flour that just missed the bowl's edge. 'I'll clean it up. Just give Ashy the spoon so he can have a turn, too.'

My boys do what they do best when I am irritated—they play nice. Cailean holds the bowl while Ashy flails the spoon around. I watch with half an eye, mind fixed on that other conversation. *Thread of propaganda.* I don't know whose propaganda it was but we—Mum, Dad, my two brothers, me—we were all complicit. None of us insisting on discussion and communication. Only from this distance can I almost admit that it wasn't that we hadn't wanted to. Just that none of us knew how.

'So that's about enough, just let me add the salt and the water and the ghee and we can take turns rolling them out.' I grab the spoon and the bowl out of a protesting Ashy's reach. Dump into the atta a more than generous teaspoon of salt and a heavy scoop of ghee. A thin stream of warm water runs from the spout of the kitchen tap and I catch it, my cupped palm a temporary vessel. The trick is to stream in just enough. Just enough to glue all these separate elements together.

Cooking can be simple like that. Life, I am learning, is less so. Standing at the sink, working the beginnings of this sticky dough with my right hand, I am able to acknowledge what before I haven't: that this recovery of mine is going to take time. That it already has. After more than thirty years spent looking for clarity, I can't reconstruct a coherent life in a day, a week, a month, likely not even a year. Just like the awkward mix of dry and wet atta and clumping ghee takes time to form a coherent ball of textural consistency, so too will my own gradual habitation of this new internal world demand an elongated period of transition. 'Can Ashy and I have a go, Mummy?'

'Sure, Buddy.' I give the dough's putty-coloured mass one good last knead. 'Just put a little bit of flour from the packet there on the bench and then you can roll a few out.' I hate transition. Hate it in all its skin-irritating and gut-destabilising uncertainty. Not that the concept is unfamiliar. Rather, the opposite. From a young age I was cajoled into an acceptance of life as a single long extension of transitory time. It is one of Hinduism's foundational tenets: to be Hindu means to believe that my soul travels on a continuum, gaining and shedding physical form. It means acceptance of lasting uncertainty. *We plant the seed, we water the seed and we tend the seed,* Dad explained in a time long past, his way to convey to his diligent young daughter the pain that is caused by a focus on aspiration. *Whether it grows to a tall tree with full fruit, or whether its first shoots wither in the soil, those things are not for you to determine.* Even then I felt the resonance of what he said, and the understanding marked me like a bruise. It was a forceful philosophy to feed a child. To remove the physical power of their influence on the world around them. Is it any wonder, then, that I now struggle to set my gaze directly upon a forward point?

It is and it isn't, I concede, train of thought abruptly short-circuited by my forced intervention in the chapatti massacre Ash and Cailean are currently carrying out on the kitchen bench. 'Boys!' I remove the rolling pin from Cailean's hand in frustration and choose not to focus on the disappointment on his small face. 'Come on. You know that's not the way to do it. Look at them, you have to be more gentle otherwise you rip holes in the dough.' I soften a little. 'The aloo is nearly ready, why don't you both climb down and play for ten minutes while I finish it off?'

It is and it isn't. Because *I* am the parent now, no longer the child. I am the adult. The one possessed of the defining role in both my own life and the smaller existences of those two little people who spend their days looking to me for shelter. I have forgotten that. So fixed on looking backward. Sideward. Anywhere but onward. So what else have I forgotten? Have I forgotten forgiveness? Compassion? Selflessness?

Have I forgotten that Parkinson's and the trauma it caused Mum and my family did not just happen to me?

I pause from the roll of chapattis to pull the tawa from a drawer and give the aloo one last stir before I turn off the heat. For that is the problem when communication is in prolonged lack: we begin to think of ourselves as islands.

'Hi, Mum. It's me.'

I don't make the call straight away. There is lunch first. My stack of fresh chapattis cooked. The boys cajoled into mouthfuls of aloo sabzi, its taste made unfamiliar by my last-minute addition of black cardamom, a savour that is more direct than the other cache of Indian spice to which they have become accustomed over these winter months of my intense cooking. The taste is not unpleasant. But it is unfamiliar. There are no outright refusals or screwed up noses. Just hesitation. An amount of increased uncertainty. It is exactly as this phone call feels to me. 'Hi, Sarina.' Mum's voice, low and flat. Parkinson's has done that, siphoned the sound of her personality, all her pitches and tones—those singsong qualities—gone. 'What are you and the boys doing?'

'Oh, nothing much really. It's too cold to go to the park so they just helped me cook some lunch and I'm about to put Ashy down for a rest. Cailean and I might do a puzzle or something.' There is silence. It makes me uncomfortable. 'Anyway,' I leap to cross the chasm, 'what's new with you?' I ask the question and force myself to listen to Mum's answer. It is so very, very hard. This is the first forward step I will take: just a call to ask how she is, supported by my willingness to actually hear her responses. For in all of these years that have passed, in all of her falls and her surgeries and just the wearing nature of days made difficult and despairing by degenerative disease, I have never done that. Not once.

Years ago now, before Cailean was born, when Scott and I were in Paris, Mum and Dad came for an extended visit that saw us all drive up one Sunday to the small holiday town of Honfleur on the Brittany coast. Little more than an hour north-west of Paris, it is possessed of the full arsenal of Gallic scenic seaside clichés: the wood-framed houses, each painted a different pastel shade; a quaint harbour lined with bistros serving *moules frites* and cider beneath striped awnings; bobbing sailboats with romantic monikers and gleaming teak decks; cobbled bluestone streets. The last was quaint, but tricky when a walk around the harbour was not so much a stroll as it was an exercise in management of Mum's signature Parkinsonian shuffle. When Dad let go of her arm for that one minute, I could have caught her. I was right there. Did I actually shy from her touch? Or did I honestly freeze? The bruise on her backside was black and equal to the size of my secret guilt, the almost-slam-of-her-head on jagged stone enough to send our party of four into mild shock. For me, the only emotion more forceful was the disgust I felt as she ate her way through fried potatoes and ice cream to anaesthetize the pain. I know it must make me sound horrid. Self-centred. Psychopathic. Fuck, how could I even stand myself? The fact was that I couldn't. I didn't want to. It isn't so confusing. What internal warring could possibly compete with that of a daughter seeing her mother break down before her eyes over days and months and years?

Shame so all-encompassing I could barely admit to being myself.

'Your father and I are coming up to Melbourne next week to see the neurologist, we were thinking we might stay the night in St Kilda and see you and the boys? Maybe take you and Scott out for dinner at Lau's?' I force myself to acknowledge the hesitation in her voice; the way she has of trailing each sentence off at its end so as to make the request seem small. I manage to keep myself steady before the metaphorical hand she holds out. Without my irritation to fall back on, I become defenceless. And to be defenceless in her presence is to be dangerously close to distraught. 'That sounds nice.' Tenor of my voice too- bright so as to hide its shake. 'I'll have to see about a babysitter, though. I'll need to let you know in the next few days.'

I hang up the phone soon after, exhausted. The strength it takes to re-establish ways of thinking and feeling around the prospect of interaction with Mum is immense. My complete emotional reprogramming, its calibration demanding of continual maintenance as she remains caught on the steepening slope of disease. My limbs shake at the prospect. I think I cannot recalibrate. I know that I must.

This is the turning point I have dreaded. Reaching it is the thing that will have me freed.

ALOO SABZI
Fried and spiced potato

I make this dish as a reassurance on days when I risk forgetting the strength I contain in myself.

INGREDIENTS:
½ kilo of potatoes
vegetable oil for deep frying
1 ½ tablespoons of ghee
1 teaspoon salt
1 teaspoon cumin seeds
1 ½ teaspoons ground coriander
⅓ teaspoon turmeric
⅓ teaspoon Kashmiri red chilli
10 grams of gur
1 black cardamom pod

METHOD:
Dice the potato into 1-centimetre cubes. If I have time, I will fry the potatoes in vegetable oil and then drain on a kitchen towel before cooking with spice. (It makes for a richer dish.)

Heat ghee in a medium sized pan. Add the spices and sauté on a medium heat until fragrant. Add the aloo pieces. If already fried, cook for a short 10 or 15 minutes or until the potato is well coated and infused in spice. If adding raw potato pieces, cook for at least 45 minutes, adding drops of water at times when the potato threatens to stick to the pan and burn.

Serves six as part of a Kashmiri meal.

CHAPTER 12

Kamargah

Kamargah is different in almost every respect
to any other Kashmiri meat dish that our
family ate. Its method adheres to few culinary
conventions: cooked in milk, with no ghee
or gur or turmeric. No browning of meat
or heated spice in a sizzling pan. For these
differences it is prized as a dish that blurs
and softens the bounds of tradition.

MUM AND DAD DIDN'T MAKE it to the neurologist, the result
of a mix up between a new receptionist and a bulging
appointment sheet. And so we didn't make it to dinner.
When Mum calls to relay the news a few days later, I am
ambushed by an alien sense of disappointment; I say
alien because, for so long, catch-ups with Mum and Dad
have been events to be avoided. So it isn't until the sensation of disappointment washes over me that I realise

how much I had wanted that meeting—how much of me longs to move forward. I had got it in my head that dinner at Lau's, talk over soy-steamed Barramundi and sticky Chinese pork ribs, would have been the occasion to mark the beginning of my transition. For that phone call to Mum has split open the ground beneath my feet; life feels enormous and new and the scale of it is mystifying. So while dinner may be cancelled I am driven to create some occasion to mark the change.

It is why I now find myself here: pulling into a parallel park on Hopkins Street in Footscray West, headed to a market I have never visited through a tangle of congested streets rarely driven in order to buy an ingredient I never cook for a dish that I have never eaten.

I have come to the Footscray market to buy lamb ribs: though the South Melbourne market is a scant ten-minute walk from our door, the suburb's growing reputation among wealthy couples and young affluent families has combined with the commercialisation of Melbourne's café and cooking culture to push market food prices to an extreme—even when it comes to purchase of formerly cheap and undesirable cuts of meat. My winter malaise has fed a reluctance to work and that has had a catastrophic influence on my bank account; as a freelance journalist, I am responsible for generating my own content. Long-standing relationships with three or four great women editors in some of Australia's biggest circulated newspapers and magazines means I have a great platform, but without the energy or focus to generate proposals, the work is not forthcoming. And so, having dropped the kids at childcare and spent a morning knee-deep in pitch proposals, I am out to explore a less expensive source. Of course, this is not my singular propulsion, even if it is the only impetus I will readily admit.

I check my time on the parking meter before I grab my wallet and phone from the car console, beep the Golf's remote lock and walk inside. The market is cold, being little more than an enormous concrete slab walled by uninsulated tin. The produce, however, is mesmerising. Towers of eggplant, okra and strangely knobbled Asian vegetables in shades of green, I cannot find the words to name: though the Footscray market has an Indian contingent, many of the stall holders are of South-east Asian origin. To walk here is to enter into a kind of Little Vietnam and though my strange new expansion has me tempted to buy—to experiment—I remind myself of my bank account's depleted status. Necessities only. So restrained, I head instead toward the frigid stalls of meat. Cold before, I am freezing now. The late August skies have been threatening all day and, though I dressed this morning with an eye turned to the gloom, my layers fail to combat the dual force of winter *plus* industrial refrigeration. I pull my turquoise and black Gujarati wool shawl closer around my neck, the one Mum bought for me at the Gujarat Emporium during the few teenage years I spent living in Bangalore. Along with the embroidered patchwork jacket we bought that same day, it is one of my favourite pieces of clothing. Both are old now, and frayed, but they survived my Erica-inspired exodus of clothing and I am inclined to view that as a sign. That these are parts of me I would keep close.

'What can I get you, Love?' Having no real experience of this market at all, I present myself to the busiest butcher I see. Behind the counter works a frenetic crew of Anglo Saxon faces: three stringy women with deeply lined skin work the counter, wrapping and serving the produce sliced by four burly and beer-gutted guys working behind. The refrigerated glass display case must be eight feet long and contains every conceivable cut and quarry: sinewy skinned rabbits, goose-pimpled quail, murderous red slabs of bovine flesh trimmed with yellow fat alongside paler, politer triangles of neatly sectioned pork chops. The line of customers is three-people deep but the tempo of service is brusque and efficient. Quickly it is my turn. 'Do you have lamb ribs, by any chance?' I have spent my few waiting minutes visually taking apart the cabinet. Pork ribs are there. And beef. But the experience of cooking this dish is new enough without an added element of free-form decision-making. I feel that, in this instance, I must be precise.

'Not ready cut but if you wait a few minutes I can get the guys to slice you up some?' I nod: 'That'd be great if they could—maybe two kilos?' She turns her back on me without answering: 'Steve-o!' It is the theatre of pure working class Australiana as she yells at one of the men carrying carcasses from the cool room. 'Can you get us some lamb ribs for this one here? 'bout two kilos.'

In all these recent months I haven't cooked meat. I grill sausages and lamb chops and steaks on the barbecue beneath the shelter of our narrow awning just outside the back door. But I haven't *cooked*. There is nothing of me in the charring of flesh. Everything that I need can be spliced together with ghee and spice in a vegetal symphony of pot and pan. It is not that I am vegetarian—rugged and cold climes that somewhat limit vegetable farming mean that, historically, Kashmiris are a carnivorous bunch. It is something else: meat is heavy and cooking it is complex—I have been keen to keep this weight of effort outside of my kitchen. For *salan* dishes in the Kashmiri tradition are neither light nor simple. They are regal pots of mutton or chicken cooked for hours, textured with ghee and up to a dozen components of ground and whole spice. But as my barriers have fallen, so too, has my resistance: I am more willing than before to accept that this journey might be about more than just the restoration of me.

'There you go, love.' A heavy pack of meat and bone wrapped in butcher's paper lands on the counter, a boxing glove-thud of dead flesh hitting zinc. 'Great.' I thank her and offer her my card. Hold my breath and feel relieved when the green tick signals the purchase has gone through. It is very hard for me to let Scott in on the day's hunt.

The thought, as I return to my car and slot the key in the ignition, does not come out of nowhere: he is my cause, today, these ribs are for him. And to cook them is to step boldly across deeply unstable ground. *Vegetarian Indian again?* These had been the first exasperated words out of Scott's mouth when I had presented his *thaali* three nights ago, the evening I had made that first outreach of a phone call to Mum. It had made me immediately defensive. Having only so very recently become comfortable with a kind of ownership of the Ganju legacy, I'd felt his question as a hatchet. It was the singular comment Scott has made that could be construed as direct culinary criticism in the months since my interplay with spice began. *That's just not enough food for me.*

Backed out of my car space, I navigate my way through an illegal U-turn in the midst of dense traffic.

It was the emotion contained within his speech that had initially taken me by surprise. As if the absence of meat on his plate was a personal affront: me, so determined to cement a link to my own culture but in doing so forgetting that he has cultural needs of his own; meat and three veg that represents the comfort of his urban fringe Anglo upbringing, just as these *sabzis* speak to mine. Not knowing what to think of his comments I hadn't meaningfully responded, other than to ensure the next night's dinner was a medium-rare cooked steak.

It wasn't until I woke this morning—hurt wiped clean by distance and sleep—that I came to understand the thing that was there in his tone but hidden by words unsaid: having finally found a place for myself within this food, I have not been willing to risk an upset of my new tender balance in order to let him in. I make the food that sustains *me*. This morning I recognise by the degree of my own guilt that Scott's three-word entreaty wasn't anything as one-dimensional as complaint: after all, disgruntled husband could be easily disregarded. Scott was asking me to let him in.

This afternoon—stuttering home through a dire mess of on-ramps and off-ramps that shoot in all directions from the shoulders of the Bolte Bridge—I hope to use my new energy to undo a small fragment of that damage. To begin to rebuild a relationship with my husband not based upon my need to use him as the scaffolding that reinforces my dreams and holds up my life.

Yet I don't want to make this sound as if it has been an easy decision. It hasn't. The ability to perceive Scott's hurt and act generously in response doesn't mean I am unaffected. Right now, driving home with two kilos of meat in my car, I am incredibly agitated. A few kilometres from South Melbourne and I am forced to stop at yet another red light; the anger it provokes in me provides a timely release for this disturbed mix of acceptance and roiling frustration: 'Oh fuck, come oooooon,' I mutter. I want to blame *him* for my current discombobulation. I want to blame him for not being strong enough to carry me through. For exerting his own demands upon *me* during this tentative and terrifying time of transition. I want to. With all of my will I desire it. But I can't. Because even so mired I can see that blame and reliance and need has ruled my life for far too long. 'Finally!' My foot on the clutch presses flat at the flash of the traffic light to green and I push the car back into gear, almost rear-ending a slow-moving refrigerated meat van in front. The irony forces a moment of levity.

In any case I am finally moving forward. That momentum now needs to be my focus. I must offer support to those who I have accused in the past of not holding me. Carry them into this new world that I am cooking up in my suburban kitchen. Should I fail to incorporate thoughts of my husband into this Hadean stage of my new topography, it will not be me who is forced to leave him behind. But Scott who will be forced to leave me.

Mum had been married before. Her first husband was named Alberto Montezano, a Spaniard she met in Europe while travelling when in her early twenties. She was holidaying with a close girlfriend; he was, at the time, in exile from Franco's Spain. I imagined him as a man on the run: dark and swarthy, lean and Latin-handsome. Mum married him in Melbourne after blackmailing Grandpa into buying Alberto passage on a ship; if Alberto couldn't return, threatened Mum, then neither would she. It was a romantic gesture of passion and heart that could have signified the solidification of a grand and enduring marriage. It *could* have, except for the fact that Alberto's attraction to the go-go girls, who danced in the Melbourne nightclub he managed, meant Mum's investment in him wasn't returned.

I loved these stories of her life that occurred before we were in it. To me they made her seem impossibly glamorous. Perhaps it was for this reason that I absconded with this memory of Mum's—re-wrote its ending in order to claim a piece of her history for my own: for at some point in my girlhood I began to dream that I was not Indian, but that I was Spanish and Alberto was my father. My imagination instigated a glitch in time that allowed me to present as a product of her first marriage, wedged impossibly as I was between two half- Indian brothers.

Contrary to later years this strange transference of identity wasn't about escape; at that point I had nothing to run *from*. It was as if this was my way to find expression for a part of me that felt unique—that was not attached to a handed-down heritage framed by thousands of years of tradition and myth. I lost my fascination with *Bharatnatyam*, a classic and beautiful form of Indian dance, and developed a sudden yearning to learn flamenco; felt that, should I just be given a pair of black tap shoes, castanets and a flouncing red dress, then my body would instinctively know to do the rest.

Such fantasy. It was as if the only way I knew how to express my idea of a divergent self was to inhabit another character entirely, so deeply ingrained was the notion of what it meant to be a Ganju. I couldn't fathom that there might have been a less radical way to find the root of my own nature. Our practices and our spirituality were set. This was who I was. It wasn't that I was told metamorphosis wasn't possible. It was more of a presumption transposed upon me: the idea that the identity I had inherited would always be enough.

I have not thought about any of this for years. In fact had entirely forgotten how deep this need for creation of my own philosophical foundation once was; how rooted it had been in my developing psyche. Now. Here. Today. I can only think that my brain regurgitates the memory as a comfort, standing, as I am, nervous and hesitant before my kitchen bench.

For I arrive home from Footscray just before the clouds unleash. The lamb ribs are unpacked from plastic and paper and placed on a chopping board. My jacket is thrown over the back of a dining room chair. I crank the heater in response to the torrent of heavy rain on our tin roof and hear the sound of the ducted unit kick in—it will take a few minutes for the warmth to spread through the house and, in the meantime, I keep my shawl wrapped about my shoulders. Maternal comfort.

The pot is pulled out from the drawer and I line up the spices by the stovetop.

'Okay,' I mutter to myself, flick my hand through Ammi's sheaf of papers, 'where's that recipe…'

To remember the Spanish fantasy of my girlhood is a comfort because it donates much-needed perspective: reminds me this drive to search for personal meaning within family philosophy is not new. It is not a reaction to change, I rationalise, moving toward the fridge to retrieve two litres of milk, but a progression towards a more fully inhabited life. 'Think of it as picking up where you left off,' I coach myself, twisting off the plastic blue lid, as if I can make the transmission smoother by simply saying the words out loud. Maybe it works. For even with each and every one of my nerve endings flailing and alive, some stable inner sense tells me I'm on the right track if only for the dish I have chosen to cook.

Kamargah.

'Okay, so milk and meat together, heat on low. What spices do we need, here? No coriander? Okay, then. Cumin. Black cardamom. Here we go…'

It is a dish I have never seen prepared or eaten. Its savoury profile carries no embryo of memory, nor weight of emotional significance. Strange contrast, then, to the half-dozen meat dishes once cooked by Mum and Dad and Ammi that speak directly to the flavour of my childhood: meals whose savoury tonalities are so deeply embedded in my psyche, I am almost certain that I could cook them without guidance. Seeking a dish to offer Scott, *aloo ki salan* might have been the most obvious choice: this is the meat dish Dad most often cooked for the Friday night Indian feasts that marked Scott's and my courtship and my favourite dish of childhood—aloo and diced lamb steeped in an immodest dress of spiced-ghee gravy made rich with the aroma of marrow and bone. Or keema, another from the canon: a spiced lamb or mutton mince that is first browned and then cooked in the full barrage of Kashmiri spice—whole cumin, ground coriander, chilli, turmeric, fresh ginger, dried ground ginger, salt, a little gur, whole green cardamom pods and perhaps even a touch of ground fenugreek finished off with the last-minute addition of *garam masala*. Even *salan wala chawal*—a relatively simple one-pot meal of meat and rice strident with black cardamom that serves as a kind of Kashmiri fast food; *salan wala chawal* is traditionally served simply with sliced cucumber or a dollop of plain yoghurt, raita at most. It was what Mum and Dad reached for when either time or motivation was in short supply.

Kamargah is not possessed of the same storied past, and owes little to classic method. It is lamb ribs simmered in milk, for one; to combine meat and dairy makes for an unusual cooking method as applied to a savoury Kashmiri dish. Then there is the curiously modest cache of spice: a heaped teaspoon each of cumin seeds, *garam masala* and Kashmiri red chilli, a more modest teaspoon of ground ginger, a quill of cinnamon, six cloves and a single pod of black cardamom. There is no inclusion of turmeric or gur. No ground coriander. The spices are not brought to popping life in a sizzle of ghee. Yet within these gaps of unfamiliarity is where my new links to Ammi and Mum and three generations of maternal cooking lineage take root. As a result there is the delicate savour of a new legacy in the plate I will offer to Scott tonight.

'Right, then, spices done. Leave the lid off, I think, probably evaporate the milk faster...'

For *kamargah* is a dish for weddings, a dish for celebrations; it is a dish a wife cooks to reassure a husband who rightly fears his wife might leave him behind as she cooks herself towards change.

'...Guess I'll just turn the heat to low...'

Nothing to do but wait, now: Ammi's recipe instructs low heat over four or five hours or until the milk condenses down to a spice-rich caramelised coat worn by pull-apart- tender meat. The seconds pass slowly: my odd stir of the pot, the clean up and reordering of the kitchen. I note the time—barely 2 p.m.—when all is finished and put away. Note, also, how that span of empty hours *feels*. For it is in the spaces in between where I have found the real challenge of cooking creeps in: in the spare minutes of loneliness that bubble alongside a gently simmering pot; in the void of loss as rice drains and cools; in the spitting anger of self-blame as ghee hits the surface of a thick-bottomed pan. Empty minutes that gape as a child's hungry mouth. *Kamargah* offers opportunity for a sea of such tick- tocking disquiet and yet today all I feel is the deep stillness of oceanic calm; perceive the swirl of spice on milk as a bloom of possibilities. For events and emotions have begun to coalesce. Fragments of my life previously wrenched apart are—as if magnetised—being drawn closer together. I use the word *magnetised* with intent: the movement in no way feels as if its push belongs to me.

Scott and I make love that night, for the first time in months. In that way my *kamargah* had proved itself just the impetus for change I had dreamed it might be. *Wow, what's that smell?* It was the first thing I'd heard after the jangle of Scott's keys in the front door. *I could smell it half-way up the street!* I accepted his kiss in the kitchen and watched as he moved to take a taste from Cailean's *thaali*, both boys home and bathed and seated up for dinner at the table. *It's* kamargah, *slow-cooked Kashmiri lamb ribs,* I told him, and relished the reaction as the milk and spice-softened meat touched his lips—the way his eyes closed for just a fraction of a second before popping open, wider then. *Did you really make this?* He reaches for another bite. *This is incredible!*

I served Scott a *thaali* and watched as he and the boys proceeded to eat, though I myself did no more than pick morsels from Ashok's plate. It wasn't that I didn't feel hungry. More that the only nourishment I desired to consume was the joyful reaction of my husband to this new taste of me.

To this new taste of us.

And now here I lie, hours on, in the aftermath of a rekindled emotional and physical moment of togetherness, struggling to sleep. I find it difficult to identify what it is that keeps me awake.

'Mummy?' Cailean's voice startles me, his form by my bed a slight outline in the darkness. 'Mummy, I had a bad dream. Can I come and cuddle with you?'

I slip from my covers in order to scoop him up and carry him back to his own bed, not wanting him to disturb Scott: stress makes it difficult for him to sleep and tonight appears to be a rare exception. 'It's late, darling,' I say as I walk with him back into his room and tuck him beneath the blue and green fish-patterned doona, 'but I'll lay here with you for a minute.'

I snuggle down beside him. The both of us curled together beneath the sturdy timber headboard lined with Cailean's dreams: favourite storybooks; his small Tour de France figurines; the plaster of Paris dragon and castle we painted together on one of his rare sick days; the Robert the Bruce statuette that was a gift from Scott. It feels safe. My hand reaches out to draw quiet shapes on his thin naked back. 'Can you tell me a talkin'eez?' The small voice comes out of the darkness. A talkin'eez is a made up bedtime tale: a talking story. It has become a pre-sleep tradition over the span of his few years. Tonight the offer of its presence feels as an appropriate antidote to sleeplessness, both for him and for me. 'Okay,' I concede, 'just a quiet one.'

His silent anticipation opens up a portal that awaits only my first few lines in order that we both drop in. 'Once upon a time,' I whisper, conscious of Ashy's sleeping form on the other bed a scant two feet away, 'there was a little boy called Cailean. Cailean was a normal little boy but for one thing—at night, when eeeveryone else was asleep—Cailean would escape to the world of dragons...'

These stories always begin with Cailean and the power of his own secret magic. They are the secular fairy tale counterparts to those same Hindu myths told to me: lands of possibility and secrets and strange interchanges between beings capable of transcending the bounds of Nature's Laws. But in these free-form verbal adventures, Cailean is never faced with impossible compromises and unexpected outcomes. I thought I was protecting him. Only now do I perceive that my desire to keep his adventures free of any moral or emotional ambiguity says little about my instinct to protect him and a lot more about what that security had meant to me.

'...Myro the dragon was an unusual beast: though tough and fiery on the outside, on the inside, in his heart, all he ever wanted was to be loved. He hated that he scared little boys. So when Cailean stood before him and refused to be afraid Myro's heart grew big…'

Refused to be afraid. And then all of a sudden I see it—the fear that keeps me from sleep. I see how I have, within reach, almost everything that I said I wanted. I have ownership over familial recipes. I have a deeper understanding of my own internal landscape. I have a door open to a new kind of relationship with my husband. I have the impression of a possible future with Mum. I have all of this. *Close.* And yet I am terrified. I am terrified because to embrace this growth means to find myself on my own. To see that faith, like life, is not the fairy tale: Shivji and Brahma and Vishnu, Scott, my parents, even Erica—they do not exist to ensure my Cinderella finale, to manifest via mantra and magic wands my idea of what a comfortable future might be.

'And so, with dawn breaking, Myro carried his new friend Cailean home through rainbows and purple clouds. Slipping in the window, he dived back under his doona just as light broke over the world…'

They provide no protection. When a marriage stutters and stalls. When a mother falls ill. When a daughter loses her way. They provide no protection, I realise, for what they are there to provide is love. And the rest? The rest is determined by me.

'…and no one had even known he was gone. But Cailean knew. Just as he knew it would be up to him to make sure all the secrets within that magical world were kept safe from anyone who might harm the place he had found.'

The story is finished. I tune my ears to Cailean's energetic body and hear his slow, deep and even tenor of breath. Asleep now, I can slip from beneath his covers and make my way back to the warmth and shelter of my own. Once settled I reach out to touch Scott's naked back. Confirmation of his sturdy physical presence. So felt, I close my eyes and finally give in to sleep. I go to sleep knowing it is not my *fate* that needs be assured and unchanging, just my connection to the deities and loved ones who consent to stay beside me as I come upon it.

KAMARGAH
Kashmiri lamb chops

I have always found difference in myself difficult to accept, particularly if I feel it pulls me from a shared history with the people I love. When such emotions rise inside me, I cook *kamargah*: a gentle reminder of how an alternative approach can marry with tradition in order to form a more textured whole.

INGREDIENTS:
1.3 kilogram lamb ribs
1 ¾ litres full-cream milk
1 ½ teaspoons cumin
6 cloves
1 heaped teaspoon garam masala
1 heaped teaspoon salt
1 heaped teaspoon Kashmiri red chilli
1 teaspoon ground ginger
1 quill cinnamon
* note

METHOD:
Place the lamb ribs in a large pot and cover with the milk. Add all the spices at once. Bring the pot to a simmer and

then turn to low heat, cooking for around 4–5 hours or until all the milk has evaporated.

Serve.

Enough for eight as part of an Indian meal.

* Traditionally, these ribs will be fried in a *besan* flour mix once they are slow-cooked. For me this last step destroys that feeling of soft nourishment and so I refrain.

Coriander

Coriander seed is my unsung keynote
spice. Soft and citric, it holds the memory
of the past I can't forget and frames
the future I have to learn to see.

I AM DRIVING TO WEST Footscray in lunchtime traffic for the second time in as many weeks. It is a Tuesday, ten days after I made *kamargah* and ten days before Ashok's second birthday. Equidistant between the past and the future. Cailean has been dropped to the house of his best friend for an afternoon of play. Ashy is strapped into his car seat. The two of us are making our way towards a lunch date with Baba and Ammi, a stand-in for the dinner that never eventuated. Though nervous, I try to be calm as I negotiate traffic lights and parking cars and darting pedestrians. Calm: a deceptively benign way to classify a hard-fought state of being. For much has happened between that phone call I made to Mum and now.

Hello, Lovely. Erica's face had been fresh and smiling at the outset of my session with her last week. It had been a fortnight or so since I last saw her, but the demeanour and welcome greeting is the same every time. *How ARE you?* I was good and I knew that I looked it—vermillion tights, violet heels, embroidered braid skirt and clashing pink argyle sweater that fitted my body as a '50s fly girl. Though spring wouldn't officially get underway for another week, a run of unusually mild weather had lightened and lifted the mood of Melbourne. *I'm great,* I said as I kicked off my heels and hoisted up onto the bed, and I was.

'You 'right there, Mashy?' I lift my eyes from the road to check on Ashy in the rear-view mirror—he woke up early this morning, and I am keen to ensure he doesn't fall asleep. 'I hungry,' is his slightly cranky response. 'Well that's lucky because we're going to have lunch in a minute! Nearly there,' I reassure.

I watch the numbers flash by on the shopfronts to the right as we drive, though my thoughts remain focussed on the past. *I'm getting a feeling of tightness in your throat,* was Erica's entrée, her hands occupied with the dab of one—no, two—essential oils along my clavicle; a strangely soothing mix of orange and patchouli that calls to mind a little lunch at a spiritual convention, *are there some words you don't want to say that need to be expressed?*

Her question was nothing that I hadn't myself considered: I had noted my own conflict caused by opposing urges. My drive, on the one hand, to burrow down into this fresh state of acceptance. And on the other? A compulsion to address a sense of embedded frustration that the new harmony in my own home didn't appear to have redressed. 'Looking for number 604, Ashy. Five-zero-eight. Six- zero-zero. Here we are!' Seeing we are close I swing the car left and pull up to park on a dead-end street, shawl blown about as I reach in to unbuckle Ashok and pick him out of the car. I keep him hoisted against my body as we cross the road, in part for his warmth—even with the sun out, spring winds in Melbourne are notoriously brisk—and in part for a last minute grab at comfort: I am coming to this lunch with my shields down and all the softness of my underbelly exposed by those unsaid words Erica sensed and that I have carried here to be said. Not until I push beyond Dosa Hut's door to the jingle of bells and survey the space—no, they are not here yet—do I put Ashy down. He immediately runs for the counter and begins to pull at a container of straws.

It was my friend Jennifer who recommended this place. Married to a south Indian she has the goods on a few of the better dosa restaurants around Melbourne. Though I had planned to suggest Flora's in the middle of the CBD, Mum and Dad's aversion to city traffic and parking made this joint, on the outskirts of suburban Melbourne, a simpler choice. And from what I can see of the magnificently thin tubular pancakes on large rectangular *thaalis* at various tables around the small canteen-style restaurant, it won't disappoint.

It isn't until Ashy and I have made ourselves comfortable upon a banquette along the back wall that I hear the clangy push of the door just about drowned out by the boom of Dad's voice. I've barely had time to take in the vadas kept warm under heating lights in the display deli or the Mahabharata-thick menu listing every kind and combination of dosa and idli mixed through with the odd Hyderabadi biryani. Ashy, however, has been quick on his almost-two-year-old feet to grab a drink from the fridge full of serve-yourself mango lassi. 'Lift your feet, Jenny! That's it. Now stop. Don't shuffle. Here, give me that bag, you can't *carry* so many things.'

I get up from the banquette just as he looks up from his focus on Mum. 'Sar-i-nnna.' Dad speaks my name in that low and familiar three-syllable way, his hand gripped to the inside of Mum's elbow as she shuffles with difficulty through the slender corridor created by a room full of tightly packed formica tables: any narrowing of her immediate surrounding is a threat to Mum, her body and her perceptions confused by the infringement of external objects upon her personal space. 'Hi, Sarina.' Today, with my defences deliberately disabled, I hear Mum's voice as an open call that waits to hear my echo. I hear it in the same way as I understand: it has always been this.

'Hi, Mum. Hi, Dad.' I come out from behind the table to give them both a one-armed hug and a kiss that is as highly charged as it is brief. This is the first time I have ever suggested to my parents that we eat an Indian meal together. Do they themselves take note? It took Scott to make me aware of the significance as he left for work this morning, a comment thrown out in that eerily perceptive way of his. Certainly, there is the distinct feeling that it is not only me who has come with an agenda. It is tangible in the way we interact. The nature of our conversational tone that feels a little like a first date: tentative and reaching. The slightly theatrical way Dad and I effuse on the look of the food, the authenticity of the menu. Even Mum, prickling with an unusually heightened sense of presence that suggests someone only waiting for the right opportunity in order to speak.

'Anup,' she cuts into Dad and I discussing paneer versus egg dosa, 'did you give Sarina the present?'

'What pres... Oh, the *dhania*?' He reaches awkwardly to unhook Mum's bag from the back of his chair before pulling out a package from inside. 'We stopped in Werribee on the way here.' Ashy grabs at the book-sized plastic bag containing an infinite tumble of silvery beige dried coriander seeds as Dad passes it to me. 'Mine!' he says, pulling the package. 'Give him his biscuits, Anup,' directs Mum. Like a magician Baba pulls a packet of Britannia orange creams from the apparently bottomless expanse of Mum's leather satchel: the small packs sold at every Indian grocer from Defence Colony market to suburban Melbourne. Dad opens the packet and passes it across to his sweet-hungry grandson. Ash gives up the pack of *dhania* in a breath.

'You told me you ran out the other day,' explains Dad as I accept the gift. 'When I bought a packet for myself I got one for you, too.' I remember in an instant: I had called Dad late one afternoon last week as I stood before a chopping board decorated with bright white cauliflower florets. In the aftermath of my *kamargah* triumph I was experimenting with cooking gobi for dinner. I had begun the ritual whump of teaspoons of spice into sizzling ghee only to find—halfway through—that my plastic container of coriander seeds was empty. I had turned the heat off and, without thinking, picked up my phone. *Is there something I can use to replace* dhania *in a* gobi *sabzi? I've run out.* Dad hadn't skipped a beat. I'd wondered about sumac but had decided it was possibly too tart. *Don't try to replace it,* he'd advised, *use methi instead.* And so I'd done as he had suggested, turning the heat back to low and substituting dried and ground coriander with dried and ground fenugreek. It hadn't really worked. *Dhania* is soft and citric. *Methi,* bitter. The sabzi*'s* aftertaste had been astringent.

'Thanks, Dad.' I am touched that he remembered. I reach down to stash the bag of seeds in my own satchel sitting at my feet before turning back to the menu. 'With the kids and work and everything I haven't had a chance to drive to Carlton or Balaclava to get anymore. It's always such a hassle trying to get through city traffic, especially if I have to take the kids. Anyway,' I look up at Dad's face again, force myself to remain open in the sweep of vulnerability and keep my gaze tied to his, 'thank you.'

'Okay, Ashok, are we going to get you a dosa for lunch?' For once I don't anger at Dad's disabling of the moment. Nor his raised-volume enthusiasm as the soft-faced and slow-paced south Indian waitress finally consents to take our order. Gentle communication is all so new. All three of us are made jumpy by its rawness. Only Ashy is unaffected and the innocence of his actions draws us in: in Ashok's unconscious grab for Mum's lassi, his unthinking spill of my water cup and his impatient knock and wobble of our table each time he climbs from the banquette to the floor and back up again, this little boy gives Mum and Dad and me the reality of a solid and familiar pattern of behaviour to encircle.

Ashy's movements lull us, so in the end I cannot tell you exactly how the conversation begins. It's as if someone—Mum. Dad. Me—says the words that cast each of us into our own verbal free fall. For the first time in forever, the individual bubbles we occupy have each swallowed the others whole until the space we exist within becomes singular. There are no walls and no distinctions. No outlines. It is just Mum, Dad and I. Three monikers contained within the same sentence. And suddenly we are no longer talking dosa*s*, but instead I am being asked all the reasons why I have not allowed my parents to see inside my private internal landscape. 'It's like you never tell us anything.' Mum's voice breaks from the weight of words as they are cast out of her mouth. 'We don't know what happens to you anymore.'

'That's because I haven't wanted to tell you.' I see Mum and Dad visibly recoil. My words are hard for them to hear. The tone of my communication that is coloured with no hesitancy and great cause. Perhaps they had expected easy-to-sympathise sorrow. But this new strong part of me knows: *sad* is not what this conversation needs to be. 'I haven't *wanted* to tell you anything that's happened in my life. I tried. But every time I did, you just tried to deflect my pain, tried to attribute some piece of its occurrence to my actions. No,' I cut Dad off firmly as makes to leap in, my voice curt, 'when I call you to tell you I've had a bad day or that one of the boys is sick and no one slept, I don't need you to start telling me all the things I'm doing wrong. *Have you tried homeopathy? I don't know why you don't just call Dr Raj. Dr Raj's medicine fixed Mother's bad tummy in two days.*' My voice gets a little mean. I hear it. Breathe out. Do my best to bring it back. 'All I want is for you to acknowledge me. To *hear* me. To tell me that, yes, it's shitty that I had a bad day. That I must be tired having been kept up half the night with a sick child. I can figure out the solutions. All I want from you is some support.'

'But we don't do that, Sar-i-nnna.' Dad's tone as he speaks is unequivocal. 'Ganjus don't *do* sympathy. We do action. Sympathy is useless…'

'But it's not sympathy!' My words that interrupt his, come out with force, a near-shout. I don't register the stares from diners so feel absolutely no compulsion to lower my voice. 'It's EMPATHY I need.' I feel like a frustrated teacher trying to teach a first grader why sticking scissors in his mouth is a bad idea. For a couple nearing seventy who have spent the better part of their lives living with disease, you'd think they might have the full spectrum of emotional language refined to an exquisite depth of comprehension. *But maybe*—whispers the voice of compassion somewhere inside—*maybe being so mired in pain's grip makes the perspective required for understanding impossible.* 'Empathy means placing yourself in someone else's shoes, hearing their pain and acknowledging where they are. Empathy is connection. Connection comes when we feel heard by the people that love us. No,' I say again as Dad tries to speak, louder this time, my body an aggressive lean forward across the table, 'you and Mum asked for the information so please let me finish.'

I hold it all there for a second. Breath held. Body tense. Silence loud. And then a whoosh of air is pushed out of my lungs in a rush. I flop back against the banquette. Give a now-cranky and food-covered Ashy my roll of photos on the phone to scroll through. And somehow find the wisdom to come at the conversation from a different angle.

'Let me tell you a story.' I am quieter now that I sense I have their attention. Food ceases to hold us. We all sit in front of near-full *thaalis* of soft and sour dosa with all of the accompanying chutneys though none of us makes a move to eat. 'When Scott and I first got married I used to make him big meals because that was how I knew to give love. But he would get cranky at me because, after expending so much energy cooking, I always felt too bothered to cuddle with him on the couch. We used to fight about it.' I look outward from behind the screen of memory to find their eyes trained on me, though there is too much going on in my own heart for me to be able to read the crash of emotions that push them wide. 'Then one day when we argued about it again he said to me, "If cooking these big meals means you're too tired to show me affection, I'd rather have toast." The thing is,' my voice is softer now, my eyes moving between two faces that have—over my life—felt alternately as home and as exile, 'when you love someone you can't give love to them based on how you feel comfortable giving it; you need to give love to them based on how they best receive it. It is then that a person feels *heard*. And that is all any human being wants. Just to be heard.'

I hadn't realised but, somewhere in those last few sentences, the tears have come. I cry out my final four words. Dad's eyes are shiny, lids pulled back wide; he looks disarmed—a slight quiver of his jowls the only movement of a body not pitched forward to counter-argue, but softened into acceptance. Mum doesn't even attempt to contain herself—I hear her barking sobs as an admission of grief and guilt. Her hands stiffened by Parksinon's shake. Her face slackens. Sounds that come from some place deep, bend her shoulders forward so that the chest that once cradled me becomes a hollowed scoop of sorrow. And I feel for her. I do. But I don't want to live with this dysfunction anymore, constantly going over what is already done. So I sit. I let the moment fill the space. My only movement is to pull Ashok into my lap, to reassure him, bewildered as he is by the emotional intensity. And while I am happy for the comfort of Ashy's bulk I refuse to hide behind it, to diminish the quality of this moment of vulnerability. For today I choose to see Mum and Dad's pain as a reflection of mine and—in that togetherness—establish our family's progress.

We walk out of the restaurant a short time later as a six-legged single entity: Dad and I bolstering Mum as Ashy babbles away, walking behind. I have never offered my arm as a walking aid voluntarily to her, but that sense of awkwardness rooted in words unsaid is banished, now. I feel lightened. Relieved they have absorbed my feelings as healing and not failure. That I can now stand in a position of being Mum's emotional support, knowing she can also be mine.

As I drive home soon after, Ashok buckled up and asleep, the memories of our shared parting hug and Dad calling out to me as he steps into the car—*I love you!*—holds fresh in my mind. I feel the kind of buoyant hope that comes when a great weight has been lifted: I move more freely in a present that no longer seems congested with the detritus of my past.

In many ways the changes wrought by that lunch are so momentous that I cannot immediately digest the significance of its impact upon me. But in one way it is clear: coriander begins to find its way into everything. Sprinkled across lamb chops with salt and pepper and olive oil. In a slow-cooked Le Creuset pot of fleshy pork chops flavoured by lemon rind, salt, black pepper, garlic and paprika. Even in the *chownk* for my daal. About the only thing I refrain from adding it to is my chai, though given its current hold over my imagination perhaps that development will only be a matter of time.

Having never considered this particular spice and its importance to me before, its reintroduction to my kitchen via the plastic bag gifted to me by Dad has placed it at the forefront of my consciousness. So intrigued, I begin to pay attention to *dhania's* savour in a way I have failed to do before. I note that the colour of the dried seeds may appear in one instant as tarnished white gold and the next as gossamer silver. That it grinds to fragrant dust the shade of warm peanut. I stick my nose up close and inhale, surprised to experience the aroma as soft and lemony with a tail of warming earth—devoid of the dusty, gritty notes its ground appearance would seem to suggest. Does it seem strange that I have never before stopped to smell the spice I have spent these past months adding liberally to each and every Kashmiri dish? That I spent even longer years before eating? Yes and no. I am possessed of a natural journalistic curiosity when considering the effect of exterior influences upon my life. It is only the deep importance of my own interior world that I seem somehow pre-programmed to ignore.

So it follows that the outcome of the phone call, when it happens, catches me entirely by surprise. Part of it is that I am manifestly unprepared: in the four days since my dosa lunch with Mum and Dad I have woken every morning breathing the heady oxygen of contentment at their changed attitude towards me. The sense of accomplishment stems from an acknowledgement I feel I have extracted—that they are now armed with knowledge of *how* to love me. As such I feel cherished. I feel safe. I feel no hesitation in answering the call when I see their number flash up on my mobile phone midway through Saturday afternoon.

'Hi Mum!' My voice is bright despite my fatigue; Cailean had brought home a hidden stomach bug from childcare yesterday that chose to reveal itself around midnight; the type of grotesquely viral gastro that cuts its annual swathe through schools and kindergartens with spring's arrival. Having only given up vomiting close to 5 a.m. this morning, he has just drifted off into another of the day's fitful sleeps. A space I, too, would love to occupy if only I could manage two things: primarily, to convince an energised Ashy to lay down arms, but also— and perhaps less achievably—to rid myself of the concern that Cailean's still-intense stomach cramps might point to the beginnings of a more severe case of dehydration.

'Hi, Sarina.' I am livened by the call: lifted by the fact I immediately hear in the sound of Mum's voice that she is similarly excited to communicate with me. 'What's happening?'

'Oh, well, kind of nothing and lots all at once, actually.' I scratch my mind for somewhere to begin. 'Scott's working the whole weekend so the boys and I are just hanging out, but Cailean's sick so that's thrown a bit of a spanner in the works...'

'What's wrong with Cailean?' asks Mum. And then, out of the background. 'Hi Sar-i-nna, I'm just cooking up a feast!'

'Oh, hi Dad!' His voice doesn't throw me; Mum and Dad always talk with the phone on speaker. I can see it: Mum sagged into a seat at the dining room and Dad working at his chopping board in the kitchen behind. Dad becomes excited when he cooks and loves to verbalise the process: what spices he is using and why, how he is choosing to innovate some new taste within a traditional dish. I don't consider that his comment requires a response. 'Sorry Mum, what did you say?'

'I said, what's wrong with Cailean?'

'Oh, well he came home from kindergarten fine yesterday afternoon, he was a little tired but nothing unusual. He ate a normal dinner and had a bath and then went to bed but then woke up crying at midnight and basically started vomiting from then until 5 o'clock this morning. I'm a bit exhausted, quite frankly, but I'm a little worried about him, actually, because he hasn't been able to drink much and has been super lethargic all day...' It feels so good to download my concern that I don't notice at all the emotional static that begins to build on the other end of the line.

'Did you give him *Amritdhara*?' It's Dad. Clearly following the conversation, the changing volume of his voice tells me, he's left his kitchen post to walk his way closer to the phone.

'Um, yeah, a couple of times,' I respond, referencing the Ayurvedic herbal remedy made in India that was given to us as kids in order to cure everything from stomach ache and vomiting to constipation and congested lungs, 'but in the end he just couldn't keep anything down.'

'Have you called Dr Raj?'

'Dr Raj?' Dad's chosen homeopath bases himself in a small office in the middle of the city where it is not only impossible to park but inevitable that I become stuck in horribly dense city traffic. 'No. I mean, it's Saturday…'

'He has his phone on all the time, Sar-i-nna.'

'I know but how would I even get there? I can't take

Cailean out of bed and cart him across town and Scott won't be home from work until after 5 o'clock…' I hear myself. And all of a sudden I stop. 'I'm not doing this.'

'What do you mean you're not…,' But I can't let him finish.

'I'm not DOING THIS.'

My voice shakes. I am violently upset that we have slipped back into this dynamic. Instantly! I am incredulous. Incandescent! Blood roars in my ears with a velocity that drowns the crash of my grief. The rest of the argument passes in a blur of angry and indignant words, culminating in my abrupt end to the call. I feel trapped. Hounded. Cornered. There is nowhere for my riot of emotion to syphon. The only possible release is in honesty, but how adept have I ever been at allowing that? For I've feared all along that refusal would be their last fall back. Why else have I proceeded with such wilfulness to build up a fortress of alternative support—the cooking, the spices, the spiritual endeavours, the *memories*. All those memories I have harvested and implanted and endeavoured to tie myself to via recreation of savours that once defined Mum and Dad and me—tastes that told the pre-Parkinsonian story of our lives together.

Enacted consciously or not, that dosa lunch had been the last effort to draw Mum and Dad up beside me.

I can't do that, Sar-i-nna! Ironically, Cailean's paralysing stomach cramps had ceased completely without aid or warning almost immediately in the moment I pushed the button to end the call. Sitting now with him and Ashy in front of *Cars,* watching the movie for the billionth time, Dad's words come back to me. *I can't do what you want. How is it useful, Sar-i-nna? If you tell me you have a problem then it doesn't make sense to me that I wouldn't try and fix it.*

I'm not a robot. I heard the pain in his voice. The frustration. I'm asking for something Dad can't give. Support, yes, but something more—that Dad anchor both himself and Mum to *my* side of the life and death divide; the anger he feels that he cannot make it so. Dad and I, who reflect back at each other the rabid futility that consumes us as we watch disease tear away large chunks of the woman we love. For where Mum and Dad are conjoined by marriage and love and choice and will and the natural order, Mum and I are not. She is my mother. All these years I have been unable to reconcile the loss when she chose—as it appeared through the lens of my own immature grief— disease over me. I know Dad is prepared to follow her down the rabbit hole of ill health, to tie himself to her as she is eventually led into darkness in a way that I cannot. For all the bitching and the bickering and the *Jenny-pick- up-your-feet,* theirs is a passionate love story.

And finally I accept that it excludes me.

'Okay, little Monkeys,' I slide from beneath the tangle of our limbs, drop a kiss on both their heads, though neither lifts their eyes from the screen, 'you guys stay put. I'm going to potter in the kitchen.'

The intensity of my thoughts means I can't sit still. So potter is what I do. I fuss with the dishwasher. Pull out some leftover sabzi*s* in readiment for steaming when it's time to prepare dinner. Only when the minutiae of domestic chores is completed do I pick up a *katori* of ground coriander left over from an earlier cooking session. I bring it to my nose, as if its scent might absorb the tears. *Dhania* that contains the seed of who I am: the soft and citric taste of my own self-determination. I knew of its existence—of my separateness—that day oh-so- many years ago when I walked out on Mum and left her collapsed in a heap upon her Kashmiri wedding carpet.

'Mummy, can I please have some cut-up apple? I'm hungry.' Cailean. I put the *katori* of *dhania* down. Ignore the knot in my throat as I grab an apple from the fruit bowl and a knife from the knife block.

But what I couldn't accept then is what this phone call has forced me to acknowledge now: my parents don't want to move towards me if it means loosening the grip they have on each other. Therefore, they will forever belong in my past and there is no reconciliation that can make it otherwise. I take the snack to Cailean, he still pale and wan, and note with abstract awareness the black hole of resigned loss that spreads outward from my gut: hope is dead. And yet I feel bereaved in a way that is clear and coherent: I am stricken but not lost. The tenor of *this* grief that is deep and conscious and welcome and good.

CHAPTER 14

Paneer

Paneer is a dish of concentrated process:
milk that is boiled, split, hung, sliced
and fried. A food transformed and
reconfigured that is then cooked through
with spice upon a low and steady burn.

INDIA IS NOT THE HOME I remember. I had spent days preceding our trip prepping Cailean for the sights that would greet us upon our midnight arrival into New Delhi airport: the monstrous crush of people; the shouting and pushing and grabbing for bags as a legion of taxi *wallas* fight for fares; the great cacophony of humanity, in other words, that has always been such a powerful external stimuli—a way for me to cement this country and hold it in my imagination. But the only sensation to assault me upon entrance into the arrivals concourse is my own intense disorientation. Nothing is as it was. The airport is almost completely void of sound—a quiet hush of space and spare white surfaces. The neatly dressed man who holds a sign that bears my name fights no mob in order to be seen. GANJU, reads the sign: Dad, who has planned and paid for this trip, had let me know this driver—my cousin's—would be the one to meet us upon arrival. The driver, I don't know his name, places our minimal luggage on a trolley that steers smoothly beyond the automatic glass doors and into the cold quiet of the night.

In all of this unexpected experience it is only the city's familiar smell of woodsmoke and diesel fumes that grounds me. Seven years since I have come and, in that regard, nothing has changed. Yet if not for my specific olfactory remembrance heightened by the January cold, I could squint my eyes and almost be in LAX: the no- parking buffer zone, the lines of low-lying concrete bollards, and the bright neon lights that illuminate the *uniformity* in it all. It is not the scene I had attempted to recreate for Cailean as the Singapore Airlines jet came in to land and yet, of the two of us, it is only I who grapple with the disparity between my remembrance and this reality. The whirr of my brain recalibrating expectation as we follow our driver to the car is of such force, I am almost certain it could be heard out loud.

'Anup *Sahib* is waiting for you at Eco Options,' the driver speaks to me for the first time as he starts the engine. He seeks my eyes in the rear-view mirror. I nod my understanding and gratefully accept his offer of a cold bottle of water wrapped in a small towel as Cailean buckles his belt. I take a sip and pass it to Cailean as the car kicks into motion. Only as we drive beyond the airport's bounds does my picture of this city refine to a singularly recognisable tableau once more. 'Look, Mummy!' Cailean's voice is excited. 'Cows!' He is up on his knees, twisted in his seat belt, both hands pressed to the window and face set upon the Barnum Brothers streetscape outside. My watch ticks towards 1 a.m. but the level of roadside activity belies the late hour. We travel through the heave and thrum and surreal excitement of New Delhi and nothing is still: cows form a bovine cavalcade on the dirt and concrete pavement; trucks whose rear bumpers are painted with pink, yellow and blue lotus flowers thunder past, horns bleating; streams of chappal-shod young men in slim brown pants and woollen jumpers hold hands as they slouch and loiter on their way to God knows where.

'Whaddya reckon, Monkey?' I look straight at Cailean as I toss out the question, car humming along congested roads, eager to share his experience. And yet I can see from his face that my enquiry hasn't registered. He is transfixed; all five senses zeroed in on the new and strange world outside his passenger window. I feel something fierce at Cailean's rapt interest and watch his eyes widen at India's hypnotic absurdity with vicarious delight. This is what I had wanted him to witness—the sheer and confronting wonder of it all. As we turn left off the Gurgaon highway and into Ayanagar village, reality's screenplay turns increasingly rural: the road narrows to single-car width and turns from asphalt to dirt; shop-fronts are smaller, roller doors pulled down against the night; human activity on the streets is diminished away from the centre of the city.

'Look! That's the White House! That's Bapu's old house, Baba's brother; the house where Daddy and I got married!' This time my words hook Cailean's attention. 'Where?' he asks, head that turns left to right, his neck a swivel. 'There! See? Behind. The two-storey one with the black gate?' He smiles over his shoulder at me, 'Oh I see it!' Cailean is kneeled up with arms hooked over his headrest, body facing backward in order to view what must appear to him as a monument to his parents' past lives. He watches the house like that, through the car's rear window, until it becomes a marker in the distance. Until we turn a corner onto a narrow and deeply rutted road. Until the building fades from sight.

This trip back to India has not come out of the blue. Dad had spoken of his desire to bring us all together on home soil since before Cailean was born. I had shot any such suggestions down—between work and two pregnancies and international moves it was simple to defer. But when Dad insistently broached the idea again in late October, as he and Mum were planning their annual three-month New Delhi return, I found myself conceding. It wasn't so much that I gave in to his demands. More that, Dad's desire to have his grandsons experience this part of him married with my own willingness to return to New Delhi after a six- or seven-year absence. This trip was driven by all and yet, on the surface at least, seemed to provide complete satisfaction to none: Mum and Dad wanted me to bring Ashok which, without Scott's help—he being tied to his store—I refused as too difficult; I wanted to stay for less time which—as they were paying for the tickets— Mum and Dad refused as too brief. Strange as it may sound, this equity of disappointment feels as progress, and not just for the channels of communication it opened. It feels as progress for it places us on parallel ground.

The victim-perpetrator dynamic is dead.

But I am freed from such thoughts as my eyes open on this first morning. Freed by the heady assault of sound and scent that has continued, unceasing, since Cailean and I woke from a jet-lagged sleep to realise ourselves slipped between latitudinal lines. This is what I experienced from my bed; gentle clatter of spoon against pot; water running and ragas playing; switch and clunk of the geyser; rhythmic slap of thongs against cement floor, thin millimetres of rubber sole that arrest the seeping cold of an early January day; cardamom-scented chai thinner than the heavy weight of dust and ash and incense that permeates the air. Every sensory recollection a link in some way to my past.

Even this, the spread of Amul butter on Cailean's toast, a recreation of the taste of New Delhi mornings once given to me. 'Peanut butter on your toast, Monkey?'

'Yes, please, Mummy!' I step around Ramu, our long-time family help, busy preparing vegetables for lunch under Dad's direction, and carry Cailean's first meal in my country towards the round timber table: two slices of peanut butter toast, a sliced yellow guava with mottled skin that is soft and sweet, and a tall, cold glass of banana lassi. But it's not him who I watch eat, it's *me*; an echo of the girl that I was projected and shape-changed into the form of a boy. For this is the exact breakfast I ate at my own Ammi's breakfast table, down to the sugary white sliced bread and marked guavas. The feeling of transference is peculiar in the extreme, not for the comfort it brings—the oddity of the experience doesn't allow for ease—but the accompanying sense of dislocation.

Over the next few days the present and my past transpose repeatedly, in almost everything that Cailean and I do: in a sunset exploration of Mum and Dad's bare and rubbly rooftop; side-of-the-road ice cream pit stops at shops laid upon hard-edged white granite steps in dusty car park clusters; in the soccer we play behind crumbling monuments in the Lodhi gardens. Each incident a vignette that layers one more frame atop my collective memories. The outcome of what feels as a stack and slot of experience is that my past draws up in a rush. So fast does this entangled mess of now and then catapult to the surface that, in any given moment, I am not entirely sure from where the resonance originates: to which Sarina does *this* sensation of déjà vu connect? The young girl? The teen? The bride?

In all of this I am not at all sure of Cailean's position. What he senses. What he knows. The only certainty is his increasing determination to create boundaries he will not be moved beyond.

'Chai-tanyaaa,' Dad turns to face Cailean and me, side by side in the very back of the seven-seater jeep somewhere towards the beginning of our first week there. Dad hires the car each day from a local Ayanagar entrepreneur— replete with driver—on the days an outing is planned, 'come and buy some *phool* from the market with Baba.' *Phool.* Flowers. Cailean knows the word. Just as he knows others. *Bacche.* Child. *Oopar.* Up. *Niche.* Down. *Joota.* Shoes. *Band.* Close. Dahi. Yoghurt. *Pani.* Water. *Kishmish.* Sultanas. *Doodh.* Milk. In Hindi, Cailean has the vocabulary of a two-year-old. Much the same one that I possess, minus, perhaps, a few key sentences and the odd scattershot of more sophisticated words.

'Mummy,' Cailean directs himself to me, eyes huge in his delicate face, hands clutched around his lunch-box filled with snacks, 'I don't want to get out.' His Baba insists. For some stupid reason I do, too. I insist. Dad insists. The car is stationary, pulled over to the side of a ludicrously dusty and hellishly congested road. Our windows are closed. We are on our way to Sohna and the ashram, around an hour further south beyond our own Ayanagar outpost that skirts the southern edge of New Delhi proper. The illusion of urban organisation is non-existent. Here, the highway bisects a crowd of shanties. The village market is in full swing. Skin-and-bone dogs lay at irregular though frequent intervals in ditches and upon dirt hills. Local women in extraordinary saris haggle with the men stationed behind wooden carts piled high with bananas! Grapes! Red carrots! Round garlands of marigolds threaded on white string!

But Cailean won't budge. He is frozen. Overcome by his proximity to such intense visual and aural stimulation: the unfamiliar faces, the exotic scene, the cacophony of Hindi. My little Paris-born, Melbourne-raised, chapatti- loving five-year-old who is stunned by the implication that, by accident of birth, he should feel a sense of belonging to these people and this language. India is a part of him, though not in the same way that it is a part of me. Later I will marvel that he knows this from the beginning. Will envy such clear perception, and wonder from what unravelling such definitive self-knowledge might have saved me.

'I don't want to get out.'

In the end we can't make him. Just as I cannot force him to sit still before our family guru in the way that I once did as a girl his age. Instead, upon arrival at the ashram a short time later, we do our *pranaam*; take our morning chai and prasad of *laddus* made in the ashram kitchen and leave Mum and Dad and Nand Baba, our family guru, to their spiritual conference. Together, Cailean and I wander the grounds. I show him the temple. We play on the lawn where peacocks preen, and Cailean struggles to believe he can come within a hand's reach of such exotic beauty. We wash our hands with soil and water by the kitchen door in preparation for lunch.

Eventually Mum and Dad finish their conference. Or they have had enough. I don't know which. What is clear when we all pile back into the car—the day now set well into mid-afternoon—is that a disturbance has occurred. 'But that's not the *point*, Jenny, he shouldn't have said that. And in any case that just isn't true.' Names are mentioned. Perceived wrongdoings recalled. Mum replies. Dad rebuts. Cailean and I talk among ourselves. Seated with a fatigued Cailean in the very back seat, I choose to deliberately remain detached from their conversation. It is easier to relax because I have Cailean's lead to follow. On the hour-long drive back towards Ayanagar, too tired and disinterested to engage in stories of angst that do not encircle him, he instead attacks a large pile of pistachio nuts; the only food remaining in the lunchbox supply of familiar snacks we carry wherever we go. I join him. We spend the drive home like this. Shelling nuts. Ignoring speech. Heads bent close. Popping the sweet green kernels into our mouths.

I am making paneer. In India particularly, preparation of food is a signifier of sanctity and social occasion. Today this dish will aid in establishment of both: Nand Baba is coming to perform a special puja in Mum and Dad's house and lunch will form a part of the occasion. This event is no simple thing: as a travelling Hindu man of God, Nand Baba is required to observe a litany of strictures whenever he moves outside of the ashram. The impetus to ensure that none of Nand Baba's religious codes are impinged upon falls to us, the devotees who will host him. It is an immense pressure; to fail our guru would not only impact our *karma*, but his, too. The list of protocols to which we must adhere is long. Everything used to make the lunch must be new: new pots, pans, utensils, *thaalis* and *katoris*. The entire house must be minutely cleaned. There can be no meat or eggs or fish kept in the house and any trace of it must be removed. I cannot use garlic or onion, though my style of Kashmiri cooking does not, in any case, demand it. Similarly, no impure foods can be consumed by those cooking, either *before* cooking or for the entire day thereafter. So I am not simply making paneer, I am making paneer as one would make if Shivji himself came to call.

'Sar-i-na, you must wash your hands with dirt before you start cooking—I have done that this morning with all the new pots.' Washing our hands with dirt and water is one of the strictures we adhere to before entering our ashram. Today, our home is the home of our guru, and so that ritual must be established here. Dad's voice is intense as I prepare to take to the kitchen and complete my contribution. I understand why: along with anxiety leavened by the spiritual weight of the tasks we must perform, there is also the complication of ashram politics. This intense focus on ritual and protocol is a mainstay criticism of Hinduism.

'What time will they be here?' I try to keep conversation light as I begin to line up my spices on the bench: fresh ginger alongside a nuanced menagerie of heat and warmth from cinnamon, ground dried ginger, whole dried mace flower, a little dried chilli, a few pungent cloves and all my usual suspects—turmeric, whole cumin, ground coriander, salt and gur. 'The puja is supposed to start at 11 o'clock.' Dad and I both look at the clock in the kitchen as he says the words—it is already after 8 a.m.

'Anuuuup!' Mum calls from their bedroom. Dad takes one last look at what I'm doing. 'I need to go and get your mother ready.' His statement contains within it an implied question—*am I going to be alright?* 'I'll be fine.' I reassure. 'I'll tell you if I need any help.'

But just as the kitchen empties of one, it fills again with another. 'What can I do, Mummy?' Cailean and I had been playing cricket earlier, a very early match following chai and strawberry jam chapatti*s* before my responsibilities in the kitchen forced time. 'Why don't you grab your camera out of our room and take some photos?' I suggest, understanding his need for activity but unable, in this moment, to be the one to provide the entertainment. 'I'm going to be caught up cooking for a little while.'

The child he is means Cailean does exactly as I suggest. He is unobtrusive with his digital device and so I barely notice his movements as I focus on the immediacy of the task at hand: paneer hung from the kitchen tap in muslin overnight, it is now time to unwrap and slice the firm ball into edible squares ready to fry. Hot oil in the *kadai* spits as I submerge each batch, carefully turning and browning before removing the lemony cubes into a bowl of cold water. Camera in hand, Cailean drifts away as I heat spice in ghee and transform the fried cheese into a sabzi, sweet with peas and tomato and cinnamon. He circles back a little while on as the full catastrophe of guru and guru's helpers enter through the front door. Holds patiently through the length of puja and adult conversation that precludes his participation.

Cailean's lightly felt presence means it is only much later, once the monumental day is completed—house dark and three of its four inhabitants asleep—that I see from the digital cartridge I download onto my laptop his experience of the day in vignettes captured. There is no question that, at five, he is utterly technically inept; most shots are unfocussed and composed at strange angles imbued with the feel of mistake more than art—unstoried sections of rug or the intersection of timber wardrobe and white wall. But *practical* ineptitude is to be expected. What explodes my senses are the half-dozen frames that distil the purest essence of the day: Nand Baba's right hand, slightly out of focus, as he pinches between pursed fingers his first mouthful of prasad from the *thaali* we offered; warmth of a tealight candle's flickering burn cradled by the purpose-built stonewall recess as light fades; the crumple of blood red rose blooms given to us as a blessing that smudge across this picture's foreground.

I see how it is Cailean's lightness that enables him to capture the day's spiritual intensity with a few reductive scenes: powerful imagery bracketed by his many tongue- poking, face-pulling self-portraits. For while the adults were swept up in the undercurrent of protocol and ashram politics—the whispers from family members that Dad had fallen out of favour with Nand Baba; that Nand Baba was displeased with Dad's insistence that he come today, knowing that our familial links made Dad's request impossible for the ashram minders to refuse—Cailean remained untouched. I know that part of his distance is attributable simply to childhood ignorance. But that is not the sum of it.

'Mummy, why are you still awake?' The voice catches me by surprise. I look up from my laptop screen to see

Cailean's head poking out from our open bedroom door. I think it is the way he startles me that makes my voice firm. 'Why are *you* awake is the question, Monkey.' He pads over to where I sit at the kitchen table and climbs into my lap. I sense his loneliness and am immediately regretful at the tone I have taken.'I'm just sorting all your photos,' I soften. In these moments, just the two of us, we could be anywhere. South Melbourne. South Delhi. Only what is outside gives our location away and—with the exterior around this house blackened by night—there is none but us to tell.

'Do you know,' I speak softly to him, snapping down the lid of my computer and cuddling him close, 'how brave I think you are?' I feel his body tighten to attention though not a single little boy muscle moves. 'What do you mean?' Instead it is me that shifts in my seat, juggling Cailean on my lap, as I struggle to find the right words. What do I mean? I mean that, by watching my son in India, I am learning so much about myself. I am learning that just because I have a significant and powerful heritage does not mean I must find my identity entirely within it. I am learning that I needn't reflexively adopt the causes and tensions and demands of those whom I love. I am learning that it is not impossible to poke my tongue out at spiritual stricture and still experience moments of profound faith. And I am learning all of this by watching a five-year-old boy hold his ground on the points that matter to him in an environment completely removed from anything he has ever experienced.

'What do I mean? I mean,' I begin, as I stand with him in my arms and carry him off to bed, 'that even though I know sometimes, here, it is hard or strange or boring for you and yet you never complain. That I know you miss your Daddy and Hughie and Ashy.' I lay Cailean down on his bed, tuck the beautiful paisley patterned cotton quilt beneath his chin and watch as his gaze moves to the photo of Scott and his best friend Blu-Tacked to the wall by his head. 'But we'll be home soon.'

I drop a last kiss onto his forehead. Slide into my own narrow bed pushed up to abut Cailean's. *His* anchor holds me in the darkness. For Cailean is both the answer and the cause of my fluctuant movement around the theme of dislocation; the disparity that results when fresh eyes challenge old perspectives. I thought that to bring my son here would be to instruct Cailean on what India means to him. I had had no idea, I think, as I give in to sleep, the tables would turn: that Cailean would be the one to contextualise my remembered life. To help me move beyond what India has been to my past. To show me that I can create space in order to reimagine a new role for this fantastical landscape in my present.

PANEER
Fried milk cheese

For me, paneer perfectly transcribes the dichotomy between simplicity and effort: not a difficult dish, it nonetheless demands much of the cook. The reward for all of that time and attention is a meal of ethereal richness and sublime depth.

INGREDIENTS:

3 litres milk
¼ cup lemon juice
3 to 4 tablespoons of yoghurt A cheesecloth
Vegetable oil to fry 1 large tomato
20 grams fresh ginger 1 tablespoon ghee
1 heaped teaspoon cumin seeds 1 heaped teaspoon salt
¾ teaspoon Kashmiri red chilli
¾ teaspoon turmeric 15 grams gur
1 ½ teaspoons ground coriander seeds
½ quill cinnamon 3 cloves
1 teaspoon *garam masala*
1 red capsicum, sliced*

METHOD:

Step 1. Pour all the milk into a large pot turned to high heat, stirring occasionally. While this is waiting to boil, squeeze enough lemons to obtain around ¼ cup of juice. Keep this, along with a tablespoon and the yoghurt, next to the stove.

Place a colander in a bowl large enough to catch the whey. Drape the colander in a piece of cheesecloth as large as a tea towel.

When the milk begins to bubble over, quickly add the lemon juice and the yoghurt and continue stirring over high heat until it curdles. This should happen almost instantly. If it doesn't curdle after 10 seconds or so, turn the heat to low and add some more lemon juice until the split occurs.

Pour the contents of the pot into the colander. The cheese should be caught by the cheesecloth. Bring up the sides until the uncooked paneer forms a ball. Tie it up and hang for at least 4 hours. (I most often hang it off the laundry tap and leave it overnight.)

Retain the whey and set aside for later use.

Step 2. Once set, unwrap the ball of paneer and cut into 1-inch cubes.

Heat vegetable oil in a deep bottomed pan or a shallow fryer.

While this is heating, prepare a bowl full of cold water and keep by the stove.

When hot, fry off the paneer for a few minutes until golden brown. Remove it and place in the bowl of water. The paneer is now ready for use

Step 3. Finely chop or use a blender to mince the tomato and ginger together.

Heat the ghee in a pan on medium heat and add the cumin seeds.

Allow the cumin to cook for around one minute or until it releases its aroma.

Add the tomato and ginger to the pan and turn down to low. Allow it to simmer until much of the water from the tomato cooks out and it begins to resemble a thicker mix. At this point add the turmeric, gur, salt, ground ginger, Kashmiri red chilli, cloves, ground coriander and cinnamon. Continue to cook on low heat until the fragrant mix becomes a paste.

Add the paneer and the capsicum along with around 1 cup of the whey. Turn to high heat until it begins to bubble. Then turn it immediately down to low heat and leave to simmer for 45 minutes or until the vegetables* are soft and the mix is fragrant and reduced of its excess liquid. Add the *garam masala* in the last moments of cooking.

Serve.

Makes enough for six as part of an Indian meal.

* In this instance I used capsicum, however I make paneer using a range of vegetables. Sometimes, cabbage or spinach or peas. Add however much of your chosen vegetable you wish and always add to the pan at the same time as the paneer itself.

CHAPTER 15

Clove

A clove is the ultimate healing spice. An
analgesic for the pained pull of nostalgia. A
calming agent for anxiety in the present. An
anti-inflammatory for expectation's flame.

WE HAVE MISSED THE ELEPHANTS and Cailean is inconsolable.
It has been his soul desire. His monologue. His mantra.
I'm going to India and I'm going to ride on an elephant. To
arrive at the lower ground of Jaipur's Amer Fort and see
no queue clustered about the ticket booth had initially
seemed fortuitous. It is not.

We have driven in the morning to get here. Rising
at 5.30 a.m. in Ayanagar for bucket baths poured from
the plastic buckets; hot water hitting goose-pimpled skin
lathered with the scent and slick of sandalwood soap.
Breakfast of banana lassi, chai and fresh chapattis spread
with jam. Washed, fed, and bound for Rajasthan. We

turned out of our driveway at 7 a.m. to leave behind the familiar magnificence of the three peacocks who roost in trees outside my bedroom window; passed an ant trail of village children in immaculate pressed shirts, pants and pinafores en route to the highway and school bus stops. Three-and-a-half hours, Dad's computer route planner had said. But while the freeway signs suggested a travel speed of 80, sometimes 90 kilometres an hour, our driver rarely pushed the odometer beyond 55. So three-and-a-half hours stretched to four. Then to five. For *freeway* is a generous description of the road that runs between New Delhi and the Pink City. *Bullock run. Dodgem track. Construction site.* These might be more apt.

Dad was not to know and so we stretched and teased out tolerance. Mum, Dad and I attempted to encourage Cailean's patience by pointing out vignettes of rural Indian life as we passed: villagers who had laid their grain across the road for trucks and cars to crack hard hulls with heavy wheels; more cows, however, these ones with beautifully painted horns and necks wreathed with large brass bells; the startling elegance of lines of women dressed in topaz, mustard, vermillion saris walking three abreast along a road that appeared equidistant between nothing and nowhere. But they were not elephants and he was not interested.

Now it is 1 p.m. and we are here. There are no people clustered about the ticket booths. But neither are there elephants. No one speaks at first, though the force of our looking almost creates its own sound. When the silence does break, it's Cailean's voice that spills into our Jeep. 'Where are the elephants, Baba?'

His tone can in no way be construed as casual. Cailean's words are not the question they appear, but rather the bringing to light of a reality none of us want to face: the elephants are absent. The fact Mum, Dad and I are aware of Cailean's subtext is implicit in our responses. Mum prods Dad into action. Dad jumps out of the car to approach the lone man standing before a shuttered booth. I push out of the back seat with Cailean to follow; feel ever so slightly sick.

'*Haathi kahan hai?*' The question is out of Dad's mouth before he has closed the distance between our car and the ticket booth: where are the elephants? I don't understand the man's response—his Hindi is too fast, and his explanation too detailed—but it is evident from his body language that the answer is not one we want to hear. Cailean is aware of it, too, for suddenly he is howling. No words. There is nothing to say. Just full-bodied sobs. As if someone dear to him has died. I grab him in a bear hug, my grip so tight that he might not break apart. The words I whisper in his ear ascribe to no coherent form. Murmurings. Snuffles. Croons. His keening becomes louder. Dad struggles to communicate above it. We are a scene. It is India, so others gather around. Our driver gets out to join the fray. It is getting out of hand. I hoist and carry Cailean back to the car. Mum is still in her seat. She sobs—her harsh gasps the raw sound of sympathy. Cailean's resilience up to this point makes his breakdown all the more spectacular. It affects us all.

'Okay,' Dad climbs in and slams the door behind him, urgency in his tone, 'the mahout who looks after some of the elephants apparently keeps them just up the road. His brother was there. He said that if we go back there now, Cailean might be able to have a little ride.' Cailean quietens a little at this. Dad leans forward to give the driver instructions. We have to U-turn. It has already been too many hours in the car. 'Did you hear that, Monkey?' Cailean is in my lap, head buried and hiccupping as we turn back on ourselves, car bumping along.'Did you hear that? Baba found a *haathi* for you.'

Dust kicked up by the tyres of our jeep transforms the rear window into a screen that blocks even Amer Fort from view. That it recedes in our distance matters to no one. We are all intent and fixed upon a single future point—the mahout*'s* village. Dad sits forward, arm on the back of the driver's seat as they consult, car in motion. We only stop once for directions: elephants play an important role in the local economy and all here know of their whereabouts. The tension in the car is as one might imagine if Cailean's life were at stake. His dreams certainly are. In any case we are all leaning forward in our seats. Breaths held. Not until we turn off one dirt road onto another, and then another—dustier, more ditch-pocked—to see a clutch of six or eight very large, well-kept animals' stalls of brick and steel and corrugated iron do any of us in the car unclench.

Perhaps someone called ahead? The caretakers here seem to be expecting us. There is an elephant still saddled from her morning's work. For timing is what left us stranded: a little less than twenty years ago Mum and Dad brought my two brothers and me here; we climbed the long and curved path to the top of Amer Fort on a single elephant and came down that way again. But times and the treatment of animals have changed. Now the elephants work only until 11.30 a.m., baskets are limited to three passengers per elephant and only upward carriage is permitted: the force of the downward journey combined with the weight of people on the pachyderms' backs makes, over time, for a crippling work environment. 'Can we ride it?' The car is parked; the four of us step out. Only now, with the animal in sight and Baba invested in conversation with three villagers, does Cailean dare to be hopeful. I am unsure of how to answer. That is, until I see Dad reach into his back pocket, remove his wallet and pass one of the men some notes. Correct payment and then a little extra. *Baksheesh* or a generous tip, I can't be sure. In any case, the deed is done. 'Yes.' I grin down at Cailean, his hand in mine, secure in the outcome. 'Yes, we can ride it.'

The man not taking money from Dad directs Cailean and me to climb a ten-tread staircase. At its top, we leap from the small steel platform on to the back of a patiently waiting elephant. Her name is Saraswati. The mahout is already seated on a thin square pillow that rests in the hollow of Saraswati's neck, his sinewy, brown feet crooked at the base of her beautiful bat-wing ears where they meet with her head. The motion, as we move off, is disconcerting; with our own feet hanging over the basket's side it feels as if we might roll off the elephant's back with each rhythmic dip of her body. 'Whoa!' Cailean exclaims, his face a startled caricature of eyebrow-raised surprise as we both reach with nervous laughs to grab the bamboo rail in front of us. It is the only sound he makes.

Dad snaps his camera as we move off and away. Cailean and I smile and wave. But quickly enough the mahout turns us left to walk down a quiet road that skirts the village made of compacted clay dusted with fine sand. There are houses on one side—those tall, concrete rectangles with small cut-out windows painted in peeling shades of faded sea green, flesh pink and pastel lemon. The other vista is of paddocks sectioned by low stone walls and marked by small clusters of trees stuck in the landscape as twigs jammed in sand. A scooter drones past. A battered Maruti and its high-whining thrum. Otherwise there is silence, the rarest of all Indian commodities.

In between the pleasant sound of Saraswati's odd moist waffle and the base drum note of her three-nailed feet hitting hard ground, there is the turning wheel of Cailean's thoughts. I'm unsure what churns in his head.

But I know what turns in mine: I must not fall into the trap of assuming the future.

'Oops,' I say, as Saraswati turns a half circle, lurching me into Cailean. 'I think we're heading back now.'

I find self re-imagination to be a fraught business. Scattered with more potholes than the ones that line this village road. Wormed with more avenues of possibility than the wrinkles that crimp Saraswati's skin. To find myself in India at the head of a new beginning is to thrum with the compulsion to paint my future outcomes with the white wash of expectation. I know from what has gone before the implicit danger in doing so—to expect a mother's recovery, rely on a husband as saviour, to read a recipe as a scripture of hope. Just as I know from my reaction to Cailean's earlier distress that I have not entirely escaped the seduction.

For it was not the loss of his dream that threw me into such panic. It was the force of his ferocious grief— the supreme sadness of surrender. I saw then the limited agency he feels over his life. And I felt in his tears the terrifying acknowledgement that I have just as little over mine.

'How was it?' Mum's words catch us as we round the corner back to the animal sheds. Her words quaver a little, as they always do when she attempts injection of volume into Parkinsonian speech; her voice projected to reach us, perched still on Saraswati's back. Cailean gives her the thumbs up. Mum stands by the jeep, lipstick bright and wrapped in one of her beautiful embroidered shawls, having been seated inside for the wait.

Dad stands a few metres away in conversation with the mahout's friend.

'Would you like to touch this one, is it?' It is the moneyman, the one who reaches out a hand to both of us as we take the leap from Saraswati's back onto the high floating platform. At his question, I see Cailean's eyes grow wide. 'We can!' I say, encouraging him with a nod. 'Okay.' His word is fast and tight, the excitement that colours his face tinged with just the barest blush of fear. Cailean descends the stairs cautiously to the waiting elephant below. I walk by his side. Descend a different, though no less real, set of steps into the depth of my psyche. I feel the soft skin of his hand clutched in mine. Acknowledge that my overriding sense has been that I will control the reformation of the person I was into the one I wish to be. That I will do so by reimagining the pillars of my life: food, faith and family. But my human mind is fatally narrow. I can't imagine scenarios beyond the limits of my own experience. And yet to let go of that concept and release myself into the drift of what might be, feels as a terrifying uncertainty. To truly soar is to release notions of autonomy and prediction and spread sheet-surety. To fly blind in faith and presence in this potholed life.

'Go on,' I urge him softly, our feet flat on the ground a spare two feet from the great grey animal with her intelligent, long-lashed eyes. Cailean inches closer, his hand stretched toward the curl and reach of Saraswati's inquisitive trunk: still for a breath, it twitches and moves in his direction.'Whoa!' he says again, startles backward. I would step in but the mahout beats me to it. This kind, unknown Indian presses a gentle hand into Cailean's back—and keeps it there—as Cailean once again inches forward; as he sources the courage to let Saraswati twist her trunk to touch him in gentle curiosity; as Cailean steps closer still to wrap both arms around the elephant; as he moves away from me and feels what it is to soar into the stratosphere of his unimagined existence.

For Cailean had long envisioned the ride on Saraswati's back. But he never imagined this: hugging close her trunk—chestnut hair ruffled by her gentle breath—in a quiet village setting far from the competing noise and hustle of touts and tourists that crowd Amer Fort with tin dreams.

'Look here, Monkey,' I encourage, bringing the view-finder of his camera close to my face. 'Smile!'

The photographic evidence taken is not for Cailean. It's for me. Not so that I might see something of myself *in* him. Just the opposite. So that I could possess a mate-rial reminder of the moment he fully stepped into his own unknowable experience. And how, being a witness to that, forced me to step fully into mine.

'Mummy, there's a storm trooper behind you!'

We are early at Amer Fort and it feels as ours. It is not yet 9 a.m. Our second day in Jaipur. I woke early from a full night's sleep following the intensity of the day before. My sense is that I am boundless.

'C'mon, c'mon,' I skip up close behind Cailean. Dart left into a short and narrow opening that hides off to the left of the high arterial pass we occupy, 'Let's hide!'

In my hand is an imaginary light sabre. The same make-believe weapon Cailean holds before his body in a tight-fisted grip. We have been at play at least an hour now and I am not flagging. As the sun stretches higher, Jaipur's chill morning fog burns into warmth trapped above the city and the fort begins to fill with tour groups and guides. Italians, Germans, Americans, Indians from other parts keen to experience their own history. Each one of these walking swathes is—to us—an evil to be defeated. We scramble and scurry into small chambers. Hide behind latticed sandstone screens. Every evasion is a small victory. I am energised.

We have all arrived to the fort in the same way: borne high upon the roll and rock of an elephant's back. Deposited in the vast open courtyard that once served as an outdoor palace foyer. Where we go to from there is our difference. 'Mummy, the Death Star,' Cailean's voice is staccato with a strange American twang, the tone he always uses for violent or urgent play, 'I think it's down here!' We are separate from them, these crowds. Not only for the secret route we choose—a winding and partially concealed ramp-like run that descends in a serpent's twist from fortress high point to palace buttress—but for the pleasure we find in reimagining this ancient structure and making it ours.

'There Mummy, look,' whispers an excited Cailean, 'it *is* the Death Star! We found it!' Our tunnelled escape route has spat us out in a forgotten corner of the fort's walled outskirts, where workmen in lungi*s* and open shirts cart barrows spilled over with concrete dust. Cailean points to the fantasy weapon: a giant black *kadai* perched on a blackened iron tripod. The place where workers' meals are cooked, I wonder? And then: Are we supposed to be here? The bamboo scaffolding and pulled up sandstone cobbles that create tripping points at every step suggest not. But no one stops us. It doesn't cross my mind that I wouldn't *want* to be here. That, while those guided groups have travelled countless miles to marvel at the *Sheesh Mahal,* the fort's famous mirrored rooms, I have done the same to hunt down science fiction's ultimate armament as imagined by my son in the rubble of hidden renovations. 'Pe-uw pe-uw!!' Cailean reaches to his waist for the Jedi gun he uses to get in one accurate Death Star shot.

'It's a hit! It's a hit!'

I don't need to be that person anymore; the person who blindly follows the presumed path and does things the 'right' way, at least, not all of the time. So when Cailean and I laugh and shout and bolt through back laneways to be returned to the fort's main courtyard and the swirl of ever-building crowds, I accept the joy in the freedom. I accept it much more eagerly than pain, though I understand I must accept that, too. Joy. Pain. Fear. Love. Anger. Challenge. Surrender. Of them all, the last is the most difficult. And yet no other place I know provides more provision for practice than India.

'Should we head home for lunch now,' I ask Cailean, as we take a moment to breathe and cool in the shade of a filigreed sandstone pergola. 'Are you hungry? Or do you want to go for another round?'

His grin swallows the Jaipur sun, 'One more round.'

Food. That has changed, too. It has not been a development I expected, nor one that I have wanted, for that matter. If I had been asked, I would have said that I have grown to love the centrifugal force that cooking and eating has become throughout my ongoing journey. That I love the way it gathers people to me. What I mightn't say is that I am less enamoured with the side of myself that worries that the closeness of others to these recipes poses a threat. For what if they uncover my secrets? And further, what if discovery of my secrets diminishes this food's meaning? But here I have watched cooks in homes, as well as at roadside dhabas, freely give of their food knowing that who they are imbues what they cook, but that what they cook is not the whole of who they are.

The end result is that food in India is not the same as Indian food in Melbourne. I don't mean its flavour: the spice or the produce or even the methods used to cook. I mean its weight of significance. I think of how little we eat here, as Cailean and I return to the upper car park in order to find our driver and accept carriage back down to ground where the elephant ascents begin. I think of the night before, seated in the hotel dining room, just Cailean and I. He was barely recovered from the heightened emotion of the day. Those five-year-old eyes redrimmed with fatigue, exhausted, but hungry. *But I don't want daal and spicy food, Mummy.*

'The hotel, madame?' The driver asks as I close the jeep door behind us. 'No, thank you,' I look to Cailean and smile, 'just back to the bottom. We're going to ride the elephants up again.'

Dad had consulted with the hotel manager in order to have kitchen staff light stovetops at 6 p.m. that wouldn't normally be flamed into action until well after 8 p.m. But the concession was not significant enough for Cailean. He wanted Western food. Something other than sabzi and rice.

'This is fine,' I accept, as we reach the road in front of the fort's ticket booths, pushing open the car door so that Cailean can exit before me. 'We will meet you in a little while back up at the top.' The driver nods his head. 'Okay, Monkey.' I grab for his hand in happiness as I slam shut the door behind me, begin negotiating the throngs to find the end of the line. 'Let's do this!'

I know what it is to want food as an anchor. I know what it feels to reject it. What it is to build security around it. Just as I know that what Cailean wanted wasn't sausages and mash, but the bite of familiarity. But it wasn't there to be had. So to watch him last night as he chewed mouthfuls of paneer, woody and strong and sweet with cloves was to see the act of eating from an entirely different angle: food as food. Food that addresses hunger directly. India has helped me to see that food can be nourishment, unweighted by metaphor and emotional baggage. Food is not an antidote to boredom. Not a pathway toward spiritual enlightenment or the plotline for a quasi-philosophical narrative.

I know for some people this recognition is normal. For me it is as if I have shed scales and feathered wings. It is these wings that spread wide as I face the laughing ticket sellers amused by this, our second elephant ascent of the morning. Cailean blushes. I giggle with them, unashamedly, in turn. These wings I use to soar into the clear air of child-like imagination. It is my new mode of transport. A way of being that generates wonder. Wonder that generates curiosity. Curiosity that generates stillness. And stillness that ensures both the strength and presence to hold me back from re-armouring against a future I now know better than to attempt to predict.

'What was that?!' Cailean squeals. We startle at the wet spray that douses us, bodies rocking in time to the lurch of the elephant we sit atop. I look forward and then behind to see, in both directions, an almost endless line of painted and adorned animals labouring uphill under the weight of sunglass-wearing, camera-toting tourists. All of us posed against a backdrop of elaborately constructed sandstone and scrubby desert hilltop. 'I think,' I say, forming each word slowly, 'that it was elephant snot.' Cailean squeals again. I giggle in return. Just then Lakshmi—for we always ask our elephant's name—raises her trunk and showers us a second time.

In a little while this moment of magic will be subsumed by the traffic-choked drive back to our hotel in a progression so slow that each crumble and crack in the stunning ancient Pink City façade will be pressed into my memory as a lithographic print. But I now know where the *me* in that moment lives. The same way I feel that, no matter how things continue to change, I know just how to find her again.

CHAPTER 16

Gajar Mattar

Carrots and peas spiced with cinnamon
and ginger and sweetened with gur
is the vegetal taste of my childhood.
And yet how different its savour once
untangled from my lessons hard won.

I WANT A LIFE MORE than I want a memory of one. The thought doesn't arrive as that, fully formed. Until now I have not had the capacity to hold a sentence of such enormity in my heart. But what began as a pinprick of consciousness sometime in the recent past has, in the six weeks since my return from India with Cailean, evolved into a new understanding.

'What's for dinner, Mummy? Can I help you cook?'

I am back here again. Back at the stovetop in our small two-storey terrace in a South Melbourne side street, the boys alternating between tangling around my feet and playing in the courtyard outside. Cailean and I had returned from New Delhi via Singapore at 7 a.m. on a bright morning at the end of January. Scott and Ashok had greeted us, the two small brothers running into each other's arms. But the missing was not our trip's only outcome: by our absence some sorcery has occurred; both my house and my insides have been rearranged and swept clean.

'Mummy?' Cailean's repetition reaches into my fancy. 'Mummy? Can I help?'

'Yes you can, Monkey.' No agitation, this time. No words pulled tight on a short string of impatience. 'Go and get Ashy from outside and you can both help me with dinner.'

Even my children have changed shape. The formless creatures who once stood against the backdrop of my past are now diamond-cut defined against the sharp points of bench corner and knife blade. They are real and vital as they take their routine positions standing or kneeling upon dining room chairs at the cutting bench: Ashy, not yet two-and-a-half, clad in a nappy only as a concession to the late February heat; Cailean, bare-chested in patterned board shorts coloured in splashes of yellow and blue that liven three different shades of grey.

'Okay, Cailean, you can cut these carrots into chunks.' I prop before him a chopping board, a child-safe orange knife and a silver tiffin. 'And put them in this bowl here. And Ashy, you can pop the peas into this bowl,' I say as I reach around Ashy to place another, smaller tiffin to his left and the open bag of peas square before his bare and rounded belly. 'Can you do that?' I take his greedy grasp of fist into the cold plastic bag as a positive sign, ignoring that the frozen green balls mostly spill onto the floor or are stuffed into his mouth.

Mine is an entirely new landscape that only by mis-judgement would I see as unchanged. For my eyes have been opened, now, by the enormity of a new acceptance which has suffused and swallowed my brain.

In the days after our return from the Rajasthan road trip to our Ayanagar house, I had gone back to the ash-ram. I went back on my own. My intent was simple—I intended to sit alone with Nand Baba and be filled with the wisdom and wonder of God. Arising from the view-point of where I, then, stood my want seemed more a foregone conclusion than a stretch: I was in India; I felt myself freed from so much of my past; I was willing. The last, I see now, was the only real point. Yet it turns out that even when will and want run parallel, there are other influences.

Pranaam, Nand Baba. I bowed before him, my fore-head an offering upon the skin of his spread and blunt-toed feet. I felt him reach down to touch the crown of my head, and mumble a Sanskrit blessing before he greets me with familiar warmth. Namaskar, *Sarina.* And then, when I failed to rise, *Sit up, sit up.* I was dressed in cream raw silk churidars worn under a black wool sweater dress.

The chestnut fine wool shawl I favoured wrapped, like always, as a charm around my neck. I felt as the imposter I routinely did in our guru's presence: a sense of embarrassment stemming from my doubt that I was somehow not *strident* enough in my devotion. That sense magnified by the awkward thing that rose inside me when seated before Nand Baba—the sentence that, until I heard his opening communications, I had not known that I had gone there to say.

For I didn't pack myself into the jeep that morning with a question. And yet neither was I loaded with confession. Instead I had come here to test the expression of a tentative new voice that had taken root sometime since my call to spice began: *I'm not sure I believe that my faith looks like my family's anymore; so true to doctrine and convention. I want more than ritual. I want space to cultivate my own practice, to implement my own understandings.*

I couldn't gather the courage to speak those words aloud. Not in the ashram. Not surrounded by garlanded images of dead gurus and immortal deities. And so I didn't. Instead I sat as a respectful student through Nand Bada's opening questions and small talk. *So, how is Cailean liking India? Your parents told me you were going to take him to Rajasthan to see tigers and ride elephants. Did he have a good time?* I listened with cowed respect to his pronouncements upon the state of my life. *You must judge. Do not listen to your_. Your______ is wrong and you must stand up for what is right. To take no action is a sin.* I suffered with inadequacy watching ashram devotees tend selflessly and completely to the maintenance of Nand Baba's spiritual and physical needs—chai on trays, shawls around his shoulders, donations taken and the logistics of upcoming *pujas* discussed and organised—all the while excruciatingly conscious of my great doubt.

It wasn't my gods that I doubted. Not anymore. It was doubt that I could find them here. That I could hear them through the static of another's translation—my family guru whose ideas on love and compassion didn't appear to run parallel to mine. I had lasted in this space so long because it has been the cradle of faith for my family. But we all outgrow our cradles eventually.

Acceptance of growth. The third dimension whose influence will and want can do nothing to minimise.

All I knew when I left the ashram just before lunch, was that it would be my last visit. I could sit no longer and listen to another's interpretation of God if it required me to neglect or reconfigure my own intimate relationship with the divine. I climbed back into the jeep a short hour after my arrival, stomach full of chai and churning, and acknowledged that my deities no longer lived within these ashram's walls. The significance of that recognition was matched only by my immediate reaction to it: for the first time in my life I could admit to such an utterly blasphemous thought and yet not feel compelled to suppress its tracking in my head.

So it was—in that moment—that my own, private conversation with God had somehow quietly begun.

'Alright, so where are we, boys?' My focus returns to a kitchen floor strewn with peas and a benchtop cluttered with great, unusable chunks of carrot. As if the vessels of containment I had placed in front of both of them went completely unregistered. 'I'll just cut. These. Up. A little. More. Buddy.' Each thwack of my knife is a rhythm to which I push out my words, arms reaching around Cailean to slice and dice his work. 'And as for you, my little pea monster,' job done, I move to grab Ashy around the middle, dig my fingertips into his sides until he spits out a gorgeous, gurgling giggle that is as ceaseless as the tickling pressure I keep up on his ribs, 'what a mess!'

'Tickle *me*, Mummy! Tickle *me*!'

'And you!' I mock threaten Cailean, touch Ashy's feet to the hardwood kitchen floor as I now turn to grab my eldest son from his seat; to swing Cailean around the bench in a tickling, laughing tangle. 'You and your big fat carroty chunks! What am I supposed to do with those?'

'More, Mama! More!' Ashy again. They each demand their turns until I cannot hold them for dizziness and laughter. They will continue this game indefinitely if I do not plead mercy. 'Okay, okay, no more!' I half pant, half laugh out the words. 'I'm pooped! And we have dinner to make, remember? So, who wants to help me with spice?'

My two little volunteers and I crowd around the cache of Tupperware plastic and small glass jars that keep in easy working order all of my dozen-or-so regularly used aromatics. We each have a teaspoon and take turns to layer savour into a central *katori*: Cailean, cumin seeds and turmeric; Ashok, ground coriander and whole cloves; me, Kashmiri red chilli and the rest—cinnamon, ground ginger, fresh grated ginger, whole star anise. Only when I pull out the plastic tub bulging with squares of ice-cube sized gur do they clamour once again to have their turn, more for the sweet chunk they each bite out than an actual desire to cook.

'That's enough of that,' I say, mock stern, 'or all your teeth will rot.' Spice base ready, I shoo them away from the kitchen to the early evening warmth of the courtyard and the matchbox cars still set out to play. Away from the fired up gas stovetop and the equally intense burn of my thoughts.

God and I were not immediately verbal. That development has taken—*is* taking—time. But on that drive back to Ayanagar from the ashram, I suddenly felt a companionship that I couldn't remember experiencing. This sense of companionship took the form of a comfortable internal silence. As if I had spent the past twenty years of my life making other people my prison, gathering them and their chatter close so that I could not see the faults in me for the faults I saw in them. A way to distract from the loneliness and introspection that, as far as I can tell, are two of the surest pathways toward reclamation of grace. But having spent almost the better part of a year, since I picked up that first packet of turmeric, painfully and systematically untangling the lures of barbed memory and self-destructive behaviours from my spirit, the release of myself from the gaff hook of religious propriety had been the last.

'Okay,' I pause and brace myself, 'what's next…' Frying pan. Ghee. The pop of cumin.

Sorrow. Reinvention. Self-recognition.

Left with just seventy-two hours between the end of my ashram visit and my flight home, I spent the next days alternating between backyard cricket matches and ice cream runs with my son, and solo expeditions beyond Ayanagar's limits. The intent of the last took me back to the South Delhi stomping grounds of my childhood, Dad's hired driver as my guide. These were dream-like adventures. And yet it was not the staggering changes in landscape and architecture and modernisation and sheer bloody crowdedness that spun me around like a blindfolded five-year-old playing pin-the-tail-on-the- donkey. It was a deeply held recognition that the girl who crossed these *nullas* and threw firecrackers off the tops of those old family houses and bought Betty and Veronica comic books in that particularly crowded Def Col market bookstore was no longer me.

She was no longer me because I was no longer her.

The sizzle of finely diced tomato into the slurry of fat and spice sends up a hiss of pungent steam that tears my eyes, momentarily blocking my pot-stirring hand from my sight. It doesn't panic me. I know my hand is still there. The same way I knew, as I cruised Defence Colony backstreets, that saying goodbye to those distant versions of who I was didn't mean that they had gone. It just meant releasing their influence over my current life. So, on those strange and singular drives around New Delhi, that is what I did. I let me go. Without all the competing noise of other people's beliefs and opinions I intrinsically understood that my healing—my *true* healing—couldn't just be born of winding back to the day of that diagnosis. I had to go further. To the time before, when my dreams for my future did not include a sick mother and a crisis of faith. Only then could I truly be free from the crippling need to conform to an ideal of 'me', that I now know I could never have become. To do so deconstructed the 'who' I have been in a way that meant that particular avatar could never. Ever. Be put back together.

My left hand is steady as I hold the heavy wooden chopping board over the hot pan. I use my right hand to sweep into the aromatic *chownk* all those awkwardly sliced carrots and swept-from-the-floor frozen peas. And yet for all the need I had to escape where I had been, I was not at all steady in the aftermath of that pivotal New Delhi shedding.

I was devastated.

I was devastated to feel the vomit rise in my throat on my first post-India ten-kilometre run as I rounded Albert Park Lake; as if my body identified the act of running—a pursuit that has been an outlet and an escape for all of my adult life—as a sickness.

I was devastated when I sat down to my work desk to be run down by the stultifying effects of boredom; as if my mind failed to realise that journalism was both a valued career and my vessel for self-identity.

Just as I was devastated to open the closed doors of my *mandir* after all these years to find that the silent conversation I discovered in the back of a jeep leaving the closed gate of the ashram had been subsumed instead and again by a distracting white noise; as if my spirit failed to reconcile that this small timber temple was the one sanctioned place where I had the ability to reach out and touch my gods.

And I rested there. One. Two. Three weeks after my return home. I rested there until I woke one morning in the new shell of a woman I didn't recognise, only to realise that this woman's foreign body was my own. Perhaps, not so strangely, this occurrence brought more confusion and sorrow than immediate relief. I may not have liked everything about the woman that I had been, but I *knew* her. Her grief. Her frustrations. Her anger. Her resentments. And now the actions in my life that had served as quotidian markers—chiefly exercise and journalism—had been drained of meaning. So it was that it took time before the steaming hiss of loss cleared enough that I could see what was left: a kitchen whose pantry has always held spice and whose pot drawers have never lacked a pressure cooker's heavy weight. A woman who is gentle with her children and open with her husband. It took time for me to recognise myself in this woman, the new, unfamiliar version who begins to know life is best when lived for what it is and not for how it should have been.

This last has been the true sorcery.

'Okay, kidlets,' I raise my voice so as to be heard over the sound of cooking and children's chatter and the crash of cars on concrete tile outside, 'who wants to add the finishing touch?' In the end we all three do it together. I grab the *garam masala* from the cupboard, Cailean measures out the small spoonful, and Ashok tips it in. That night all four of us—Cailean, Scott, Ashok and I—eat a *thaali* full of *gajar mattar* that is complex, sweet, balanced, salty and spiced. 'You know,' says Scott later that night, as the boys are asleep and he stands at the sink cleaning up the last of the dishes, 'I could tell just by eating it who made that dish. It didn't taste like your Dad's food at all. It tasted just exactly like you.'

The compulsion to return to Erica draws over me slowly. It has been months; my last visit played out in the weeks before I left for India, sparked then by a scuttle of fear at what imminent upset I had encouraged by agreeing to the trip at all. My reasons for returning might not be based on fear but they are similarly saturated in my apparently inexhaustible need for answers.

'How *are* you?' In all the strange ways my life compass has shifted in recent weeks, the lyricism of Erica's question—the emphasis she always seems to place on that second word in order to tie me to the present—hasn't changed at all. She might ask me a simpler question, I think. Because I am still acclimatising to this new shell. Still waiting for the moment when the distorting sensation of pliability will solidify into something reliable and familiar. Something like the fit of my old skin, but less lined. Less wrinkled by worry. Tighter and more smoothed out.

'I'm well,' I finally decide. The surprisingly stable tenor of my answer feels as unfamiliar as the thing that next unfolds when I shed my shoes and lie down, a body beneath a blanket, on Erica's healing bed. For what next unfolds is silence. Big. Deep. Cavernous. Absorbent. Silence. A silence so womb-like it swallows each question that would want to push through. Questions that would speak to my future and my present and my past. Questions that have peppered these sessions with my fear and anxiety and discontent. One by one they are let go. Whisked as balloons by wind. Up, up, I imagine their trajectory, up through the ceiling of Melbourne summer cumulus and into the infinite beyond. So released,

I sink deeper. Through my body and through the bed. Collapsed upon myself as an imploded star. Until all that is left is blackness. Blankness.

My moment of peaceful death hangs suspended for a lifetime and no time at all. I barely note the click of the door as Erica exits, and yet something must register, for her departure acts as a signal.

Behind my closed lids it is Mum who rises up first. As an absence, not a face. A presence like death. I feel salty tears push into my throat as a tumour but can barely prepare for its unleash before—*phhht*—it is excised by the sure scalpel of God. Only later would I understand the moment for its figurative significance: not the death of her, but removal of the final contained malignancy of my guilt at her disease. With that gone, the future unfolds as a series of beauteous vignettes. I view Cailean, a young adolescent, on an English clifftop with the shadow of Ashy just out of frame. Myself and Scott, hearts and bodies light with love and sunlight. Cailean again, though older this time, distracted from drafting at his desk by the run of his child into his lap. A Paris apartment lined with books in a room with a skylight, and me, writing at a desk within it. My dear friend Emma; just her, for the longest time. There are others. Others that I cannot hold onto. And yet when the experience finally slows and subsides I know that—remembered or not—these visions are a part of the possibility of me. I don't have to reach out to grab them.

I don't have to work to ensure they are realised. I don't even have to believe they *will* be realised. I just need to accept that there is a lifetime ahead of unplanned pleasure and untold difficulty and it is an exercise in complete futility to presume to really know any of it. That, if I am living life truly, my skin will always feel as this—strange in its yes-no familiarity. That there is no point I can ever get to where certainty can be cemented. And that, this is why I need God; because all those spiritual silences with Shiv and Shakti and strange spirits and gorgeous Ganesh and flute-playing, clothes-stealing Krishna, those are the conversations that will keep me balanced from the inside out when the outside in is so loose and impossibly susceptible to the vagaries of fear and fate and faith.

So, right then and there, I stop asking for answers. Contradictorily—though not unexpectedly—it is in doing so that I receive a response to the only question that still matters to me in this baby-plump form: where is it that *I* find God?

The answer doesn't come on the drive home. It doesn't come in the excitement of primary school pick-up in these, Cailean's first few weeks at school. It doesn't arrive in the yoga classes I now attend as an alternative to running, nor the increasingly personal stories I pitch to newspaper and magazine editors in order to make my job feel less like journalism and more like the more intimate style of writing I crave. It comes instead the morning I sit within the frame of that sterile timber puja *ghar* and call forth the deities with my own presence. Just me. My energy and my devotion, so that even the vibration of the mantra*s* on my lips feels as extraneous sound. Though Dad always taught the enunciation of the words is what carries my love to *Bhagwan*, I drop into silence. Focus instead on the run of electricity that causes my cranium and spine to fizz; the echo of the prayers in my heart.

I stay like that for a long time. Sometimes with my eyes open. Sometimes closed. I repeat some mantras tenfold. Others I say so slowly that each syllable becomes its own distinct word. *Om. Sa. Ra. Swa. Ti.* Just as that. So that one recitation might take one minute to complete. Then I speed up. As fast as I can until I lose the connection between utterance and stillness only to ease and slow so that—in the next deep breath—my spirit and my sounds conjoin once again.

I am playing with prayer.

I do this every day when I sit in my puja *ghar*. Not every *day*: I do not have that kind of regular, consistent practice in my life. Not yet. But on the days that I do find the discipline and the courage to close the door on family life and sit in the quiet front room before my newly active temple, I take a breath and a pause to monitor and assess the best way—*today*—to communicate with my deities. It is equally exhausting and liberating, to rely on no set framework. And yet there are rewards: sometimes I can lie down still upon the grass in nearby St Vincent's garden and feel the movement in its individual tremoring shoots as I might my own breath. Other days I can find millimetres of relief between anxiety and observance—not always enough to untie the knot, but that small space of perspective alone allows hope that one day soon I might. But mainly what this toe-dipping experiment into personalised prayer promises is release from reliance: reliance on happiness, on things going my way; reliance on others for the answers I think I need.

Maybe others have those answers. It doesn't matter anymore. I am at the very beginning of becoming a self-determined entity. Of finding my own way with God. A woman wise enough to supply my own spirit with the savour of nourishment that it needs.

GAJAR MATTAR
Carrot and pea sabzi

One of my favourite sabzi*s* to cook for the boys, it reminds me of all the pieces of my heritage I wish to pass down framed within the sweeter flavour of my own relationship with faith.

INGREDIENTS:
500 grams carrots diced
1 cup peas
20 grams fresh ginger
2 large tomatoes
1 tablespoon of ghee
1 heaped teaspoon of cumin seeds
1 heaped teaspoon salt
½ teaspoon ground ginger
¾ teaspoon turmeric
3 cloves
2 green cardamom pods
½ quill of cinnamon
¾ teaspoon Kashmiri red chilli
1 teaspoon garam masala
Whey or water, around ½ a cup

Method:

Finely chop or use a blender to mince the tomato and ginger together.

Heat the ghee in a pan on medium heat and add the cumin seeds.

Allow the cumin to cook off for around one minute or until it releases its aroma.

Add the tomato and ginger to the pan and turn down to low. Allow it to simmer until some of the water from the tomato cooks out but much of the liquid remains.

At this point add the turmeric, gur, salt, ground ginger, Kashmiri red chilli, cloves and cinnamon. Cook for a few minutes.

Add the carrot and the peas while the tomato and spice mix is still quite wet, as the liquid will help to soften the carrot. Continue to cook on low heat for around 40 minutes until the vegetables become soft. If the mix starts to become too dry, add some water or some of the reserved whey from paneer if you have it on hand (look at the paneer recipe for explanation).

With around 5 minutes to go, add the *garam masala* and stir well.

Serve.

Enough for eight as part of an Indian meal.

CHAPTER 17

Cinnamon

Cinnamon is sweetness balanced. One
never craves too much, for its warmth
is grounded in woody earth.

I KEEP QUILLS UPON QUILLS of cinnamon in my pantry. I hold them in a circular glass jar the exact height of a spring asparagus stalk with its woody end trimmed. The quills whorl tightly together so that, from the top, with the lid opened, it is like looking upon an abstract of eternity: a spinning spiral of circular circumference that folds in on itself in patterned beauty. I use my quills in almost every dish. *Gajar mattar*, of course. *Kaddu.* Those *sabzis* that naturally lend themselves to sweetness. But I have begun to experiment in other ways, too.

When I was a woman refusing to cook Dad's food his constant refrain was how little time and preparation it took. Now that my kitchen is my own I know that to be intrinsically untrue: like anything in life worth keeping close, Kashmiri food demands that I hold its space through care and forethought and patience. And so I do, now. I can. It is a fine balance: mornings when I stir a small pan of oats alongside three litres of bubbling milk as I make paneer parallel with porridge; packing Cailean's school lunchbox while placing a *katori* of daal to soak. These preparations I do as part of my larger life so that the roles of carer and cook can harmoniously co-exist.

This is an important transition: my early days of flurry and excitement around stovetop and spice have taught me how quickly internal expression can corrupt into external addiction when new elements introduced into my life are allowed to morph from creative outlet to crutch. So instead of making my life about cooking, I am learning to hold a space for cooking *within* the bounds of my daily life. Letting go of obsession requires attention. Continual readjustment. Unceasing acknowledgement of loss and gain. Sometimes the day turns against me and work or physical fatigue forces me to surrender grand plans for dinner of sabzi*s* and homemade chapatti*s* to simple plates of sausage and spuds. At other times I excel, somehow managing to find time for *kamargah* and paneer and daal and *gajar mattar* to boot. But most often I fall somewhere in between; an Australian–Indian mash-up of sabzi, daal and green salad along with barbecued lamb cutlets with market-bought *roti* heated by me on a ghee- slathered tawa.

It seems, at first, such a silly little focus. Over weeks I learn that it's not. I learn that to shop weekly for fresh food—to heed levels of vegetables in the fridge and dry goods and spice in my pantry—means that, no matter the tenor of my day, I am always supplied with the basis for a meal I can cook with material and meaning. These *sabzis* are now absorbed into the form of my life. Through them I have found a sustainable source of sustenance. One that originates from some place in my distant past yet is not unchanged by my present.

Because for all of the things this food is, I have come to understand that there is an even longer list of what this food is not. It is not a life raft. It is not the scope of who I am. It is not God. It is not family. It is not me in my entirety. It is not me in partiality. It is neither rope nor release. It is not profound feeling. It is not a thing with which to be careless. It is not a power apart from me. It is not my driving cause. It is not a platform over which I have ownership, and yet neither is it an object over which I have no influence. It is not an abstract.

I understand these intricacies only because of all the ways I have *misunderstood* them before. So it is that the thought occurs: it is not the things I do right that bring me in closer touch with divinity, but my recognition of all the ways in which I have erred.

Initially, I value this acknowledgement for all the wrong reasons, for I value it as an end unto itself. It feels as a circle of completion, and if a circle is complete, then surely there must be nowhere else for me to go? What it takes me longer to identify is that like those whorls of cinnamon seen from above, I am composed of infinite loops and vortices. The linking of one only ever precedes my necessary focal shift to another. And when that circle is drawn? There are more besides. Always more. Never complete. Discs and rings and spheres and rounds.

A significant development in claiming ownership of my own nourishment is my understanding that there is no one else to blame if my life should start to fall apart. The thought is liberating. To understand that a journey that began with a bag of turmeric, a sheaf of recipes and a pressure cooker full of anguish has led me to a place where, now, food and cooking provide me with a spiritually self-sustaining practice. And that, in feeling so nourished, I find myself wanting to pull this enveloping sensation of sanctity out of my kitchen and my puja. To free my dialogue from stricture with grace and pull it up alongside me. To have my belief and my gods become part of my daily life.

But a larger piece of the draw is in wanting to physically and practically distance myself from an early childhood falsity: that a Ganju's life is always imbued with the grace and blessings of our Hindu deities. It has taken me a long time to be willing to see the subtle malevolence in this myth. It was my bedtime fable. The way in which Dad would metaphorically tuck me up into my life. And yet it was also the root cause of my world's collapse. It is not, I am beginning to discover, that the premise is wrong. More that its meaning has been foreshortened: God is with me always, yes, but only if I direct my effort to always be with Him.

When I was a young girl in that Anglo-Saxon coastal Australian town, I took shelter in the exoticism of my religiosity. I took shelter in its difference: that my gods were often coloured blue; were possessed of splays of arms holding conch shells and cosmic weaponry; were seen by Western eyes not so much as idols of faith, but mystical, mysterious and marvellous bodies of magic. The comic book nature of my deities' appearance made it safe for me to reveal my devotion among young school friends who—as far as I could tell—equated Christianity with tinsel at Christmas and chocolate at Easter. The stories of Shiv and Ganesh and Krishna enchanted them. They didn't laugh at the tika that I sometimes forgot to rub off before I walked in the primary school gate. When Ammi came to stay, my friends fell in love with her saris and her stillness and her radiant faith. In their eyes, Hinduism was little more than a world of make-believe and I felt shielded by that.

My love of the church was different. My neighbour was my best friend growing up. Marie. Her father was raised Church of England. Her mother was someone I considered to be a devout Catholic: she attended church and worked as a teacher at one of the local Catholic secondary schools. Marie herself went to Catholic schools. The traditional Catholic rites of Communion and Confirmation marked her life. And every Sunday morning at 10 a.m., she and her mother would take the five-minute trip in their white Subaru to Torquay's plain-looking Catholic Church built in a patch of gravel car park between a cluster of surf shops and the local laundromat.

Marie was an only child, then. We were eight, nine, ten, eleven. I spent almost every Saturday night at her house, stretched out on her bottom bunk in a room filled with Barbies and My Little Ponies and the fish tank that burbled away as a comfort in the dark. I'm not sure when the transition occurred but, at some point, instead of shrugging on my backpack, running across the paddock and jumping the fence home as they left the house at 9.45 a.m. for Sunday service, I would stay and travel to church with them. I didn't know any of the hymns or prayers and so, at first, felt highly conspicuous. Shamed and embarrassed. This was God with a capital 'G': to love him out in the open made me feel exposed. Very gradually I let my guard down; only once I knew that the people I shared an hour with here did not penetrate the small circle of my everyday life. So relieved of anxiety, I soon learned the blessing of the cross. The Lord's Prayer. When to interject the priest's monologue with a mumbled *amen*. I never completely shed that feeling of being an outsider, but I would follow behind Marie to take the sacrament and feel a measure of peace given by this foreign God whose importance in my life—at this young age—I had no idea how to explain, let alone reconcile. Afterwards we would head to the bakery for strawberry iced doughnuts. I look back now and marvel at what is my child-self's easy acceptance of different faiths.

These thoughts rush back in as I stand, this afternoon, on the steps of Melbourne's St Paul's Cathedral. I have caught the number one tram, walking from my office above Scott's Clarendon Street shop to nearby Park Street, jumping on for a short ride before hopping off at Flinders Street station on a whim. Ostensibly driven by hunger, my plan is for a dosa at Flora. Except instead of turning left off the cross walk, down past Young and Jackson's and onto Flora, I step right. Back up the hill I walk, ignorant of the soft autumn sun, of the force of the Swanston Street crowds I intersect. I walk back up the hill until I find myself standing on St Paul's tiered cathedral steps. Though I am inconspicuous in the thrum of a Melbourne city lunchtime, standing here makes me feel exposed; as vulnerable as a person is when stripped of artifice. To enter the church. To light a candle. To kneel upon the pew. But this isn't about conversion. That would be a problem of clear-cut magnitude.

My actions at the cathedral represent a re- acknowledgement of what the girl in me once knew. Religion is for everyone. Faith interpretations feel best when they are broad. This idea is reinforced for me continually over the next few days: wrapped in a trench coat and shawl, I walk up the autumnal wind tunnel that is Flinders Lane to have my attention stolen by the beauty of a man-sized and psychedelically coloured Ganesh painted as an intricate spray of graffiti upon an alley wall; on another day, I find Kali as an art advertisement wrapped around a lamppost.

Gods and goddesses pitched out of recognisable context.

The rush of absurdity and surprise each of these encounters brings is seismic, like running into my high school principal at a nudist camp. My idols become exposed and stripped of reference: Ganesh without the gravitas; Kali shorn of her merciless intent. But more than that, they become unfamiliar. Transformed by another's interpretation into small 'g' gods. Mini deities.

The first thing I feel at the emergence of this idea of diminished deities is remembrance of my time in Marie's Catholic Church. The way I felt in there—surrounded by the grace of God and yet unencumbered. I had rarely experienced such sublime freedom in the ashram, where five thousand years of religious inheritance pressed the sharp points of the ancestors against me. I know that Jesus is not my God. Just as I know that the Bible isn't my scripture. But I do know that stripping God and religion of gravitas and redressing these concepts with love feels like the kind of spirituality that I can live with.

I am old enough—secure enough, now—to want that: to want a faith that doesn't feel as if I am reaching to catch up with it. A faith that doesn't require me to be strident. That isn't so grand, so righteous that I cannot see myself reflected in its image. That doesn't shield my piousness because the humble nature of my belief means the issue of piety ceases to exist as a problem. I need a joyful faith. A messy faith. A faith that lets me be me within the framework I have built for myself. I need my God to have a small 'g'. It suits who I am: a half-Indian, half-Australian Hindu raised with my heart in the East and a good part of my mind in the West.

It is hard for me to think I mightn't be as God-fearing as I have always wanted to believe. But maybe I might be spiritual in my own way? The dull pain that rises from the press of my knee bones against the hard wooden pew brings me out of my trance before an answer to that question arises. I'm not sure how long I have been crouched here, almost alone in St Paul's on a Wednesday lunchtime, but the screaming pain in my joints, if not the confused thoughts in my head, tell me it's time to leave. So I loop home to cinnamon. To milk and water and cardamom stirred upon a stovetop. The bloom of turmeric. Wooded essence of cloves. A quill dropped in for warmth. This is my context. There is no one else in the house. Being midweek, the street is quiet. In the living room, a low-sitting afternoon sun holds dust mites in mid-air above the geometric patterns created by beams of light hitting polished wooden floorboards. The moment is one of time suspended, minutes marked only by the darkening stain of tea that tans milk turned over by a roiling simmer.

I leave the gur out, this time. I seek a subtle taste of something sweet. The chai I have made in the past— the chai my friends adore—is a bombastic crash of honeyed texture on the tongue; it is the Indian diaspora; a cymballed-cacophony that sounds to the beat of 100 dancing Hindu gods. This cup is not that.

How many people in the world are built in a way that allows them to encompass the brilliance of deities and kings of heaven within themselves? How many people try and fail, only to find that shame in human frailty forces them to leave it all behind? I did. I left it all for as long as I could. Only desperation brought me back. Desperation and some ember of grace that I, in my wavering belief, had not quite managed to extinguish. Is this what God wants? For us to feel as children who never quite make the grade? Me, an eternal D+? *God is good,* so the saying goes. And He is. But I'm not sure He wants us to accept the version of Him we are fed—whichever form that takes—without question. My growth and expansion requires both doubt and curiosity. One without the other is not enough: without doubt, I would not have sought to question; and yet without curiosity's flight, doubt's weight would hang eternal in my gut as a sickness.

That was where I ended up; sickened with sorrow. For while doubt was gifted to me in Mum's despairing eyes the day I gave up on God, it has taken me much, much longer to unwrap curiosity; the parcel I dragged behind as a club foot, sure that what lay inside was another form of death. I was right, of course. And death has come. In one million different ways. I have lived through multiple incarnations in these twelve months alone. The loss of every single version of myself that felt like failure. As if I never could excel in divine eyes. As if standing still was the ultimate reward. Yet I am learning to accept this dying process as a part of my life. One million deaths so far and, by the grace of my own God, there will be one million more.

In all of this, it makes sense to me that my image of God should change to match my continually altering shape. But that doesn't stop me from grasping at the idea of a face—the desire to capture a picture of the One who captures my prayers.

So, as I stand by the stove and wait for my chai to simmer, I do what has become a private game in recent days: I keep very still and try to listen to who my deity might be.

I run through the Hindu canon as I know it. Shiv, though an obvious choice, I have already counted out. Krishna, for me, is the eternal flute-playing playboy.

Lord Ram? I am too female to see myself reflected in the might of a returned warrior king. Jesus Christ is too

Christian. Brahma, so scholarly, does not appear as one who might take time to listen for individual prayers—too busy writing and revising the laws of the universe. I have never possessed a strong sense of Parvati other than in her role as Shiv's wife and Ganesh's mother. The divine feminine of Devi has resonance, and perhaps I could settle here if not for the fact of her perfection. Mary comes closer, though her pious quietude shrinks her inward to herself, somehow. Who is left? Kali with her malevolent skull necklace? Righteous Vishnu perpetuating creation? Sometimes I wonder if the question isn't just another hook to get stuck on; one created by me as a distraction from the ultimate awareness—that I may never recognize who it is that receives my prayers, and I need to live my life being okay with that. That perhaps that's God's trick: implanting that last immovable trace of doubt that will keep my curiosity alive for an eternity.

UNSWEETENED CHAI

Sometimes I begin to feel myself float away from centre. I recognise the behaviours: anxiety, chiefly, followed by a reluctance to sit still in my puja or play in the kitchen with my pots and pans. To help reset I will give up gur until I feel peace re-descend. This here is my cup of balance.

INGREDIENTS:

½ cup of water

¾ cup of milk

3 green cardamom pods, cracked open

2 shards from a whole cinnamon

3 cloves

1 star anise

½ teaspoon of turmeric

1 teabag or a tablespoon scoop of loose black tea leaves

METHOD:

Put all ingredients in a small pot and heat on a very slow simmer until the liquid is caramel-brown and viscous. Strain and serve. Makes one cup.

Gobi

Cauliflower tastes of nothing on its
own. It is a palette for spice, made
rich by its ability to absorb both light
and dark; to reflect back flavour as a
balanced, clear and coherent whole.

TIME DOESN'T HEAL. TIME TEACHES. It has taught me. I am
thirty-eight now. Three years on from the day I rose
from a pew in St Paul's on creaking knees. Four years
younger than Mum the year that Parkinson's caught her
in its reach. These numbers and records give outline to
the structural facts of my life: I am well, I feel purpose-
ful, I have a family and an existence carefully tended.
The same triplicate of fundamentals Mum once held in
her possession. So then what is the distance between us?
Who would *I* become, should that axe of illness fall upon
me? Could I forgive God? Would I know the words to

say to keep my children and my husband close? To keep them safe? Could I continue to recognise myself in the aftermath? Live inside a body that betrayed me and still find myself within it?

I'm not morbid by nature. I don't think these thoughts often. But they do, every now and then, catch me by surprise. 'You've got to teach me how to cook some of these things,' Scott said, out of the blue, last night. It was after 8 p.m. I had just handed him a cup of chai. Together we had put the boys to bed and cleaned up the clamour of pots from the night's symphony of aloo sabzi and daal and spaghetti and salad in the prosaic kitchen of our new rental: each meal is like this now, a banquet of East-meets- West love and divinity. 'If something happened to you, we wouldn't just lose you, we'd lose all of these beautiful meals as well.' Scott wasn't speaking of food, but of the soul I invest in our family table: for just as Ammi and Mum had infused their spirits into the spice jars that fed their families, so, too, have I infused mine.

It does create some concern for me; that should I be lost to illness, I am lining my own children up for the same fate. But then I think of where I am in this moment and can only wonder at the beauty birthed from unrecognised blessings. In any case, it feels healthy to consider a future without me in it: my mortality is a strengthening awareness. It's not that I ever chafed against the intransience of life, prior to now, more that I gave the idea of my human-ness credit for little, concerned as I was with *immortality*—with finding a place for myself among my deities, my gods and my goddesses, my family, my recipes; fixated upon finding protection from an outside-in faith.

From where I sit today, writing at my second-hand Singer sewing machine table fitted neatly into a corner of our bedroom, my view has changed.

Mystical geographies, ashrams and churches are gone. In their place is a rectangle of bedroom window in the small West Australian town of Margaret River filled with wind-worn cumulus. We sold our house in Melbourne to move here, and I have brought all of my new understandings with me. This afternoon those clouds move east to west in a spectrum shaded from luminescent porcelain to oyster grey. The lawn directly out front is a couch grass patchwork of frost-burnt green brought on by the nearing winter. A shrub hedge—spiny, drought- resistant—has its sole appeal in its road-blocking height. This is the bare bones look of small town regional life: the immediate landscape of our four-by-two rental in a manmade estate surrounded by south-west Western Australian bush. In the quiet of school hours, my boxy room is where I think. It's where I pray. It's where I read and draft and untangle my thoughts.

Removed from exoticism and steeped in suburbia, this is my new context. And I feel as free as I've ever been.

To write these words down is to find myself surprised anew: that I may now, here, from this position, reach within and retrieve only a sense of curiosity and wonder. A backdrop of electrician's vans and house-and-land-package-rendered-brick is not the vision of contentment I had formed. Contentment was held elsewhere: in the glamorous amalgam of a future that borrowed its environs from the globetrotting sophistication of my past. Indirectly, I equated contentment with geographic flexibility. In admitting to that connection I have succeeded in betraying the belief that underlined it: that I had always imagined freedom's spine to be held straight and by the supporting muscle of money. I know it isn't what I was taught, what I was taught being the supremacy of religiosity as the only true path to enlightenment. But from what I'd seen it was the people with who money travelled; travel looks like freedom; and that, even when still, when cemented in place by work or babies or external commitments, these people appeared relieved from worry caused by money's lack. It's a fallacy, of course. Scott and I once had money and my burden was as heavy as anyone's.

I can sit here and watch the clouds and see that now. I can say *once* because Scott and I are those people no longer. I can see that happiness finds its roots in contentment and that contentment, for me, is found in my own quiet faith. And yet, on my part, the transformation from who I was to who I now am was not without trauma.

I am highly conscious of the narrative problem created by this admission. It is disruptive, so late in the piece, to be speaking once more of failure. For one thing, it interferes with anything I would introduce now of the physical reality of this moment: the chattering sound of the boys and Scott cycling into the driveway; muffled thud of sweaty runners and heavy school bags and—as the internal door from the garage pushes open—the full volume escalation of after-school's return. And for another, it is likely to leave one feeling as if this journey with me has come to nought.

But then life *is* disruptive and all failure is not equal; it is a word that can mean gain as much as loss. Just as nought can be both end and beginning.

'Mummy!'

'Shokey!' I turn on my chair to grab Ashok as he bursts into my bedroom and throws himself at my writing table, no longer that toddler in nappies, but a strong and uniformed five-year-old with the sensuous heart of a boyhood Krishna.'How was your day? How was school? Good, great or excellent?'

'Good, great, excellent and AMAZING!' And then, with his next breath: 'Can you play with me?'

'That's WONDERFUL!' I grin, holding him back so that I can see those dark eyes; deep brown, they illuminate an arrestingly bright and beautiful face. 'And yes. If you go and get changed out of your school clothes then I can finish this sentence and be done for the day.'

It is not the isolation of far-flung regional suburbia that has freed me, I think, as Ashy runs out of my room and I turn back to my window, my laptop and to my thoughts. It is my relationship to place. Or, more precisely, my relationship with myself in any place that I am. For in the spectrum of life events, I now know the happenings that will no longer shake me. To lose my house. A business. A family member outside our circle of four. My money—all of it. To let go of a career and have it replaced by labour: cleaning, and casual employ. To lose the power of glamour and glory that frames a globe-trotting lifestyle. To lose friendships in proximity. The luxury of *things*. The security of a superannuated future. The certainty of 'never'.

I only know this because it has happened. In the three years since I stood by my South Melbourne stovetop to make a sugarless pot of chai I have grieved each of these occurrences. (Though they have rarely presented singularly. It seems that, for the main, upset arrives in multiples as a kind of domino of destruction.) I didn't expect that the need for grief would arise. Had thought somewhat naively and simplistically that being able to hear my gods outside of mantra*s* and in my daily life ensured a degree of bullet-dodging guidance; like that long-ago great-uncle of mine, the sole survivor in his blown-apart Indian Army jeep. But events to inspire grief did come. Over eighteen months and in quick succession.

The loss of a father-in-law to death, a business to gross complication and fatigue, a house to debt. The loss of old friends and a once-cherished life as we chased a job and financial security and moved to Spain. Very, very quickly—within twelve months—there was, too, the loss of that circle of new life in Spain. Loss of Scott's new job, the one that I thought would save us. The loss of effort such a move requires, and with children, and new Spanish school, and the need to contend, in Catalonia, with not one, but two new languages. There was the loss of pride as friends moved on from great jobs in the Middle East to better jobs in London, just as we lost our Spanish dream.

There was the loss of a borrowed future.

And each loss was hard. And no matter how anticipated the outcome, each loss was tearing. And at the beginning I fought in a way that prolonged the pain of every experience. But in that prolongation of pain something unexpected happened: no matter how much I railed and resisted the changing nature of my family's circumstances, a resolve was reached. And when that resolve presented itself—say, our house sold and quite literally all the money from its sale was immediately lost to the demands of debt—I still recognised myself in the body I was in and knew, in that confirmation of grounded presence, that freedom was to be found where I was. The end result being that the one thing I didn't lose in all of that time and trial was me. I never, not for a second, lost who I was or where I was positioned. Because where I was positioned was in the driver's seat of my own life, God a travelling companion by my side.

'Mummy?' Ashok's voice interrupts the run of my remembrance. 'Are you still working? Can we play puppies now?'

'What about puppies who can cook?' I ask Ashy, now out of his uniform and dressed in small black football shorts and a short-sleeved tee shirt though it's already May and the sky looks as winter. I am conscious of dinnertime, and yet the question is barely out of my mouth before I see his face fall. 'Okay, okay, puppies first, puppies first,' I soothe, and drop from my chair to my knees.

So we snout and we snort and we snuffle: me the mummy doggy, and he the puppy with his restless, vigorous demands. 'What are you guys doing?' I look up from the bedroom floor, from our canine wrestling, to spot Cailean in the doorframe. He, too, is almost unrecognisable from the child he was when all of this began: at nine years old, there is still that soft face, but he is taller, now, made curious and lean and strong and brave with surfing and new friends and challenging experiences. 'Puppies,' I smile, 'wanna play?' He does. Not too changed, then, to still revel in his younger brother's uncomplicated games.

To have God as a travelling companion. It is not a new idea, not in Hindu scripture in any case. In those days when Scott and I still attended the ashram, Nand Baba had referred to this relationship as having Hanuman on one's flag. The notion is rooted in the Bhagavad Gita: as Arjuna forged through doubt to enter into a violently moral war against his family on the battlefield of Kurukshetra, he was empowered most obviously by his chosen charioteer, Lord Krishna. But a more subtle strength was present in Hanuman the monkey god who rode, golden, on the triangle of fabric that held up the warrior's chariot until battle's end. Often Hanuman's image is drawn upon to illustrate the boons given to devotees possessed of blind faith and unswerving spiritual loyalties: Hanuman himself having been blessed with the gift of tireless physical strength and vigour for his devotion to Lord Ram, one of Vishnu's many incarnations. But other explanations are (if possible) more metaphoric: that Hanuman's presence on Arjuna's flag is a signifier of the spiritual sustenance available when we can find the courage to direct belief towards the unbelievable. That God's support is strongest when His intangibility becomes the strength we see in ourselves.

It's easy to grasp this as a child—to intrinsically understand the magic of the immaterial as being a safe place to explore developing self-perceptions. From where I crouch on the edges of their imaginations, I watch Cailean and Ashy do so now; connecting with fragments of identity—aggression and vulnerability and nurture and dominance—cloaked in the fantasy skin of puppies-at- play on a carpeted bedroom floor. It is only since I began applying that same playful spirit of make-believe to the realities of my own life that I have been able to reconnect with *my* intangible self.

I am highly aware of the difference such a connection makes, if only because it is still new: that I can find contentment with so little—a glimpse of a kookaburra or kangaroo on my morning bike ride through a fringe of bush to the delicatessen where I work three days a week, slicing cured meats and European cheeses in a converted dairy shed where locals come to buy organic flours, Asian sauces, or nuts and grains in bulk. This kind of work is a long way from the life I thought I deserved: my world has always been signposted by foreign places and enviable experiences; to have lived, throughout almost four decades, in four countries across three continents. I have acted at being a theatrical teenager in Bangalore, a triathlete in Southern California, a Parisienne in Paris, a professional editor and scribe in Edinburgh, and a travelling food writer in Melbourne. And for as long as my life was as I envisioned it—for as long as the exterior environment equalled or exceeded what I felt was my interior worth—I was content to see myself reflected in the high sheen of golden circumstance.

Little did I understand that, throughout all those years, each move, each new backdrop, was nothing other than a chance to see who I was in contrast to the physical space I occupied; that the challenge is not to adapt, but to retain that unique sense of separateness once assimilation has occurred. By the grace of a materially blessed life, I was presented with such an opportunity. Multiple times. And yet on each occasion I failed to recognise the intrinsic value contained in that wonderfully curious sense of new-arrival dislocation: for those weeks before I allowed familiarity and routine to set solid, the new world I lived in appeared just as the world always is—a stage set. And if the world is a stage, it has no meaning. And if it has no meaning, then the only meaning to be found must be found within.

'Okay, chidlets,' I intercede in their roly-poly as the emotional temperature escalates and 'puppies' begins to more closely resemble 'gladiators', 'who wants to come and help me cook?'

And therein lies the true worth of all my loss. The contradiction of success in my arena of failure. I could *do* the twelve months of spiritual introspection. I could relinquish my grip on old familial understandings and embrace spiritual epiphanies. But none of this was the end. It wasn't even the beginning. That time of spice and emotional solitude simply prepared the ground so that, when my old world was finally torn down, the clearing dust revealed a bare patch of self, readied for construction of a new foundation.

Only this foundation is not made of bricks and mortar. It is not anchored to the kitchen bench I stand at, directly beneath the white glare of an energy-saving bulb. Not to the couch in the open-plan living room I can see from my sentinel post, where Scott relaxes into a book. Neither to the dining chair upon which Cailean kneels at *his* square- foot of kitchen bench, nor the portable step that enables Ashy's reach at his. It has no hooks into the immediate landscape that feels as foreign to me as an alien planet: the heaving Indian Ocean with its undersea tempest of migrating whales and sleek-bodied sharks; white crash of waves pushing up onto pristine sand lined by brave clusters of houses disappearing into dry, dense and dugite- occupied bush.

'Ashy, if you could please carefully cut that half of the cauliflower,' I instruct, reaching over to lay a damp dish-cloth beneath his chopping board as he jumps off his stool to retrieve the transparent orange child-safe knife from the cutlery drawer. 'And Cailean,' I pause, wait to speak until he joins his eyes to mine, 'I'm going to give you my knife to use to cut the other half, but *please* be careful. It's super duper sharp.' He nods his head solemnly, and for a moment I cannot tell him apart from the little boy he once was, accepting a *katori* of sultanas on Mum and Dad's kitchen step. 'Okay, Mummy.'

The sensation lasts only a second before my tiny remembrance settles into something else. Something softer than longing and more sharply defined than memory: as I watch Cailean deftly handle the knife, the breadth evident between the nine-year-old he is and the five-year-old he was becomes the gauge that, to me, vividly illustrates his growth. As adults we lose those basic physical markers that outwardly express internal changes—to become taller, hairier, deeper-voiced or suddenly wide-hipped and large-breasted—and so our consumer culture presumes no real acknowledgement of change is required. A conflict emphasised by modern social values that reward stagnation; to settle into a house and a job and the safety of Saturday football and mortgages and Sunday night roasts relieved by annual winter treks for week-long rests in warmer climes. How do we grow in any of this? Well, the answer to that is simple: we grow in spite of ourselves. We grow old. We grow sick. We grow tired.

'Is that right, Mummy?' Cailean is halfway through, a stack of neatly cut, small white florets pushed to one side of his chopping board, a larger, still untackled clump to the other. 'Yep, perfect, Monkey.'

'I think I've finished, Mummy.' Ashok, less skilled with a knife, who still believes proficiency and speed are interchangeable. 'Not yet!' I say. 'See how those clumps are really big? These ones, and those over there,' I move certain pieces back before his hands, 'they need to be cut smaller.' They bend their heads over the bench once more, both in near-silent concentration.

In any case I don't advocate pointless upheaval. Misdirected adventure. These are only thoughts to remind me, as I turn back to the pantry and remove an old shortbread tin containing my cache of spice, that it is possible for me to fall back there again: to choose the reliability of routine over the edginess of clear sight, despite those known ill effects. And yet I cannot see myself slipping back there. I don't think that I will.

'Done!' Cailean is loudly triumphant as he puts down his knife. 'Me, too!' shouts Ashy. 'Right then,' I laugh, 'let me fry all of this off and then it's time for spices.'

It has become important for me to pinpoint the roots of my self in words void of metaphor and allegory; to be as straightforward as the sizzle of cauliflower hitting hot oil. For it's seductive to be vague about the origin of the things that matter to me: vagueness, I think, as I drain the now browned florets on the kitchen towel, being just another way to minimise connection and my responsibility towards maintaining it.

'So, then, spices... Ashy first. Take this teaspoon; we'll put it all together in this *katori*. Just a third of a spoon of turmeric—no, no...' I catch his effort, 'a third means just the edge of the spoon, the *edge* of the spoon. There you go, there you go!' My words a cheerleader's cry as Ash carefully withdraws his teaspoon from the snap-lock bag of spice and tips it precisely into the waiting vessel. 'Perfect.

Cailean next. A huge heaped teaspoon of coriander, and then another half spoon more.'

'Is that the one you can't live without, Mummy?' Cailean asks as he shovels the roughly ground dried seed from its container in to join the turmeric. 'Nope, that's cumin seeds. You can do that one next if you like.'

My foundation is contained within the deepest part of my self. The part that has no gender. That owns no goods. Has no accent or explicitly oral language. The part of me that recognises no geographical boundaries or material constriction and so is free and at home wherever I am. It is the internal gaze of which Ammi spoke and once seemed to me so impossibly unattainable.

And yet I understand, now, that to connect with my internal gaze means only to recognise my endless and undying internal character that circumvents ego and collapses me into love. That my most direct access to this connection is via the signposts of sabzi, spice and silent prayer—mirrors that reflect back the unglossed image of my soul so that, at any moment, I always know exactly where I am.

'Mummy? Mummy!' Cailean's voice reaches into my thoughts. 'Which ones do we do now?'

The very thought is a circle complete, I think, as I guide Cailean and Ashy as to quantities in the last additions of black cardamom, salt, Kashmiri red chilli and gur. I let Cailean fire up the gas beneath. Ashy looks on, a half-minute later tipping the *katori's* contents into rich and melting ghee. And then, a further half-minute on, I sweep in the cauliflower. All of it. Turned by a wooden spoon through the slurry of scent, any fleshy white untouched by the browning oil turns immediately turmeric yellow.

GOBI
Cauliflower sabzi

Rich and spicy and soft and sustaining, this gobi sabzi contains all the dark and heat and sweetness and light that is implicit in living. I note my recipe here with a significant caveat: never will I make the same sabzi twice.

Ingredients:

1 cauliflower (about 900 grams)
vegetable oil for frying
1 tablespoon ghee
1 heaped teaspoon salt
1 ½ teaspoons cumin seeds
½ teaspoon turmeric
1 black cardamom pod
8 grams fresh ginger, finely julienned
1 teaspoon Kashmiri red chilli
2 teaspoons ground coriander
10 grams gur

Method:

Cut the cauliflower into small florets. In a deep frying pan, pour vegetable oil until about an inch deep. Fry cauliflower in batches in very hot oil. Drain on kitchen paper and set aside.

Heat the ghee in a separate pan on moderate heat. Add spices and heat until fragrant but not burnt. Toss in the fried cauliflower and cook for at least a further 35 minutes on very low heat. Add a little water to the pan if it starts to stick or burn, but make sure all liquid is evaporated before serving. This is a dry dish.

Serves six in small serves as part of a larger Kashmiri meal.

Acknowledgements

CREATING A BOOK LIKE THIS, for a writer like me, has been a baptism of fire. I couldn't have brought this long-thought story to completion without support, encouragement and direction from a tight posse of personal and professional cheerleaders.

Firstly, to England and to Sally Cline and the Gold Dust mentoring program for helping me to set the foundation for this book, thank you. It took a while to get this journalist-turned-author comfortable with use of personal pronouns, but, Sally you got there.

To Emma Quilliam. Emma, Emma, Emma. My reader. My champion. My believer in the moments when I lost track of how to be my own. This book is almost as much yours as it is mine. I treasure the time, knowledge and pieces of you given to me. And James 'Jimmy' Clarke-Kennedy. It is fitting, the editor who gave me my first chance in newspapers as a nineteen-year-old kid, should also have brought his editor's eye to my first foray into authorhood.

Thank you to Urmila Dasgupta at Purple Folio for not only taking on my manuscript, but selling it.

To Sanghamitra Biswas and the team at Westland, thank you for seeing the worth of my voice while helping me to sharpen its tone. A great editor is a writer's best friend. And to Saurav Das, for a cover of exquisite beauty. Taline Malkasian and Jennifer Crescenzo, my two long-distance sounding boards when I had no hope of working out a narrative problem on my own. The generosity you both showed in letting me talk to you for hours on end means an enormous amount to me.

I'd like to thank my Spanish families. To Jennifer and Gary Parsons in Barcelona for giving over their spare room, their study and their privacy to allow me a fortnight of incredible productivity. And to the Monson-Unceta's in Pamplona. Tina and Luis, I was made to feel at home every day of the three weeks I lived with you and the kids. We not only birthed our first babies together, but Tina you helped me to gestate a book. Love you always.

To my brothers, Eeshan and Shyam Ganju for being so free with their approval and encouragement. And to Mum and Dad, because who could I ever be without you. Most importantly, to the three men in my life whose strength bolsters mine. Scott, Cailean and Ashok Lewis:

The Sacred Three, My Fortress Be.